LEAF SHAPES

Linear: *Helianthella californica var. californica*

Heart-shaped: *Asarum hartwegii*

Arc[...]

Lobed and serrated: *Boykinia elata*

Deep cleft: *Lithophragma affinis*

Compound leaves (divided into leaflets)

Palmately compound: *Lupinus stiversii*

Pinnately compound: *Lotus oblongifolius*

Leaf Attachments

Basal rosette: *Plagiobothrys nothofulvus*

Alternate: *Solanum xantii*

Opposite: *Scutellaria californica*

Clasping: *Streptanthus tortuosus*

Whorled: *Galium aparine*

On November 4, 1997, The Royal Horticultural Society in London
awarded its prestigious Gold Medal to artist Martha Kemp for her
collection of delicately executed flower drawings. Included in her
winning exhibit were this graphite rendering of the Live-Forever,
Dudleya cymosa, and the drawing of Whiteleaf Manzanita,
Arctostaphylos viscida, pictured on the title page (opposite).

Wildflower Walks and Roads of the Sierra Gold Country

TONI FAUVER

Illustrations by
MARTHA KEMP
and Peggy Edwards-Carkeet

HISTORICAL NOTES BY HELEN BRECK

Comstock Bonanza Press
GRASS VALLEY, CALIFORNIA

To my grandson,
Rio deReynier McFarland,
who spent Easter vacation hiking with me in the Red Hills.
He loved playing on the "bouncer bushes" *(Ceanothus cuneatus)*

Copyright information:
© 1998 Toni Fauver
Historical Notes © 1998 Helen Breck
Drawings signed MGK: © 1998 Martha G. Kemp
Drawings signed PEC © 1998 Peggy Edwards-Carkeet
Drawings signed ER © 1998 Emily Reid

Published by Comstock Bonanza Press
18919 William Quirk Drive, Grass Valley, CA 95945-8611
Telephone 530-273-6220
Toni Fauver, P.O. Box 2322, Orinda, CA 94563

Designed by Dave Comstock
Printed and bound by Thomson-Shore, Inc., on acid-free recycled paper

ISBN 0-933994-20-6
Library of Congress Catalog Card No. 98-74243

CONTENTS

ACKNOWLEDGMENTS

Special thanks to Helen Breck for her hard work, time, love of her subject, and the expense it took to do the historical notes for this book. Helen also spent many hours of "car botany" and hiking with me. Thanks to Helen, as well, for the introduction to our gentle and exceptional artist, Martha Kemp, who was frequently on call to draw fresh flowers from the foothills. I am indebted to Martha for her fine and exact work. I appreciate the additional drawings that Peggy Edwards-Carkeet contributed when we neared our deadline and needed extra help. Peggy herself could have written and illustrated a foothill wildflower book, with her experience as a botanist and artist and a foothill resident for many years. There are also a few of Emily Reid's beautiful drawings.

This book could not have been attempted without help from my plant-savvy friend and computer whiz, Karen Wetherell, also on call. My sister-in-law, Catherine Fauver, a professional copy editor, has also been patient and invaluable. It was fun turning her on to wildflowers on a few Sunday drives during 1998's spectacular El Niño spring.

I have met many wonderful people in the foothills during the four years I have spent researching this book. The late George Clark, the former president of the California Native Plant Society, gave me lots of tips on where to find the flowers. Al Franklin, a botanist for the Bureau of Land Management, was helpful and very encouraging throughout the project. Forest Service botanists Jennie Haas, Mike Foster, Phyllis Ashmead, and Kathy VanZuick gave helpful information and occasionally hiked with me. Frank Oyung, active in the Sierra Club from Groveland, suggested some of the good hikes. Chet Blackburn has a wealth of computerized plant lists and hiking spots he generously shared with me. Don Smith and Sue Britting helped with the Placerville chapter. Steve Diers, a ranger and naturalist with the East Bay Municipal Utility District, helped out with his maps and plant lists of the areas around Pardee and Camanche Reservoirs.

Some of the difficult plants needed experts for identification. Thank you to Glen Keator for help with several of the Brodiaea, and to John Strother for help with *Agoseris heterophylla*. The California Academy of Sciences and the Oakland Museum also have been helpful.

My longtime friends, Sandra and Bruce Beyaert, and their friend, Pat Kennerly (my new friend), hiked many of the trails with me, and Bruce also did some of the proofreading. My friend Cindy Shaw, a teacher (and a good proofreader), spent her Easter vacation hiking with me during El Niño weather. My daughter, Jeanne McFarland, a botanist, gave me valuable advice and helped with the proofreading. My friends Dolly Dreiman, Jane Owens, and Wilma Follette also helped with catching

Acknowledgments

errors. Many thanks to our friends Kay and Jim Riewerts for their help with the trails and lore of the Sonora area.

Thanks to David Comstock for designing our book and putting it together, and to his wife, Ardis, for her hospitality when we littered their home with new book material and budding ideas that the Comstocks helped bring to fruition.

Finally, thank you to our husbands, Dick Fauver, Alson Kemp, and Beau Breck, for patience, support, and the freedom to do our book.

Toni Fauver

To Helen Breck, who introduced me to Toni Fauver and set the wheels in motion for this collaboration, and to Toni, who entrusted the artwork in her book to me and gave me the luxury of working from her freshly collected specimens—thank you!

To Dr. Frank Almeda, Senior Curator and Chairman of the Department of Botany, California Academy of Sciences, who patiently reviewed my drawings and combined words of encouragement with suggestions for improvement—thank you! To Dick Wagner, Jacqueline Browne, and Carolyn Sanders, botanical drawing teacher and two fellow students, all friends, who taught and inspired me—thank you!

To many others, including David Comstock, Walt McCauley, Ron Acquistapace, Frances Wolfe, and Mary Ricksen, who helped in many ways—thank you!

To Alson Kemp, Trey Kemp, and Colin Kemp, my husband and sons, whose encouragement, support, and love gave me the security to focus my attention on this project—my deepest thanks!

Martha Gudenrath Kemp

Special thanks to my daughter-in-law, Kristen Beck, and my daughter, Amy Sullivan, for being devoted editors; to Catherine Fauver for editing the final draft; to Ian Carmichael, Professor of Geology, University of California, Berkeley, and Jean De Mouthe, California Academy of Sciences, for fact-editing the geology information and sharing their expertise; to David Comstock, publisher, for historical research guidance; to my friends Martha and Alson Kemp, whose comradeship in this project encouraged me; to my friend Toni Fauver, who has gracefully taught me how and where to look at wildflowers for 11 years; to Dolly Dreiman, a wildflower enthusiast, who kept me company as I searched for gold, ghosts, and golden poppies along Highway 49; to my devoted sister, Mary Ricksen; and my heartfelt thanks to my husband, Beau, my lifelong companion in so many adventures.

Helen Bragg Breck

INTRODUCTION

THIS BOOK IS PRIMARILY A GUIDE TO HELP YOU FIND AND IDENTIFY the spring wildflowers of the Sierra gold country. The area it covers is from Mariposa in the south to Oroville and the Feather River canyon in the north. The westernmost extension is the Folsom area at an elevation of about 600 feet to the eastern range of Bowman Lake Road and Hetch Hetchy in the Sierra at about 3,800 feet and the Sierra City area at about 4,400 feet.

There is wonderful plant diversity within this area. On the edge of the Great Valley, just as the land begins to slope up to the hills, the soil is often rocky and gravelly, fit only for grazing, thus allowing many miles of beautiful displays of spring-blooming annuals to survive and flourish. The soil often has a hardpan base, and water collects in low spots, called vernal pools. The water gradually evaporates, and as the soil dries colorful rings of spring-flowering annuals especially adapted to spend their winter under water come into bloom.

Sometimes there will be a bull's-eye effect created by Goldfields, Meadowfoam, Tidy-tips, and finally Yellow Monkeyflower or blue Downingia, the last flowers to bloom, in what was the deepest part of the pool. Or there is an outline of Yellow Monkeyflowers or white Meadowfoam along rivulets that lead to the vernal pool. The gravelly areas, which support very little grass, have beautiful displays of Brodiaea, Mariposa Lilies, and small annuals such as Butter and Eggs, Goldfields, and Sandwort.

The sloping grasslands are particularly beautiful from the Lake McSwain area, west of Mariposa, north to Nimbus Dam at Lake Folsom and from Lincoln, near Roseville, to Chico. The Sacramento area is too developed and the land east of Marysville seems to be fertile enough for agriculture so these fabulous displays are absent. All of the highways into the Sierra, with the exception of I-80 and US 50, have wonderful spring flower displays.

When the valley is left behind and the hills begin to take shape, Blue Oaks, Buttercups, and rocky outcroppings called tombstones are a part of the scene. In a few places in the lower foothills, volcanic tablelands rise above the gently sloping land. Table Mountain near Oroville and Table Mountain near SR 120 and Tulloch Reservoir are very visible examples. Many of the Bay Area's reservoirs are located in the lower foothills and have captured the major Sierra rivers where so much mining took place. The land begins to get more rugged, and chaparral species such as Chamise, Coffeeberry, Buck Brush, and grayish Foothill Pine appear.

Approaching SR 49, the Gold Country highway, the hills get steeper, and there are more creeks and rivers. At this 1,000 to 2,000 foot elevation the road cuts are frequently the "red dirt" (from iron) that is typical of this country. There may also be shiny, greenish serpentine that generally has good spring flower displays, or fractured shalelike rocks, which continue under the roadbed into riverbeds and look as if every crevice should contain gold.

The land east of SR 49 is cut by deep canyons along the major rivers that drain the Sierra snow pack. Any bridge crossing upriver from SR 49 is usually worth a long drive on a narrow road to see what is often a historic bridge, in a steep canyon, with good flowers that are different on each side of the canyon because of sun or shade exposure. The hot side of the canyons frequently has better spring flower displays because there is less tree cover. The shrubs at this elevation are beautiful. On dry slopes the white Mock Orange and Snowdrop Bush and the apricot-colored shrubby Monkeyflower are very showy, usually in May. Often there are Dogwoods in the shaded canyons. The creeks that flow into the major rivers have beautiful microclimates of Bigleaf Maple, Yew, Maidenhair Fern, Indian Rhubarb, Trillium, or Waterfall Buttercups.

The peak blooming season is generally from mid-March to mid-May, with some plants, as noted, being early or late bloomers. The first two weeks in April tend to be the best for flowering annuals below 2,000 feet. The flowers last until the soil moisture is gone. Bulbous plants respond well to increased rainfall. Perennials, shrubs, and trees with deeper tap roots are not as affected by the differing amount of rainfall and bloom fairly reliably when the weather gets warm. The year of the New Year's flood, 1997, California had all its rain at once. After that the foothills were without any rain until May, and many seedlings died without producing fruit. Spring was over (for the annuals) by early April. Conversely, the following El Niño year of 1998 produced rain and snow into mid-May and stalled spring at about 2,400 feet, when usually the plants at 3,800 feet are in bloom.

This book was completed in perhaps the most beautiful spring I have ever seen. The bulbs were magnificent, the flowers were taller than ever, and it was the longest spring I can remember. Therefore, particular flower displays I have said were fantastic may be only mediocre in a drier spring. Even another El Niño year might not produce such a spring if it is too cold or too warm at the wrong time.

We hope you will use the book as a journal, making notations beside the illustrations to help you recall a flower or an interesting sight along the roads or trails. Coloring the illustrations with colored pencils will also help you remember the flowers.

In general, the trails we have included have more than just beautiful flowers. There is usually a water feature, either creeks crossing the trail or a river parallel to it, and often there is a creek, waterfall, river, or lake at the end of the trail.

It is great fun to hike in this country and imagine what went on here in the past. Many of the trails have Indian grinding holes near a water source, and on every trail there is evidence of mining activity. Look for the flats that were home sites, the dry rock walls that were home or road foundations, the ditches that follow the contour lines of the hills, the flumes that make such easy walking today, the rocks that form the tailing piles, and the mines and air shafts themselves. Think about the hardworking people who were here before you and have left evidence of their lives. The historical notes with each chapter will enhance your enjoyment and understanding of the Sierra Gold Country as you walk the trails and wander the beautiful back roads.

DIAGRAM OF PLANT PAGES

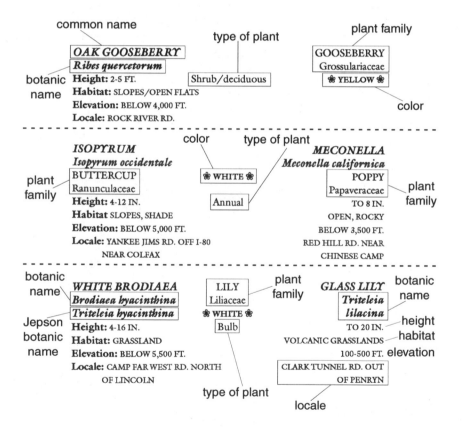

HOW TO USE THIS BOOK

Most of the plants illustrated in this book have been drawn from live material collected in the Sierra foothills. Each illustration shows several views of the flower and includes key characteristics such as glands, hairs, or seeds that are necessary for identification of a particular plant. A scale (in inches) has been placed alongside each drawing to give an idea of that plant's relative size.

The plants are **arranged by the color** of the flower: white to cream; yellow to orange; pink to rose, red, magenta, and maroon; blue to lavender; and (finally) plants lacking apparent color, such as ferns, trees, and shrubs. Within each color grouping, the **shrubs** are first; next come the **herbaceous plants** arranged by **family**, to show the similarities between related groups, by **increasing petal number** and then by **symmetry**, from regular flower shape to irregular shape, and last the **sunflower family**, because the California flora has so many we want you to be able to turn to them easily.

Each illustration is accompanied by the following information (see diagram on page x): **botanic name**, the new **Jepson botanic name** (if it applies), **common name, plant family, height, type of plant** (annual, perennial, bulb, shrub, tree), **color, habitat**, and **locale** (where to find good examples of the plant). There are also some interesting facts about the plant, such as the derivation of the botanic name, whether it is poisonous or edible, or perhaps its landscape potential.

The **botanic name**, or scientific name, usually consists of two Latin or Greek words, the first being the genus or general name and the second the species or specific name. Some names will have a third part, a varietal (var.) or subspecies (ssp.) name, for additional differentiation. The scientific name is used worldwide. In a flower book on the Swiss Alps written in German, the scientific names are the same as they are here. Botanic names are always italicized, with the genus name capitalized. Often the genus name is descriptive—for example *Chrysothamnus*, meaning gold shrub. Some genera are commemorative, such as *Castilleja* (paintbrush), named after a Spanish botanist. Others might refer to medicinal uses. Old common names have sometimes been Latinized, and some names are derived from mythology. The specific names, or species, are often descriptive, such as *albidus*, referring to white—think of albino. Interesting stories or "handles" that will help you remember the botanic names are usually included. You must know the botanic name if you are buying a native plant for your garden or are wondering whether some part of a plant has medicinal use or can be eaten.

Common names are easy to remember because they are often descriptive. However, with common names, it is sometimes difficult, without pictures, to understand what plant is being discussed. The more common a plant, the more "folk names" it will have. Look up Columbine, for example, on page 245. It has so many common names because of its wide distribution and beauty.

A **family** is a large group of plants with similar characteristics that are usually recognizable. An example is the Pea family, whose members have a distinctive flower and usually a seed pod that most of us are familiar with. Lupine is a typical member of the Pea family.

The Aster, or Sunflower, family is a very large plant family in California. Its members usually have flowers that look like a Dandelion or Daisy and seeds that look like mini-Sunflower seeds with Thistledown attached. Balsam Root is a typical composite. The Phlox and Geranium families are good examples of plants with regular flowers. The Phlox has petals united at the base forming a tube, while the Geranium petals are separate at the base.

The Figwort, or Snapdragon, family includes many showy plants. This family has irregular flowers and could be confused with the Mint family except that most Mints are aromatic. Penstemon and Monkeyflowers are typical Figworts.

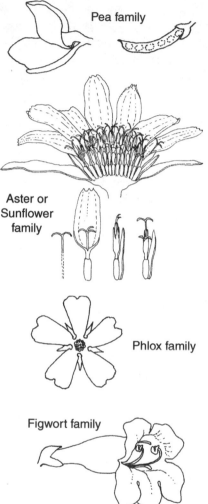

Pea family

Aster or Sunflower family

Phlox family

Figwort family

The **height** given for each plant is intended only as a general guideline, since height varies depending on available moisture, light, surrounding plants, and soil nutrients. For example, in a drought year the plants could be dwarfed. The **type** of plant, such as annual, perennial, shrub, or tree, is noted next, along with the **color** of the flower. In the valley and adjacent foothills the spectacular flower display of annuals is dependent on moisture from winter rainfall. The peak season is generally the end of March to early May, but if a plant blooms at other than peak season it will be noted.

A further aid to identification is the **habitat** in which the plant is generally found. The foothills have many different habitats. The moist riparian areas, such as river and stream banks, are stabilized by Bigleaf Maple, Alders, and Willows. Other moist habitats include seeps, vernal pools (see Phoenix Park, pages 40-41), and meadows (see Discovery Trail, Bowman Lake Road, page 71). Downingia and Meadowfoam are typical vernal pool plants and Yellow Monkeyflower also indicates moisture. The dry habitats include slopes, grasslands, road banks, dry forests, and chaparral, shrubby and almost impenetrable, typified by the presence of Manzanita and Chamise. Gravelly, rocky areas such as Table Mountain and areas with rock outcroppings such as Knights Ferry Trail are yet another foothill habitat, where the bulbs and Birds Eye Gilia thrive. Rock habitats consist of large rocks with nooks and crannies where plants such as Saxifrage, Heuchera, Sedums, and Dudleya can grow. Many plants thrive in the microclimate created at the base of rocks; moisture runs off a rock and collects under it, creating a reservoir for plants. Also, some plants choose the sunny side of rocks for the reflected heat, and others choose the north side for cool shade.

The **locale** for each plant will allow you to set out on a treasure hunt for a certain flower that perhaps you have heard of and would like to see. Many of the locales mentioned are described in more detail in the trails section.

To help you identify plants more quickly, attach a colored index tab at the beginning of each color section of the illustrations. If there is a page you refer to often, such as the glossary, flower key, or plant index, turn the corner down or put a tab on that page too. If you are vacationing in the area and have the time, color the illustrations with colored pencils. As you hike, make notes beside the illustrations about flower colors, the weather, the trail, or your companions. The plants and their names will be more memorable to you.

Happy hunting. Remember: "Take only pictures, leave only footprints."

NOTICE
All
WILDFLOWERS
are for viewing and
enjoyment by everyone.
**Collecting, picking,
or removing any
plant or vegetative
material is a
violation of
36 CFR 327.14(a)**

TRAIL WISDOM

THE ADVICE BELOW WILL HELP MAKE YOUR TIME ON THE TRAIL pleasant and safe. Happy trails! Wear hiking boots so you won't slip on the trail. Bring plenty of water and food. Layer your clothing, including a windbreaker. Bring a hat (to get wet in a stream if it gets too hot) and a scarf useful as a sling or bandage, or to put wet around your neck to cool off. Many of the gold country trails involve walking down into a canyon and coming back out in the hot afternoon.

Your daypack should contain: a first aid kit (with special medication for those who are allergic to bees and tweezers or a tick-removing implement), a compass, insect repellent, Wash and Wipes, Kleenex, a hand lens, a whistle, a knife, matches, maps (if you are going to hike off the described trail), food, and some hard candy or energy bars. Binoculars for bird watching or identifying cliff-hanging plants are handy. In this country it is fun to have a gold pan, trowel, and vial along also.

Stay out of the mines; the vertical air shafts are not easy to distinguish and the supports are often rotten in the mines. Read the trail descriptions carefully so that you don't end up on a trail that is too long, too steep, has a steep drop-off, or has a creek to ford that is impossible until late spring. Unfortunately there is Poison Oak (page 103) on all the trails below 3,500 feet. Make sure you recognize it with and without leaves. Former roads and some of the trails that are well maintained are not such a problem; however, bring Wash and Wipes or an alcohol swab with you and use it right away if you realize you have brushed the plant. An allergist told me the toxin bonds with the skin in three minutes.

Watch where you walk. Once the weather warms up there could be rattlesnakes on the trail. Wear ankle-covering boots and loose pants. On a hot day the snakes like the shade of the Silver Bush Lupines at the edge of the trail, so tap ahead with a stick if you can't see the ground where you walk. This same stick can be useful rock-hopping across a creek or warding off a mountain lion. The Tahoe National Forest botanist advised bringing your dog (where allowed) as "cougar bait," because the dog is in the position a lion prefers. She also said not to hike alone and to make lots of noise. If you meet a lion, don't run, don't bend over, don't turn your back; look big, and put children on your shoulders.

Ticks are a problem until the rain has stopped. Use insect repellent and do a "tick check" if you feel a tickle, and check at the end of the hike also. Ticks find their way under your clothes. Pull the tick straight out using tweezers with constant pressure but without twisting.

GOLD, GHOSTS, AND GOLDEN POPPIES
by Helen Breck

IN 1848 GOLD WAS DISCOVERED IN THE SIERRA NEVADA FOOTHILLS. California's destiny was shaped by this discovery, and by those people whose ambition, courage, greed, and sense of adventure emboldened them to "see the elephant"— a much-used expression of the 1850s, meaning to encounter and experience it all. In 1849 that flood of gold seekers known as the 49ers crossed deserts, breached the Sierra Nevada mountain barrier, or sailed around the Horn to make their fortunes in California.

The Gold Rush lasted only ten years, until 1858. During that time, prospectors moved from one gold-rich strike to the next strike, from one makeshift camp to another. Little remains now of the Gold Rush decade except "ghosts" of the past—stone and brick remnants of mining camps and towns and scarred hillsides. Today, the California golden poppy and other wildflowers grow over these remnants, replacing the traces of past fortune with nature's immutable bounty.

GOLD

Imagine that the earth's crust consists of floating rafts on a sea of very thick viscous material called the mantle. As the "rafts" (plates) grind against each other, one is subducted (one plate slides beneath another) as in California, where the Pacific plate slides beneath the North American plate. The collision compresses and thickens the crust as it is forced into the earth's mantle. Here the crust heats up and melts to form magma. Geologists estimate that some 150 million years ago the magma rose into older pre-existing rocks and continued for the next 80 million years. For millions of years molten rock cooled and crystallized into solid rock, which became the Sierra batholith, the world's largest block of granodiorite, commonly called granite. The older pre-existing rocks eroded, exposing the underlying granite. This process created the Sierra Nevada.

As the granite magmas of the ancestral Sierra Nevada cooled, hot fluids penetrated the cracks above the cooling magma bodies. As the fluids cooled in the crevices and fractures in the rocks, they became light-colored quartz veins with flecks of gold and sulphides; these are the gold-rich veins (hard rock deposits). Volcanoes began erupting about 30 million years ago, burying the Sierra in a thick layer of lava, ash, and mud flows. About 3 million years ago the modern Sierra Nevada, nearly 400 miles long and 60-80 miles wide, rose along earthquake faults, tilting the old land surfaces westward. Glacial action carved, scoured, and eroded the Sierra at least three times in the past 2 million years. New swift streams cut deep canyons, exposed ancient river beds, and deposited gravel, rocks, sand, and gold in the foothill stream beds.

The Gold Country can be divided into two regions, the Northern Mines area and the Southern Mines area. In the Northern Mines area, stretching from Sierra City to Auburn, placer miners traced gold-rich gravels that are a part of a prehistoric river system. As the volcanic layers eroded, gold-bearing gravels were exposed. There were also hard-rock mines with rich quartz veins, such as the Empire Mine in Grass Valley. The Southern Mines area stretches from Georgetown to southeast of Mariposa. After surface placers in river and creek beds became unprofitable, the miners turned to hard-rock mining. The Mother Lode, a particularly rich vein running from Georgetown to Sonora, was the geographic heart of the Gold Rush.

THE GOLD RUSH

On January 24, 1848, in Coloma, California, on the South Fork of the American River, James Marshall was deepening a tailrace (water channel) for the sawmill he was constructing with his partner, Captain John Sutter. In the water he discovered shining particles which proved to be tiny pieces of gold. These pea-sized nuggets would soon set the world on fire with gold fever. The news spread. Sam Brannan, publisher of San Francisco's first weekly newspaper, the *California Star*, and another weekly, *The Californian*, reported the discovery in March. Brannan, an entrepreneur, also owned a store at Sutter's Fort and by May, after stocking the store with picks, pans, shovels, and tents, he was waving glittering gold samples aloft and shouting to all who would listen, "Gold! Gold from the American River." President Polk, in his last address to Congress in December, confirmed the report of California's military governor, Colonel Richard B. Mason, and announced enthusiastically, "There is more gold in the country drained by the Sacramento and San Joaquin Rivers than will pay for the cost of the war with Mexico."

Within a year of the discovery, and with dreams of fortunes to be made, men were deserting their land, their ships, and their families to seek gold, and the world rushed in to California's gold country. Wagon trains left from Independence and St. Joseph, Missouri, then the western edge of the United States. Most of the 49ers came from the "states," but shiploads of men also came from Europe, South and Central America, Australia, Hawaii, China, and Mexico. For many emigrants, the trip west was difficult and sometimes deadly, as the perilous journey and diseases like cholera and yellow fever took their toll. But the 49ers came by the tens of thousands. California's population grew in the Gold Rush decade from approximately 14,000 to 350,000. While some made fortunes, most did not. When the California Gold Rush drew to a close, many prospectors moved on to the rich Comstock Lode silver strike centered in Virginia City, Nevada. However, gold mining in California continued until 1942, was suspended during World War II, and was resumed after the war, but on a small scale.

MINING METHODS

At first, prospectors used a simple knife to extract the readily available gold from stream and creek beds. Very soon, they devised various methods of using water to concentrate the gold. Gold is nineteen times heavier than water, is heavier than most other metals, and it naturally sinks to the bottom of a pan, a rocker, a sluice box, a river or stream.

In the **panning** process, the miner gently rotated a saucer-shaped pan partially filled with gravel and water; the lighter gravel washed out with the water, leaving the heavier gold in the bottom of the pan. A **rocker** is a crude machine consisting of a sieve-bottomed hopper on a rocker. The operator rocked the machine as he fed earth and water into the hopper; the earth washed through the sieve onto a slanting apron with ridges, which caught the gold but let the lighter water, gravel, and earth wash out. Sometimes miners joined together to dam and divert rivers and streams during periods of low water flow so they could work the exposed streambeds.

The **Long Tom** consisted of two parts: a 12-foot long wooden trough in which gravel was washed and a riffle box in which gold was collected. **Sluicing** is an improved version of the Long Tom that can process more gravel in less time by introducing a continuous flow of water into a series of open-ended riffle boxes, called sluices, neatly fitted together like a flume. Miners shoveled dirt in from the sides.

A steady supply of water was needed for this process. In 1850, at Coyote Hill, Nevada City, the first ditch was dug to supply water for miners; it was two miles long. Later, water companies built dams and hundreds of miles of ditches and flumes (inclined chutes) to supply water to miners whose claims were far removed from streams.

But this kind of surface or **placer mining** gradually played out and became less profitable. Miners then turned to **hard-rock mining** of gold-rich quartz. They dug deep shafts and tunnels to reach veins or pockets of gold ore. Hard-rock mining required huge investments in equipment to sink shafts, raise ore, and build stamp mills, which crushed the ore. Mining partnerships and companies consolidated in order to finance this expensive process. Some miners used an *arrastra,* a primitive mule-powered device, to crush ore. This was a shallow circular pit with a rotating post to which heavy beams with heavy stone blocks were attached;

mules rotated the beams, crushing the ore mixed with water. Whether the ore was crushed in a mill or an arrastra, the crushed ore was washed in sluices or pans to retrieve the gold.

Another expensive method was **hydraulic mining**. In 1853, in Nevada City, Edward E. Matteson invented a water cannon—a giant rawhide or canvas hose with a nozzle that could shoot a high-powered stream of water into a hillside and dislodge the gold-bearing earth and gravel. An extensive system of reservoirs, flumes, and ditches was built to carry enormous volumes of water and funnel it into smaller and smaller pipelines leading into the nozzle, called a **"monitor"** during and after the Civil War. Hydraulic mining clogged rivers and streams with debris, causing flooding and pollution downstream. As a result of such destruction, a federal judge prohibited this mining method in 1884. Many of the ditches and flumes can still be found today throughout the gold country.

GHOSTS

The placer miners moved from strike to strike along the rivers, streams, and creeks, setting up tent encampments and shanty towns as they rushed to each new discovery. These temporary living quarters were short-lived. Fires, wind, and rain destroyed all but a few of the earliest wooden structures. After the fires, people began to build more substantial buildings of stone, adobe, or brick, and some of these remain—Wells Fargo buildings, Masonic and Odd Fellows and Grange halls, and churches. The "ghosts" of the gold country are the remnants of graveyards, stamp mill foundations, rusted mining machinery, stores, saloons, Chinese-built stone walls and corrals, ailanthus trees (the Chinese Tree of Heaven), and the huge mounds of mined or dredged gravel. They are the visible reminders of the feverish and hopeful history of the 49ers, the men and women who dreamed of and searched for gold.

GOLDEN POPPIES

For the past 150 years Mother Nature has slowly healed many of the mining scars by covering the gold country with trees, shrubs, and wildflowers. Today, many of the ghosts of yesterday are seen along the walks and roads of the Sierra gold country. Where there was once gold in the hills, today there is the golden poppy, California's state flower.

> Poppies, golden Poppies, gleaming in the sun,
> Closing up at evening when the day is done.
> Pride of California, flower of our State
> Growing from the mountains to the Golden Gate.*

---

*"Poppies, Golden Poppies" by Leila France, in *California Wildflower Songs*.

MARIPOSA AREA

Best for Children: Hites Cove (older children), El Portal
Best for Botanists: Hites Cove, Briceburg, SR 49
Best Displays: SR 49, Lake McSwain (early spring), Hites Cove, Briceburg
Best Hikes: Hites Cove (to hotel site), Foresta Falls

HISTORY: In 1806 Gabriel Moraga named a small creek El Arroyo de las Mariposas ("butterflies" in Spanish) because of the many beautiful butterflies he had seen on an exploratory expedition. In 1847 Colonel John C. Frémont purchased part of an original Mexican land grant, called Rancho Las Mariposas, for $3,200 from Juan Bautista Alvarado. Frémont's grant was a "floating grant" with undetermined boundaries at the time of purchase. After rich placer mines were discovered in the Mariposa region in 1849, Frémont "floated" his rancho boundaries to include gold-rich placer areas. Frémont—famous western explorer, California military governor, first California senator, presidential candidate—made his headquarters and built a home in Bear Valley, northwest of Mariposa. Little remains of his presence except for a few streets in the town of Mariposa named for family members—Jessie Street for his wife, Bullion Street for "Old Bullion," Senator Thomas Benton, his father-in-law. In 1863 Frémont sold his rancho for $6 million, but he lost most of the money in a railroad speculation.

When California became the 31st state in the Union in 1850, Mariposa County covered 30,000 square miles, one fifth of the state. It was one of the original 27 counties. In 1852 the county seat was moved from Agua Fria, a ghost site today, to the town of Mariposa. The handsome 1854 county courthouse is the oldest continuously operating courthouse in the state.

East of Mariposa lies Yosemite Valley. Yosemite was explored and named by Major James D. Savage and Dr. Lafayette Bunnell, of the Mariposa Battalion, while pursuing the Yo Semite Indians there in 1851. Savage's first trading post was at the confluence of the South Fork and the Middle Fork of the Merced River. Although Savage had several Native American wives, conflicts with the Indian tribes forced him to move. Savage also had trading posts at Big Oak Flat, originally called Savage's Diggings, and at Fresno Flats, later called Oakhurst, which is the terminus of SR 49, the gold country highway.

West of Mariposa lies the ghost town of Hornitos—"little ovens" in Spanish. The name refers to piles of mud and stone, which look like little ovens but are actually above-ground tombs. Mexican miners, who had been ousted from the nearby town of Quartzburg by American miners, settled the town of Hornitos, although little remains of it except some brick and stone skeleton buildings, such as Domingo Ghirardelli's general store. After selling this business in the late 1850s, Ghirardelli moved to San Francisco to establish the famed Ghirardelli chocolate enterprise. For a short time in 1853,

1

John Studebaker worked here as a blacksmith but soon moved to Hangtown (later Placerville) to build wagons and wheelbarrows for the miners. In 1858 he and his "poke" (a pouch full of earnings) left for South Bend, Indiana, where he established the wagon company that later became the Studebaker Automobile Company.

Farther west, some French sailors who had jumped ship in San Francisco became prospectors in 1849 on the Tuolumne River's rich placers. They called their settlement French Bar. The tiny settlement grew to more than 4,000 people and became a thriving trading center and major river crossing. In 1854 French Bar was renamed La Grange, and from 1856 to 1862 it was the Stanislaus County seat. In 1862 the county seat was moved to Knights Ferry, which, along with the miners' departure for more lucrative strikes elsewhere, contributed to the decline of the town. Today, piles of gravel tailings left from the 1930s dredging operations are the ghosts of La Grange.

MARIPOSA, located at the junction of SRs 140 and 49 on the route to Yosemite, is at a 1,953-foot elevation and has a population of about 1,800. Don't miss the Mariposa County Courthouse, one block east of SR 49 on Bullion Street between Ninth and Tenth streets. The California State Mining and Mineral Museum is worth a stop; 2 miles south of Mariposa on SR 49, at the fairgrounds.

NORTH OF MARIPOSA ALONG SR 49 TO COULTERVILLE

There are marvelous wildflower displays among the rocks, serpentine seeps, and chaparral along SR 49. It is easier and safer to stop at most of these displays while driving north. Note your mileage from Mariposa and be aware of the white county mile markers so you can anticipate when you might want to stop. Pull off to let cars behind you pass; then if you "brake

for flowers" you won't upset anyone. This road usually has good wild-flower displays from mid-March to mid-April.

1 mile north, Bomprezzi Road Tidy-tips, Bird's Eye Gilia, Goldfields, Delphinium, Monkeyflower, Blue Dicks.

Co. marker 21.50 Beautiful swales just north of Mykleoaks.

3 miles north of Mariposa Beautiful calendar photo stop with Meadow-foam.

Bear Valley (site of Frémont's floating land grant) Beautiful pastures.

Co. marker ESA Environmental Sensitive Area, Serpentine Soil. Notice the greenish-blue wet look of the serpentine rock. Pull out at the gate and take a peek, without trespassing, at the *Lewisia rediviva* in the rocks at the top of the road bank. There are Sandwort and Buckwheat here also.

Co. marker 31.50 Rare Stinging Lupine or *Lupinus spectabilis*. Don't pick—it is rare and the hairs are irritating to the skin. The New Year's 1997 floods caused good germination but then the four-month spring drought caused many seedlings to die without blooming. However, the heavy rains of El Niño brought up many seedlings and they put on a wonderful show, to the delight of the author, who feared the demise of Stinging Lupine in this area. It usually grows on the little serpentine mound on the west side of the road but the rare lupine was widespread in this area in 1998 as a result of El Niño.

Shilling Road and SR 49 A splendid wildflower display.

Co. marker 40.50 At the top of the hill. Rare *Fritillaria agrestis*, Caespitose Poppies, and Lupine.

HIGHWAY 140 EAST OF MARIPOSA

BRICEBURG Visitors' Center is located about 20 miles from Mariposa, at the bottom of the long grade below Midpines. Stop at this new visitors' center to pick up a plant list, and then continue across the bridge. This was the site of the Yosemite Valley Railroad, which operated from 1906 to 1945. The William Brice family ran a store that served the mining families, the railroad, tourists, logging interests, and the construction crews who built SR 140. Max Brice, whose father died in 1917, ran the business from the age of fourteen and sold the property in 1989 to BLM. (For more history see Giacomazzi in the bibliography.) BLM has established several camps along this 6-mile stretch of the Merced River. It is a good road for car botanizing or a good place to walk and take pictures of the abundant flowers and enjoy a picnic along the river.

PLANT LIST

Wildflowers Along the Merced River below Briceberg, compiled by the Wildflower Action Committee of Mariposans for Environmentally Responsible Growth (MERG), is available at BLM Briceburg Visitors' Center. (The complete list is not used here.)

Shrubs	Blue Elderberry	*Sambucus caerulea*
and	Buck Brush	*Ceanothus cuneatus*
Trees	Buckeye	*Aesculus californica*
	California Bay	*Umbellularia californica*
	Chamise	*Adenostoma fasciculatum*
	Coffeeberry	*Rhamnus californica*
	Deer Brush	*Ceanothus integerrimus*
	Flowering Ash	*Fraxinus dipetala*
	Mountain Mahogany	*Cercocarpus betuloides*
	Poison Oak	*Rhus diversiloba*
	Squaw Bush	*Rhus trilobata*
	Toyon	*Heteromeles arbutifolia*
	White Alder	*Alnus rhombifolia*
	Yawning Penstemon	*Keckiella breviflorus*
	Yerba Santa	*Eriodictyon californicum*
White	Caterpillar Phacelia	*Phacelia cicutaria*
	Chickweed	*Stellaria media*
	Dudleya	*Dudleya cymosa*
	Fairy Lantern/Globe Lily	*Calochortus albus*
	Lacepod	*Thysanocarpus curvipes*
	Jimsonweed	*Datura meteloides*
	Jewel Flower, Creamy	*Streptanthus tortuosus*
	Mariposa Lily	*Calochortus venustus*
	Milkmaids	*Dentaria californica*
	Miner's Lettuce	*Montia perfoliata*
	Popcorn Flower	*Plagiobothrys nothofulvus*
	Soap Plant	*Chlorogalum pomeridianum*
	Sierra Manroot/Wild Cucumber	*Marah horridus*
	White Nemophila	*Nemophila heterophylla*
	White Whorl Lupine	*Lupinus densiflorus*
	Woodland Star	*Lithophragma affine*
Yellow	Blazing Star	*Mentzelia lindleyi*
	Foothill Lomatium	*Lomatium utriculatum*
	Golden Brodiaea/Pretty Face	*Triteleia scabra*
	Goldfields	*Lasthenia californica*
	Gum Weed	*Grindelia camporum*
	Monkeyflower	*Mimulus guttatus*
	Pincushion Flower	*Chaenactus glabriuscula*
	Pseudobahia	*Pseudobahia heermannii*
Orange	California Poppy	*Eschscholzia californica*
	Caespitose Poppy	*Eschscholzia caespitosa*
	Fiddleneck	*Amsinckia intermedia*
Pink to	Manzanita	*Arctostaphylos viscida* ssp. *mariposa*
Red	Redbud Tree	*Cercis occidentalis*
	Clarkia, Bilobed	*Clarkia biloba*
	Clarkia, Elegant	*Clarkia unguiculata*
	Clarkia, Winecup	*Clarkia purpurea*
	Farewell to Spring	*Clarkia dudleyana*
	Filaree/Storksbill	*Erodium cicutarium*
	Indian Paintbrush	*Castilleja applegatei*

Indian Pink	*Silene californica*
Jewel Flower	*Streptanthus tortuosus*
Purple Milkweed	*Asclepias cordifolia*
Purple Owl's Clover	*Orthocarpus purpurascens*
Red Maids	*Calandrinia ciliata* var. *menziesii*
Shooting Star	*Dodecatheon hendersonii*
Twining Brodiaea	*Dichelostemma volubile*
Whitestem Hedgenettle	*Stachys albens*

Blue to Lavender

Baby Blue Eyes	*Nemophila menziesii*
Bentham's Lupine / Spider Lupine	*Lupinus benthamii*
Bird's Eye Gilia	*Gilia tricolor*
Ball-Headed Gilia / Globe Gilia	*Gilia capitata*
Bush Lupine / Silver Bush Lupine	*Lupinus albifrons*
Fiesta Flower	*Pholistoma auritum*
Foothill Penstemon	*Penstemon heterophylla*
Hansen's Delphinium	*Delphinium hansenii*
Harvest Brodiaea	*Brodiaea elegans*
Ithuriel's Spear	*Triteleia laxa*
Miniature Lupine	*Lupinus bicolor*

BULL CREEK ROAD from Briceburg to SR 120 (15-20 miles) is not for the timid. When crossing the Briceburg Bridge, look up at the switchbacks. The road is actually well graded and peaceful, but be sure to have plenty of gas, courage, and a detailed map of the area between SR 120 and SR 140. The flowers can be seen easily from the car (men like this adventure). Paintbrush, Pseudobahia, and Bush Poppies are on the road banks, and there are fields of Baby Blue Eyes and a pretty meandering creek suitable for a picnic, once you are out of the Merced gorge. The Old Yosemite Road, Moore Creek Road, and Greeley Hill meet Bull Creek Road in the vicinity of Bower Cave, where there is a nice flower walk down the North Fork of the Merced River. This area is discussed in the Groveland chapter.

HITES COVE TRAIL starts at the confluence of the Merced River and its South Fork, and is one of the best wildflower hikes in the Sierra foothills from late March to early May. This is Redbud heaven. The trail has spectacular displays of Caespitose Poppies, Bird's Eye Gilia, Tidy-tips, Chinese Houses, Farewell to Spring, and much more, making it a delight for all. Park opposite Sisóchi Gallery (formerly Savage's Trading Post) along the river; then go into the store to register for a walk on the trail and get something to drink, film, and a copy of *Wildflowers of the Hites Cove Trail* by Steve Botti and Ann Mendershausen. Watch for orioles in the vicinity of the store. The trail is better in the morning because of afternoon heat in the canyon. The former hotel site at Hites Cove is about a 4-mile walk. There is a nice picnic area of big flat rocks on the river a little more than 2 miles along the trail, and you will have seen most of the flower species by the time you reach river level. **No plant list—***buy the book and* *help the Merced Canyon Committee!* The book is very good and has pictures and a checklist. If you can't get the book the Briceburg plant list will help.

EL PORTAL has a walk behind the school that leads up to the ridge just west of the school. You'll see beautiful wildflowers on the way up the hill. There used to be a trail up and behind the ridge above the school, but except for the stile up in the saddle way off to the right of the school, the trail has pretty much disappeared over the years and the rocks are over-grown with Poison Oak. Driving down from the school, turn right, go to the west side of the same ridge, and watch for Harlequin and Spider Lupine in the gutter. As you near the waste-treatment plant, you come to a fire road you can walk up to see different flowers than those on the school side of the ridge. Look for Yellow Pincushion Flower. Many of the plants are the same as on the Briceburg list except that you are in them, not walking along a road. Harlequin Lupine or *Lupinus stiversii* is not on the Briceburg list.

Moss Canyon can be reached by driving to the top of the road beyond the school. A fire road leads up onto the ridge to your left and into Moss Canyon. A boardwalk runs along the creek (unless floods have carried it away). Poppies, Lupines, and other wildflowers that like rocky areas are on the hot slope as you enter the canyon. How many shades of green do you see on the hill across the canyon? This was the question the teacher of a watercolor class asked at this exact location. It was fun to try and put them on paper. A forestry professor would ask the students to name the plant species that make up the mosaic of green across the canyon (an actual question in another location).

Foresta Falls, along old Foresta Road, are located behind the little town of El Portal. This road used to be open to cars but now is restricted to bikers and hikers. Crane Creek can be heard about 2 miles up the road and the waterfalls about 3.5 miles up the road. Park in town near the train display. You will enjoy walking past the quaint cottages with their pretty gardens.

WEST OF MARIPOSA

HORNITOS LOOP. The drive down the **Old Toll Road at Mt. Bullion** goes through a habitat called hard chaparral, which consists of fire-adapted species. This particular hard chaparral is composed of Man-zanita, Chamise, and Bush Poppy. Stump sprouting is the way these shrubs respond to fire. Or the seeds may lie dormant on the soil until there is enough heat to crack them and allow moisture to enter and growth to begin. Often an area like this has an understory of bulbous plants such as *Calochortus, Zigadenus,* and *Brodiaea* just waiting for a fire to burn off the shrubs and allow the bulbs enough sunlight to bloom. This is happening now along SR 120 above Moccasin as the result of a fire a few years ago. Soon the chaparral will have grown back enough to shade the bulbs. It will be interesting to see whether the plants that have seeds that germinate as a result of a fire, as with some Ceanothus species, or the plants that sprout, such as Chamise, will outcompete the other plants for sunlight. Additional plants along this road are Monkeyflower, Ithuriel's Spear, Vetch, Tree of Heaven, and Fiddleneck. Hornitos has lots of very picturesque ruins. You will want to spend some time there reading the historical notices. Leaving Hornitos on J16, the Bear Valley Road, look in the trees along the creek for heron nests. On the north side of the road you might see the fairly unusual Oakleaf Gooseberry, or *Ribes quercetorum*. There is a beautiful drive of 10 to 15 miles to Lake McSwain on the Hornitos Road.

LAKE McSWAIN AND LAKE McCLURE have absolutely beautiful wildflower displays on the rocky road banks. This is perhaps the earliest blooming good plant display in the Sierra Gold Country, because of the low elevation and the dark, southwest-facing rocky banks. Watch for the Meadowfoam below the road just after the entry station. Whorled Lupine, Spider Lupine, several Blue Brodiaea, Fiddleneck, Poppies, and Chinese Houses are a few of the plants to be seen here. Use the Briceburg plant list (pages 4-5) to help determine others. The road is wide and very peaceful early in the year so it is a good place to car-botanize.

   Directions: From Turlock on SR 99, take J17 east and turn left on SR 59. In Snelling 59 becomes Merced Falls Road. When Merced Falls Road turns left, go straight, following the signs to Lake McSwain. From Merced on SR 99, it is 27 miles on the G Street Snelling Road to Lake McSwain. The drive from Lake McSwain to Hornitos is between 10 and 15 miles along Hornitos Road (J16) to an interesting town with photogenic ruins.

BEN HUR ROAD is located 2 miles south of Mariposa, near the fairgrounds. This 17-mile back road has beautiful rock outcrops and rock walls (generally it was the Chinese who did this fine rock work in the 1850s and 1860s). Creeks cross the road in several places and there are canyons and good valley views. The flowers include many of the usual lower-foothill varieties, such as Popcorn Flower, Fiddleneck, several species of blue Brodiaea, Baby Blue Eyes, and Chinese Houses, to name a few. When Ben Hur Road ends, you can go right on the unpaved Preston Road, which becomes Raynor Ranch Road to Le Grand, and west on Le Grand Road to SR 99. Or you can go left 7 miles to Raymond, which was once the end of the Southern Pacific spur line that took tourists to Yosemite. In Raymond take Road 600, right on Road 603, which becomes Avenue 26, and go west into Chowchilla. Have a map of the area, plenty of gas, food, and water. The back road will take about 3 hours, depending on how many plant and photo stops are needed.

GROVELAND AREA

Best for Children: *North Fork of Merced River, South Fork of Tuolumne River, Hetch Hetchy*
Best for Botanists: *North Fork of Merced River, Marshes Flat Road, Preston Falls Trail*
Best Displays: *Marshes Flat Road, Preston Falls Trail, Hetch Hetchy*
Best Hikes: *Preston Falls Trail, Cherry Creek Intake, Hetch Hetchy*

HISTORY: In late 1849 or early 1850, Mexican miners found rich placer deposits in Groveland and settled there. Groveland originally was called First Garrotte (which in Spanish means execution by strangulation or hanging). The name originated from stories about a much-publicized hanging that circulated through the mining camps. So rich were the gravel deposits in this area that at first mining claims were limited to a space ten feet square. In 1851 they were extended to fifty yards along a creek. Covetous American miners drove out the Mexicans and the name was changed to Groveland in 1875, to give the citizens a more respectable post office address.

West of Groveland is Big Oak Flat, where Major James Savage—trader, miner, and soldier—established a trading post in 1849 called Savage's Diggings. When he left a year later, the camp was renamed Big Oak Flat, for a huge oak tree believed to be the largest in California. Unfortunately, miners killed the tree by digging gold out of its roots. Placer mining in Groveland, Deer Flat, and Big Oak Flat yielded an estimated $25 million.

Farther west, SR 120 follows the steep old wagon-train road of the Gold Rush down Priest Grade, descending 1,575 feet in less than 2 miles to Moccasin Creek, once a rich placer area. Piles of rocks beside stream beds testify to the 49ers' backbreaking work wresting gold from the gravel. Today, the Moccasin Creek Power Plant, part of the Hetch Hetchy Aqueduct,

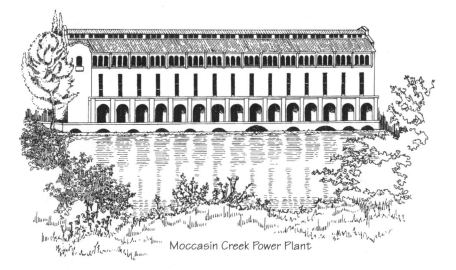

Moccasin Creek Power Plant

8

straddles the creek. In 1913 the City of San Francisco, by an act of Congress, acquired the water rights, and by 1923 the Tuolumne River was dammed, its water filling the Hetch Hetchy Valley at the western end of the Grand Canyon of the Tuolumne River. Damming the Tuolumne River west of SR 49 also formed Don Pedro Reservoir in 1923. The dam was reconstructed in 1971. In dry years, as the water level in Don Pedro Reservoir drops in late summer, the ghostly remnants of an old mining camp, Jacksonville, appear along the banks of the reservoir.

GROVELAND, located on SR 120 to Yosemite, is a small town with wonderful recreation nearby and good restaurants. People from the Bay Area have retired in Groveland, and many activities are available. Wayside Park, on the north side of the road, was the site of the Hetch Hetchy Railroad yard. The Sierra Club meets there for its weekly hike.

WEST OF GROVELAND

DON PEDRO RESERVOIR, MOCCASIN RECREATION AREA, just off SR 120 northwest of the fish hatchery, is easy to find and has a nice picnic area and a trail with good flowers. The trees in the area are Blue Oak, Black Oak, and Foothill Pine. Shrubs include Coffeeberry, Toyon, and Poison Oak. Some of the wildflowers are White Fairy Lantern, Miniature Lupine, Sky Lupine, Ithuriel's Spear, Caespitose Poppy, Purple Sanicle, Popcorn Flower, Goldfields, Plectritis, Lomatium, and Fiesta Flower.

MARSHES FLAT ROAD is off SR 49 opposite the Moccasin Power-house. The road climbs steeply for about 1.5 miles up to the flat. Many people prefer to walk the road. The most spectacular display of flowers occurs within the first few miles off SR 49. Once you reach the farmhouse, you have passed the best displays. Indian Pinks are the most notable and plentiful flower on these road banks. Some of the other spectacular road-bank plants are Tarweed, Chinese Houses, Clarkia, and Spider Lupine. Ithuriel's Spear, White Brodiaea, and Royal Delphinium are spectacular growing together as the road begins to level. The meadows in the flat are white with Meadowfoam until the grass gets too high. The countryside is lovely for the 9 miles to SR 132.

Directions: Just off SR 120 on SR 49, across from the Moccasin Powerhouse, Marshes Flat Road leaves 49 going west uphill. About 8 miles later Marshes Flat Road becomes Blanchard Road, then turns left onto Granite Springs Road, which ends at SR 132, the Old Yosemite Road between La Grange and Coulterville. This looks like a nice bike road heading west from the top of Marshes Flat if a shuttle could be arranged.

PRIEST-COULTERVILLE ROAD is a beautiful wildflower road that leaves SR 120 at the top of Priest Grade and ends in Coulterville 10 miles later. Some of the showy flowers along the road are Valley Tassels, Spider Lupine, Hog Fennel, Miniature Lupine, Popcorn Flower, Shooting Stars, Goldfields, Buttercups, Fiddleneck, Ithuriel's Spear or *Brodiaea laxa*, Blue Dicks, and Bird's Eye Gilia.

Don't miss the historic Moccasin Powerhouse at the bottom of Priest Grade, at the intersection of SR 120 and 49. Good photos can be taken from SR 49 across the water at sunset.

LA GRANGE OLD BRIDGE WALK trailhead is right across the street from the store in La Grange. Walk down to the bridge and then go upriver. This is a good early-season walk. Plants include Onions, Chinese Houses, Caterpillar Phacelia, Blue Dicks, Clarkia, White Shooting Stars, and Fiesta Flower. The hike joins an old road that used to be part of a park and it ends at a private farm, so you will have to retrace your steps when you reach the farm.

The drive from La Grange on the Old Yosemite Road, SR 132, to Coulterville is lovely. The 23-mile drive goes past Lake Don Pedro and Lake McClure reservoirs. It is beautiful country, with scattered fields of flowers, but the road has some tricky corners so take it easy. Just as you approach SR 49, notice the unusual road cut and rock outcrops. The green rock is mariposite. You often see it in monuments or added to walls.

NORTH FORK OF MERCED RIVER OR DIANA'S POOLS NEAR BOWERS CAVE This 1.2-mile walk past waterfalls and wildflowers is a nice area for children because the river is small. There is also good fishing. The trail starts on the south side of the road just before the bridge. Half a mile into the trail are some waterfalls, and just beyond is the confluence with Bean Creek. Walk a little way up Bean Creek for another set of waterfalls. The special plants of this walk are Skullcap, or *Scutellaria angustifolia, Adiantum jordanii, Fraxinus dipetala, Lupine stiversii, Scutellaria angustifolia,* and *Silene californica.*

Directions: Take Moore Creek or Buck Meadows Road (2S05), across the highway from Buck Meadows General Store, south about 6 miles to the T intersection with the Greeley Hills Road. (Have you noticed the Indian Pink along the road?) Turn left and continue toward Bower Cave. In about 0.4 mile there is a concrete bridge. Park on the left side of the road, cross the road, and go through the gate. An alternative road, especially if you're returning to the Central Valley, is to follow Greeley Hill down to Coulterville on SR 49.

RAINBOW POOL, SOUTH FORK OF TUOLUMNE RIVER CASCADES Rainbow Pool is a wonderful stop for a swim and a picnic on the way to Yosemite when the weather is warm. It is a good flower stop in the spring as well. Our trail follows a service road, a little over a mile round trip, for access ports to the Hetch Hetchy Aqueduct, which is located below the pool. Before the 1997 New Year's flood you could park at Rainbow Pool, cross a bridge over the waterfalls, and walk down to the service road, passing under SR 120, but the bridge was washed out and may not be replaced. This is a very exciting walk along the cascading South Fork of the Tuolumne, but don't bring pets or children. The road, which has been damaged by floods (it includes a little rock-hopping), ends at the confluence with the Middle Fork of the Tuolumne. Rainbow Pool used to be the site of the Cliff House Inn and the tollgate for the Old Big Oak Flat Road. There are two species of Clarkia, Lacepod, Chinese Houses, Sierra Plum, Mountain Mahogany, Flowering Ash, Buck Brush, White Nemophila, Indian Pink, Popcorn Flower, Western Buttercup, and Shooting Star.

Directions: Drive on SR 120 about 13 miles east of Groveland or 2.75 miles east of Buck Meadows Lodge. Just before crossing the high bridge, turn right through the green gate and drive down to Rainbow Pool. If the bridge has not been repaired or the green gate is closed, hop back in your car and drive over the highway bridge, turn left on Cherry Lake Road, take another left to the parking lot above the river, and walk down the access road. Don't miss seeing Rainbow Pool or taking the walk down to the confluence.

SOUTH FORK OF TUOLUMNE RIVER is a peaceful 1.5-mile section of the river. The trail is 3 miles round trip with little elevation change. This is a popular fishing spot. The trail starts at the gate of an old, unmaintained road along the north bank of the river and ends at a large primitive camping area after about a mile. Little creeklets provide extra water for Columbine and Azalea. A surprising plant in a forest opening is Five Spot Nemophila. There are also Lupine and Woodland Star. Continue beyond the campground until you come to a fork in the trail. Take the left fork (the right one ends at the river), until you cross a creek and reach some big flat rocks that are ideal for a picnic

Directions: Drive on SR 120 8.5 miles east of Buck Meadows to the concrete bridge of the South Fork (about a mile beyond the Yosemite Mini Mart). Just before the bridge, on the left, is a closed green gate. Park here.

PRESTON FALLS TRAIL, 8.4 miles round trip, starts at a 2,400-foot elevation and has a high point of 2,700 feet. The varied habitats of meadows, riparian, rocks, and forests produce wonderful flower diversity; add to that the distraction of ghosts, ruins, waterfalls, and fishing pools and the hike does not seem that far. About 2.5 miles up the trail the river passes through a narrow black rock canyon and the trail runs along its upper edge. When you see the Preston house, listen for the evening grosbeak; perhaps Mrs. Preston grew Sunflowers for its ancestors. The house is near the falls. It took 3½ hours for one group of intense flower followers to get to the falls, but it was quicker coming back. This is my favorite trail in the Southern Mines country.

PLANT LIST: mid-April to mid-May

Aesculus californica	California Buckeye
Apocynum androsaemifolium	Dogbane
Arctostaphylos viscida	Sticky Manzanita
Artemisia douglasiana	Wormwood, Mugwort
Asclepias cordifolia	Milkweed
Asclepias fascicularis	Narrow-leaf Milkweed
Calandrinia ciliata var. *menziesii*	Red Maids
Calochortus venustus	Mariposa Lily
Ceanothus cuneatus	Buck Brush
Cercocarpus betuloides	Mountain Mahogany
Chamaebatia foliolosa	Mountain Misery
Clematis lasiantha	Virgin's Bower
Collinsia tinctoria	White Chinese Houses
Dichelostemma capitata	Blue Dicks
Dryopteris arguta	Wood Fern
Dudleya cymosa	Dudleya
Erigeron foliosus	Fleabane
Eriodictyon californicum	Yerba Santa
Eriophyllum lanatum	Woolly Sunflower
Eschscholzia lobbii	Frying Pans Poppy
Fritillaria micrantha	Brown Bells
Gilia tricolor	Bird's Eye Gilia
Helenium biglovii	Sneezeweed
Hypericum anagalloides	Tinker's Penny
Keckiella breviflora	Yawning Penstemon
Linanthus dichotomus	Evening Snow
Linanthus montanus	Mustang-Clover
Lithophragma affine	Woodland Star
Lotus humistratus	Hill Lotus
Lotus scoparius	Deer Weed
Lupinus albifrons	Silver Bush Lupine
Lupinus benthamii	Spider Lupine
Lupinus bicolor	Miniature Lupine
Lupinus stiversii	Harlequin Lupine
Mimulus guttatus	Yellow Monkeyflower
Mimulus moschatus	Musk Monkeyflower
Montia perfoliata	Miner's Lettuce
Nemophila heterophylla	White Nemophila
Nemophila maculata	Five Spot Nemophila
Nemophila menziesii	Baby Blue Eyes
Orthocarpus purpurascens	Purple Owl's Clover
Phacelia cicutaria	Caterpillar Phacelia
Philadelphus lewisii	California Mock Orange
Pityrogramma triangularis	Goldback Fern
Plectritis ciliosa	Valerian
Rhamnus crocea var. *ilicifolia*	Redberry

Rhododendron occidentale	Western Azalea
Sambucus caerulea	Elderberry
Silene californica	Indian Pink
Tauschia hartwegii	Hartweg's Tauschia

Directions: Drive east from Groveland on SR 120. Shortly after you pass Buck Meadows, the vista turnout, and the long bridge at Rainbow Falls picnic area, turn left onto Cherry Lake Road and follow it for 5 miles to a signed road junction at the edge of the Tuolumne River canyon. Take the left fork down to Early Intake Powerhouse (3.5 miles). Cross the bridge and turn right, up past the Kirkwood Powerhouse, until you come to the trailhead parking.

CHERRY CREEK INTAKE TRAIL is an absolutely beautiful hike, with the white water of Cherry Creek below you and lots of beautiful flowers on rocky cliffs beside and above you. Originally this trail may have been a flume, and when the dams were built on Cherry Lake and Lake Eleanor the trail was probably redesigned to aid in construction of a tunnel that carries water for power. There are two adits (that were used to bring waste rock out of the tunnels within the mountain) along the trail, several creeks cross it, a small waterfall falls onto it—with a piece of metal over the trail so walkers won't get wet. What luxury!

A few of the more noticeable plants are Hartweg's Iris, Alum Root, or *Heuchera micrantha*, Indian Pinks, Wild Ginger, and Naked Broomrape, or *Orobanche uniflora*, which is parasitic on the Sedum. It is about 2 miles round trip to the intake house, which seems to be in bad shape as a result of the 1997 floods. One access to the river is by going down the steps of the intake shed to a slab of granite beside a roaring creek that runs for about 100 yards in a sluice-box-like canyon. Or you can go back up to the trail, upstream past the weir, to some rocks that are a safer place for a picnic. Stay away from the water; the chute below the weir looks deadly. Look uphill to your right and you can see a pile of rock that was removed through an adit at that level. If you are curious you can drive up and walk in about half a mile to the adit. There are good canyon views.

Directions: Follow Preston Falls directions. After crossing the bridge by the Kirkwood Powerhouse, turn left and continue for a mile or so, then take a side road on the right leading uphill. If you come to the Cherry Creek Bridge you have just missed the turn. Go up the dirt road (#1N45) and take the left turn downhill. There is a small parking area near a fig tree. The tree surely has more to do with flume ghosts than with power-plant ghosts of the 1920s. If you want to see the upper adit, just continue up the dirt road a little more than a half mile to the parking area and walk a short way to the adit.

CARLON FALLS is reached by a 2.5 mile round trip walk through a

White Fir and Cedar forest, along the South Fork of the Tuolumne River, to an impressive waterfall. The trail is fairly level except for a few detours uphill to avoid log jams and slides from the 1997 floods. A few downed trees, as well, make this trail into a par course. At times the trail runs right beside the river. If you are a fisherman, it is torture to be without a rod when you can see the fish swimming against the sandy bottom. The former inn, whose remaining foundation is being gobbled up by a Cedar root, must have catered to fishermen. Our friend Bruce Howard tells of a mechanic at Carl Inn in 1926 who repaired Howard's car. He said there was also a little golf course here. A few of the botanical treasures along the trail are Trillium, Azalea (usually late May bloom), yellow *Viola lobata* and *Viola glabella* or Stream Violet, Columbine, Bleeding Heart, and Snow Plant. An added bonus, if the violets are still in bloom, is finding Morels and Yellow Coral Fungus.

Directions: Drive 10.5 miles east of Buck Meadows on SR 120 and turn left onto Evergreen Road. The South Fork of the Tuolumne River is within a mile. Pass the campground and cross to the far side of the bridge to reach the trailhead.

HETCH HETCHY AREA at an elevation of 3,812 feet has the feeling of Yosemite with its granite walls and waterfalls. The trail (which blooms in late May) to spectacular Wapama Falls, which drop 1,400 feet on the north shore of the lake, is a round trip of 6 miles with a 200-foot elevation gain. Cross the dam and the road tunnel to the Tueeulala and Wapama falls. Often the trail is closed at the falls due to high water. This same trail continues on to Rancheria Creek, bad bears, and the high country. Hetch Hetchy is derived from an Indian word meaning quail.

Directions: Take SR 120 to Evergreen Road (1 mile west of the Yosemite Park entry station). Along the 7.5 miles to Camp Mather there are beautiful meadows filled with Tarweed (*Madia sp.*), Lupine, and Yampa (*Perideridia sp.*). Turn right on Hetch Hetchy Road, where you change habitats almost immediately to rock gardens and canyon views for the next 9 miles. Once in a while there is a spectacular view of the reservoir with its granite walls, huge lake, and two waterfalls.

SONORA AREA

Best for Children: Columbia, Knights Ferry, Red Hill Road (Hike)
Best for Botanists: Red Hill Road, Wards Ferry
Best Displays: Red Hill Road, Knights Ferry, Wards Ferry, Westside Railroad Grade
Best Hike: Red Hill Road

HISTORY: In the summer of 1848 Mexican miners from Sonora, Mexico, settled the area known as Sonoran Camp, later shortened to Sonora. Americans heard of the rich diggings and arrived in early 1849. By the fall, thousands of Argonauts (gold-seeking men of '49) from Central and South America, Spain, China, England, Hawaii, France, and the "states" had set up their tents and camps on the hills and were mining the rich placers. The camp became the wildest and richest of the Southern Mines.

Sonora became the county seat when Tuolumne County was formed in 1850, and it served as a supply and trading center for miners on the road south. In 1850 Mexican miners ousted from Sonora by American miners discovered gold in Columbia. These diggings were extremely rich. Again the Mexicans were ousted, and the camp became known as Hildreths Diggings, then American Camp, and then Columbia, "Gem of the Southern Mines," on April 29, 1850. The town was incorporated in May of 1854.

In 1851 the miners organized to provide a steady supply of water for washing the gravels in order to increase production. They formed the Tuolumne County Water Company, which built a ditch that eventually extended to the South Fork of the Stanislaus. With a steady supply of water ensured, the camp's gold production averaged $100,000 per week. Although the mines began to decline by the early 1870s, it is estimated that the area produced $87 million in gold (worth today about $1.26 billion). In 1854 a fire destroyed the town, but brick and stone buildings with iron shutters and doors quickly replaced the old wooden ones. Some of them still stand today. In 1945 the State of California created Columbia State Historic Park to preserve and restore what was left of Columbia's golden years.

Chinese Camp was a placer mining center settled by Chinese miners in 1849. The camp was a haven for Chinese who had been cast out of other mining camps or had been employed for a pittance by Englishmen to work in their mines. In its heyday, the population was nearly 5,000. In 1856 two rival Tongs (secret Chinese societies) had a disagreement, and a fullscale Tong war ensued, with over 2,000 participants. Fewer than 10 were killed or wounded. Today, the Chinese Tree of Heaven is evidence that Chinese once mined this sleepy little townlet.

SONORA, at an elevation of 1,825 feet, is the business and shopping center for the many tiny towns located within 30 miles. Modesto and Stockton, much larger towns in the Valley, have fog in the winter and heat

in the summer, making Sonora a pleasant alternative. The population of about 4,200 and all the people coming into town for supplies lead to much congestion on the narrow streets. A mall is located just southeast of town, and through traffic to the Sierra and points north such as Columbia is somewhat diverted from the downtown area. The Tuolumne County Courthouse and some other structures from the Gold Rush days remain as museums and places of business. There is a Heritage Home Tour of some of the Victorian houses.

NORTH OF SONORA

COLUMBIA STATE PARK is a well-preserved Gold Rush town which children really enjoy. There is a pretty garden near the ice cream store with a beautiful Lady Banks Rose covering one side of the building. Every year the town has a Victorian Easter parade and Easter egg hunt. Just northeast of the town, uphill from the school, you will find the Karen Bakerville Smith Memorial Trail, a 40-minute self-guiding loop trail.

Directions: Drive 2 to 3 miles north of Sonora on SR 49, then right on Parrotts Ferry Road. Follow the signs to Columbia.

WEST OF SONORA

KNIGHTS FERRY bloom time is mid-March until the soil dries out. The displays of Poppies, Lupines, Popcorn Flower, and Fiesta Flower are absolutely beautiful in early spring. The Visitor Center is loaded with information, pamphlets, and maps. There are picnic tables and swimming holes. Photographers will strike it rich with the bright yellow-orange Poppies and Silver Shrub Lupine in front of the old covered bridge. History lovers enjoy the ruins of Tulloch's Flour Mill as well as the bridge, which dates back to 1863. An older bridge, started in 1857, was swept away in the 1862 January floods. Dr. William Knight and his partner, James Vantine, operated a ferry here in 1848, charging as much as $200 for a crossing.

This is a flower chaser's paradise, with a few unusual plants such as Button Willow, a shrub with ball-like flowerheads found fairly near the water in late May and June, and bluish Fiesta Flower, *Pholistoma auritum,* on the main trail up in the rock and oaks beyond the covered bridge. A short wide trail leads upstream from the covered bridge, past beautiful swales of blue, yellow, white, and lavender wildflowers. The picnic tables in this area are shaded by oaks and nestled among huge boulders. In late March and early April, the Fiesta Flower is found here, as well as the sweet sounds of the orange-crowned warbler. A path through a gateway of boulders invites river exploration. Across the river is a concrete aqueduct that comes out of Tulloch Reservoir a few miles upstream. This area is operated by the U.S. Army Corps of Engineers and Stanislaus River Parks, (209) 881-3517.

Directions: Knights Ferry is 12 miles east of Oakdale, just off SR 120. It is on the north side of SR 120 and is well signed. It has two parking areas, and a Visitor Center on the north side of the Stanislaus River. The Yosemite AAA map shows lots of alternative roads home, one of the prettier being through Copperopolis and down SR 4. Red Hill Road off the La Grange Road is a must-see in spring and only about 15 minutes up SR 120 from Knights Ferry. An alternative road to Red Hill is the pretty drive on Rock River Road and Willms Road (see page 21), which starts just across SR 120 from the Knights Ferry Road and ends at Green Springs Road; a right turn on Green Springs ends at the La Grange Road. A right turn onto La Grange and you are almost at Red Hill.

TWO MILE BAR is about half a mile below Tulloch Reservoir Road off the westbound-only lanes of SR 120. This is a nice location for a picnic, fishing, or rafting. Enjoy a slow drive down the Two Mile Bar Road, where you'll see blue Ithuriel's Spear, Buttercups, Fiddleneck, Yellow Monkeyflower, Goldfields, and Meadowfoam. A Tree of Heaven, *Ailanthus altissima,* grows near the flume on the trail down to the river. There is a nice view of the river with the black bluffs above it. Wouldn't it be wonderful if the Palm Tree could tell us the history of this site? There is a huge bed of Fiesta Flower underneath the Blue Oak near the former home site.

TULLOCH RESERVOIR ROAD is a quick, beautiful flower stop in an interesting geological area. Admire the tableland across the river and keep in mind that these flat tablelands were once rivers of lava in a canyon. The former canyon walls and surrounding land eroded, leaving the hard black volcanic rock. As the road approaches the canyon, the road banks are full of flowers.

White	Yellow	Pink
Meadowfoam	Monkeyflower	Tomcat Clover
Woodland Star	Fiddleneck	Chinese Houses
Caterpillar Phacelia	Mule Ears	Twining Brodiaea
Jewel Flower	Tarweed	Cranesbill
Whorled Lupine	**Orange**	**Blue**
Popcorn Flower	Sticky Monkeyflower	Blue Dicks, Ithuriel's Spear
Lace Pod	Caespitose Poppy	Spider Lupine, Sky Lupine
Valley Tassels		Fiesta Flower

Directions: Tulloch Road is about 4 miles below the O'Byrnes Ferry Road, where SR 108 and SR 120 are totally divided. It is best approached driving west; crossing the westbound lanes is tricky. Once on the little Tulloch Road, it is about 1.5 miles to Flower Curves. This is also the access to Table Mountain. It is not posted, however, and may be private land, so further information is not included.

RED HILL ROAD is one of the all-time great wildflower spots in California, as long as you don't get there too late in the spring. It is very rocky, so the area dries out quickly except where the serpentine seeps occur. Mid-March and the first week or two in April are usually good, though sometimes the season is longer. Notice the old stone corral just as you turn onto Red Hill Road from the La Grange Road. Soon there is a lavender mist on the ground created by thousands of Bird's Eye Gilia, along with a bright yellow road border of Monkeyflowers. At the top of the hill, if your timing is right, there is brilliant yellow *Coreopsis stillmanii* contrasting with the soft gray of *Ceanothus cuneatus*. If you are too late for the big flower displays, stop in the parking lot near the bathrooms and look for pink *Lewisia rediviva* on the serpentine (greenish rock) mound. When the creek crosses the road, look for Five Spot growing on the uphill side near the fences. This is BLM property and they have a superb plant list, (916) 985-4474. Both BLM and the California Native Plant Society are considering putting in a nature trail.

Trails: In early spring take one of the loop trails near the kiosk and bathrooms. *Be sure to check the map at the kiosk before your hike;* this area is extensive, with few landmarks other than views of the distant Don Pedro Lake. The Soaproot Ridge Trail will take you onto the ridge behind the parking area and bathrooms, where you have the option of taking the overlook loop (the plants are not as varied), which returns to the Ridge Trail in the valley to the southeast. Continue on the Ridge Trail over several ridges with creeks and wildflowers until you come to an important trail intersection, at the most likely picnic spot (about an hour from the start). A nice creek, a barbed-wire fence on your left, and a *right turn* onto the Verbena Trail will help you identify this important junction. The Verbena Trail follows the creek to the right (it has Spice Bush and a fancy

18

horse trough along the creek) and intersects the Old Stage Road Trail. *Take the right fork on Old Stage Road Trail to return to the parking lot.* The left fork of the Old Stage Road Trail will eventually take you to the Six Bit Trail, which with a right turn would take you down to Old Don Pedro Road. This is a fairly long walk and would need a shuttle.

PLANT LIST: mid-March to mid-April

White	*Brodiaea hyacinthina*	White Brodiaea
	Calochortus albus	Fairy Lantern
	Calochortus superbus	Mariposa Lily
	Calystegia occidentalis	Morning-glory
	Ceanothus cuneatus	Buck Brush
	Chlorogalum pomeridianum	Soap Plant
	Clematis lasiantha	Virgin's Bower
	Collinsia tinctoria	White Chinese Houses
	Lupinus densiflora	White Whorled Lupine
	Minuartia californica	Sandwort
	Navarretia squarrosa	Skunkweed
	Nemophila maculata	Five Spot Nemophila
	Meconella californica	Meconella
	Orthocarpus attenuatus	Valley Tassels
	Phacelia cicutaria	Caterpillar Phacelia
	Thysanocarpus curvipes	Lacepod, Fringepod
Yellow-Orange	*Eschscholzia caespitosa*	Caespitose, Tufted Poppy
	Eschscholzia californica	California Poppy
	Eschscholzia lobbii	Frying Pans Poppy
	Mimulus aurantiacus	Sticky Monkeyflower
	Dudleya cymosa	Live-Forever
	Platystemon californicus	Cream Cups
	Blennosperma nanum	Blennosperma Nanum
	Chaenactis glabriuscula	Yellow-flowered Chaenactis
	Coreopsis stillmanii	Coreopsis
	Eriophyllum lanatum	Woolly Sunflower
	Grindelia camporum	Gum Weed
	Hypericum perforatum	Klammath Weed
	Lasthenia californica	Goldfields
	Layia fremontii	Fremont's Tidy-Tip
	Lomatium utriculatum	Foothill Lomatium
	Madia elegans	Tarweed
	Mimulus guttatus	Yellow Monkeyflower
	Orthocarpus erianthus	Butter and Eggs
	Parvisedum pumilum	Little Sedum
	Pseudobahia heermannii	Foothill Pseudobahia
	Ranunculus californicus	California Buttercup
Pink to Red	*Lithophragma parviflora*	Prairie Star
	Eriogonum latifolium	Nude Buckwheat
	Lewisia rediviva	Bitter Root
	Montia perfoliata	Miner's Lettuce
	Allium peninsulare	

19

	Sidalcea calycosa ssp. *calycosa*	Checker Mallow
	Sidalcea hartwegii	Checker
	Calycanthus occidentalis	Spicebush
	Castilleja applegatei	Applegate's Paintbrush
	Castilleja foliolosa	Fuzzy Paintbrush
	Brodiaea volubilis	Twining Brodiaea
	Clarkia biloba	Clarkia, Farewell to Spring
	Clarkia purpurea	Winecup Clarkia
	Heuchera micrantha var.*erubescens*	Alum Root
	Linanthus ciliatus	Whisker Brush
	Trifolium hirtum	Rosy Clover
	Plectritis ciliosa	Plectritis
	Scrophularia californica	Bee Plant
	Dodecatheon hendersonii	Shooting Star
	Trifolium tridentatum	Tomcat Clover
	Calandrinia ciliata var. *menziesii*	Red Maids
Blue-	*Delphinium hansenii*	Hansen's Delphinium
Purple	*Gilia tricolor*	Bird's Eye Gilia
	Brodiaea laxa	Ithuriel's Spear
	Brodiaea multiflora	Wild Hyacinth
	Brodiaea elegans	Harvest Brodiaea
	Gilia capitata	Capitate Gilia
	Lupinus benthamii	Spider Lupine
	Lupinus bicolor	Miniature Lupine
	Triteleia bridgesii	Bridge's Brodiaea
	Sanicula bipinnatifida	Purple Sanicle
	Trifolium depauperatum	Cow's Udder Clover
	Vicia sativa	Spring Vetch
Greenish	*Ailanthus altissima*	Tree of Heaven
	Pellaea mucronata	Bird's Foot Fern
	Pinus sabiniana	Gray, Ghost, Digger, Foothill Pine
	Rhamnus crocea ssp. *ilicifolia*	Redberry, Buckthorn

Directions: Red Hill Road is located 2 miles south of SR 120 and SR 108. Turn right after Green Springs Road on La Grange Road (J59) and then left in a mile onto Red Hill Road. Just after the turn, be sure to notice the Crimea House Historical Marker and to the right the beautiful round stone corral, probably built by the Chinese in the 1850s. Drive along Red Hill Road, or get out and walk in various parts of the area. About half a mile after crossing the creek, turn right at the junction with Sims Road to get to Chinese Camp and SR 120 and SR 49. When the Chinese-style houses and school come into view, watch for Star Lily (*Zigadenus fremontii*) in the fields along the road.

ROCK RIVER ROAD has a 300-foot elevation change in the 7-mile walk. It would be a delightful downhill bike ride if you have a shuttle. This can also be driven. There are wonderful tombstones, rock walls, pastoral scenes, and valley views with splashes of color from Goldfields, Lupines, and Popcorn Flower. Be considerate of the ranchers; don't trespass, climb on the rock walls, or block the road. An unusual plant of the area is the shrub Oak Gooseberry (*Ribes quercetorum*).

Directions: Take Green Springs Road off SR 120 (8 miles from Knights Ferry); after a mile, turn right onto Rock River Road. If you miss Green Springs, take La Grange Road and turn right onto Green Springs and left onto Rock River Road. An alternative is to take Willms Road, opposite Knights Ferry Road, to Rock River Road. Sometimes the "Road Closed" or "Flooded" doesn't mean it. You decide.

NEW MELONES DAM, TUTTLETOWN RECREATION AREA, HERON POINT TRAIL, is under the jurisdiction of the Bureau of Reclamation Central Valley Project. Along the entry road are Chamise, Fiddleneck, Popcorn Flower, Buckwheat, Yerba Santa, Manzanita, *Ceanothus cuneatus*, Blue Oak Woodland, and Poppies, plus bluebirds and acorn woodpeckers. Near Acorn Campground on the main road, Linaria, a colorful snapdragon (non-native), was a surprise. There are nice views and good birding.

Trail: The 3-mile loop trail starts on the north side of the Heron Point parking lot and meanders above the lake, with views to the west, then rounds the point to the north side of a hill, providing some nice diversity within the Blue Oak woodland habitat. The trail ends at Acorn Campground and involves a short walk back down the road to Heron Point. The treasures of the trail are: Golden Brodiaea, blue Hound's Tongue, and white Globe Lily or Fairy Lanterns.

This trail was built without a budget, by convict labor, and directed and planned by Ranger Paul Barney. Contact the New Melones Lake Office, (209) 536-9094, for a plant list.

Directions: Turn north either on Rawhide Road below Jamestown or on SR 49 out of Sonora and continue north about 5 to 7 miles to Tuttletown, where you make a left turn down to New Melones Lake and Heron Point.

EAST OF SONORA

ITALIAN BAR ROAD is a delightful wildflower road. It is 6 miles to the Stanislaus River. Lemon-yellow Tuolumne Fawn Lily, *Erythronium tuolumnense*, is spectacular in mid to late March, along with the Shooting Stars, Isopyrum, and other early plants. It is worth a return trip a month later to see a new set of plants. Italian Bar Road exits north out of the state park in Columbia. It becomes a fairly steep but good dirt road, with pullouts. The best of the flowers occur before the bridge. After the Stanislaus River the road gets steeper and has bad potholes in some areas. Jupiter must be a ghost town; don't hope for a cold drink there. It is a pretty back road, beyond the river, with good flowers (more Fawn Lily), beautiful canyons, and crashing creeks and rivers. It is about 25 miles from Columbia to Twain Harte and takes about 2½ hours for flower folks to drive. Take food and water and enough gas. An OHV area along Deer Creek has some unusual plants. The Forest Service is talking of creating a nature trail along Deer Creek. The exciting flowers of this drive are: white Fairy Lantern, Yellow Pussy Ears, Tuolumne Fawn Lily, Isopyrum, and pink Phlox.

SOUTH FORK ROAD, TWAIN HARTE TO THE STANISLAUS RIVER, is a beautiful Dogwood drive. Take Confidence Road to South Fork Road from SR 108 or Joaquin Gulch in Twain Harte to a right on Middlecamp Road and turn left onto South Fork Road. It is about 6 miles down to the river through Dogwoods and big conifers (primarily White Fir). Some of the understory plants are False Solomon's Seal, Yellow Pussy Ears, Hartweg's Iris, Shooting Stars, Dandelion (*Agoseris retrorsa*), and Bracken Fern. One can walk upriver, staying within the highwater mark, or downriver where there are some picnicking sites. Near the river are Alder and Cedar trees, as well as pink-flowered Wild Currant (*Ribes nevadense*), Columbine, Red Monkeyflower, Miniature Lupine, Buttercups, Woodland Star, and White Nemophila. Italian Bar Road begins on the far side of the bridge and goes to the left in a gentle climb out of the river canyon. Columbia is about 25 miles and 2½ hours from here on a pretty road with big potholes, flowers, views, canyons, and creeks.

TWAIN HARTE FLUMES have sparkling white dogwoods in bloom that contrast against the green of Ceanothus and the mixed conifer forest, with a groundcover of Mountain Misery.

Directions: Exit SR 108 and turn left onto Confidence Road. Continue to Middlecamp Road and South Fork Road, where there are paths along the Confidence Ditch or flume.

LYONS RESERVOIR is located just off SR 108. Turn left at the sign for Lyons Reservoir just above Mi-Wuk Village and Sierra Village. A 2-mile road runs down to the pretty reservoir. A few of the special plants along the road and in the reservoir area are *Heuchera micrantha*, which resembles Coral Bells, Woodland Star, and False Solomon's Seal. There are two species of *Ceanothus, Ceanothus integerrimus*, or Deer Brush, and the prostrate Squaw Carpet, or *Ceanothus prostratus*. Look for the small, hanging red and white flowers of Gooseberry on spiny arching stems. The gooseberries are ready to pick for jelly in the fall. This is a good spot for fishing, picnicking, or exploring. Be sure to walk over to the old arched dam, which was a WPA project. You can walk below the dam, on the near side, and see the waterfall in the canyon. Near the dam, also on the near side, you can spot the Old Pickering Railroad trail that comes up from Twain Harte. A 5-mile right-of-way along the former railroad bed is said to be a good bike trail. The Twain Harte end of the trail is on Confidence Road just off South Fork Road.

SOUTH OF SONORA

OLD WESTSIDE RAILROAD GRADE TRAIL out of Tuolumne City has spectacular flowers and views. The southwest exposure produces flowers from mid-March to early May. Walk until you are tired or the old railroad ties get too bothersome and then turn back. Bring water—there is always one more curve ahead to lure you farther than you had planned. The Westside Railroad operated from 1900 to 1960 as a logging system, with 70 miles of mainline from Tuolumne to within 6 miles of Hetch Hetchy and over 250 cumulative miles of temporary spur grades, some of which are now open for hiking and cycling. The Bush Lupine is spectacular. Bring a camera because you will probably want to be photographed beside these beautiful plants. Look for Twining Brodiaea and the Purple Owl's-clover. This vegetation is typical of a south-facing road bank.

Directions: Take SR 108 past Sonora to E17 or Tuolumne Road to Tuolumne City. In Tuolumne City take Carter Street to Buchanan. Park at the intersection of Miramonte and Buchanan near the trailhead.

WARDS FERRY ROAD is one of the most beautiful flowery roads in the foothills, with hillsides of flowers and beautiful canyon views. The Sonora side of the canyon is warmer and drier than the Groveland side, as is shown by the plant material. Among the plants on the Sonora, or north, side of the canyon are Whorled Lupine, which can be found in various colors, pink, white, pale yellow, and lavender. The brilliant blue graceful wands of Spider Lupine are beautiful against the yellow and orange of the Tarweed, Woolly Sunflowers, Pseudobahia, and Caespitose Poppies. There is white Pearly Everlasting, Mustang-Clover (*Linanthus montanus*), and Mariposa Lilies. On the south side of the bridge are pinkish-white Hansen's Delphinium, Tomcat Clover, Chinese Houses, Fairy Lanterns, Spicebush, Elderberry shrubs, and Grapes, to name just a few. With so many beautiful plants to see, don't forget to notice the old bridge site and the dry rock wall foundations of the road and of the smaller bridges.

Directions: You can reach Wards Ferry Road from either Tuolumne City or Jamestown to Big Oak Flat on SR 120. Take Yosemite Road out of Tuolumne City or Algerine Road out of Jamestown to the Wards Ferry Road. Allow about 45 minutes to an hour to drive this narrow paved road. It is 17 miles from Jamestown to Groveland. The beautiful displays of flowers don't really start until you get into the canyon on the narrow road.

JACKSON AREA

Best for Children: Indian Grinding Stone State Park, New Hogan Reservoir, Calaveras Big Trees, Natural Bridges
Best for Botanists: Electra, Camp Nine Road
Best Displays: Electra, Camp Nine Road, Daffodil Hill, Sutter Ione Road, Milton and Southworth Roads
Best Hikes: Pardee Dam, Calaveras Big Trees

HISTORY: Jackson began in 1848 as a place to find water, not gold. Mexican miners, on their way from Sacramento to the Mokelumne River mining area, called the year-round spring they found here Bottilleas (Bottle Spring). By 1849 the name of the camp had become Jackson in honor of Colonel Aldan Apollo Jackson, a miner who moved on to establish the town of Jacksonville on the Tuolumne River.

In 1856 Andrew Kennedy, an Irish immigrant, found a gold-rich quartz vein on a hill north of Jackson, which, along with other nearby claims, became the Kennedy Mine in 1860. About the same time, two black miners, James Hagar and William Tudor, found gold quartz on the other side of the hill and sold their claim in 1860 to a company which was purchased in 1893 by the Argonaut Mining Co. Until they were shut down in 1942, the Kennedy and the Argonaut were two of the deepest and most productive quartz mines in the world. In response to a federal law requiring that refuse from hydraulic mining be impounded, four "tailing" wheels, 58 feet in diameter, were installed to lift the mine waste across two hills and dump it in Indian Gulch. Today, two rusting wheels and the head frame of the Kennedy Mine remain, the ghosts of once prosperous gold mining activity.

In 1846 John A. Sutter was the first white man in the area that later was named for him. In 1848, after gold was discovered in Coloma, he returned to mine the Sutter Creek area. With little gold to show for his efforts, Sutter left the area and never mined again. In 1851 rich quartz deposits were discovered and hardrock mining replaced the modestly successful placer mining. From the late 1850s until 1872 Leland Stanford, a Sacramento grocer, financed and held the controlling interest in the gold-rich Lincoln Mine, which was located between Sutter Creek and Amador City. Its proceeds underwrote many of his financial, political, and educational pursuits.

South of Jackson, in Calaveras County, thousands of miners sought their fortunes in the gold-rich gravel bars in the flats, gulches, and creeks. The area also drew journalists and novelists who wanted to witness and record the Gold Rush phenomenon. Bret Harte, who visited in 1855, brought the county recognition with his geographically fanciful stories. In 1865, while sitting in an Angels Camp saloon, Mark Twain picked up the gist of his famous story about "The Celebrated Jumping Frog of Calaveras County."

24

John and Daniel Murphy opened a trading post on Angels Creek and by enlisting Native Americans to work their mining claims they soon made a fortune. In 1849 they left Murphys Camp, never to return. About 20 miles northeast of Murphys stand the largest living things on earth, the North and South Groves of Calaveras Big Trees (*Sequoiadendron giganteum*). John Bidwell was the first white man to visit these giants (1841); A. T. Dowd of Murphys is credited with bringing recognition to the North Grove in 1852.

JACKSON has a population of 3,900 and is at a 1,200-foot elevation. It has the feeling of a nice old established town, with good restaurants, a charming old hotel at the end of Main Street, and interesting antique stores. Jackson is lots of fun during the Spring Jazz Festival, generally held the last Sunday in April, when every bar on the main street has a different band and your drinking cup is the entry ticket. For more information call the Amador County Chamber of Commerce, (209) 223-0350.

KENNEDY TAILING WHEELS PARK, consisting of 10 acres, is 2 miles north of Jackson on Jackson Gate Road (a northern extension of Main Street), past the Serbian Church. Chinese Houses cover the shaded banks of the parking lot. The two huge tailing wheels, one on either side of Jackson Gate Road, are remnants from the Kennedy Mine. Tailing wheels were installed because of environmental concerns; stop at the information kiosk to learn more. Frame the weathered wood of the massive wheel with the lacy oak leaves and delicate grassland plants for a wonderful photo. Call (209) 223-9524 for above-ground mine tour.

SUTTER CREEK is a small, pretty one-street town with covered side-walks. The population is 2,000 and the elevation is 1,200 feet. It has lovely old homes, some converted into bed and breakfast accommodations, with old-fashioned gardens and picket fences.

WEST OF HIGHWAY 49

SUTTER IONE ROAD leaves SR 49 on the north side of town heading west toward Ione. A short way out of Sutter Creek, turn right on Tonzi Road. There is a creek along part of the road, fields of Popcorn Flower, Shooting Stars, Brodiaea, White Nemophila, and Yellow Monkeyflower, and rivers of Buttercups and Mustard. The stark vertical rock outcroppings are called tombstones. This is old California with beautiful dry rock walls. Be gentle with this old road; don't trespass, pick flowers, or block the road while taking pictures.

In about 4 miles, turn left on Paine Road, where there are Goldfields nestled up against the gray chaparral. Some of the white-flowered shrubs of the chaparral in this area are Chamise, Buck Brush, or *Ceanothus cuneatus*, and Elderberry. The pale lavender-flowered shrub is Yerba Santa. There are large Valley Oaks and smaller Blue Oaks. The serpentine outcroppings are loaded with yellow flowers: Goldfields, Cream Cups, Purple Owl's-clover, and Blennosperma, a tiny yellow composite that looks as if the flower had been sprinkled with salt. Stop and check out the bright yellow little Frying Pans Poppies in the ditch along the road.

CAMANCHE RESERVOIR, SOUTH SHORE RECREATION AREA, MOKELUMNE COAST TO CREST TRAIL has a 3-mile segment of trail just west of the entry station on the south shore. Several different habitats are found along this trail, the most unique being the thin rocky soil before you reach Camanche Creek. This area is about a mile and a half to two miles in along the trail. It blooms early in April and has beautiful displays of Goldfields, Cream Cups, Bird's Eye Gilia, Blue Dicks, and White Hyacinth. The botanical treasure of this area is pink Bitter Root on the rock outcroppings. A few of the other showy plants along the trail are white Shooting Stars, Frying Pans Poppies, Twining Brodiaea, Larkspur, and Golden Brodiaea.

Directions: Take SR 12 off SR 99, east of Lodi. Soon after SR 12 (which eventually leads to San Andreas) and SR 88 split, watch for a left turn onto South Camanche Parkway, then another left or really straight (South Camanche turns right) onto Pattison Road, which turns left onto Wade Lane. As you approach the entry gate, notice the horse crossing sign and the gate to your left. This is the trail, but you need to go through the gate, get a permit, and park at the trail staging area. South Camanche Road has a spectacular late bloom of yellow Mariposa Lilies (*Calochortus luteus*) and Sticky Monkeyflower shrubs.

CAMPO SECO ROAD between Camanche and Pardee reservoirs is a beautiful little road with at least one photogenic stone ruin.

PARDEE DAM was completed in 1929. It is a beautiful gravity-arch dam with elegant old light fixtures that contain aged purple glass. Pardee and

Camanche reservoirs, under the jurisdiction of East Bay Municipal Utility District (EBMUD), are designed for boating, fishing, camping, and horseback riding. Hikers can use the horse trails, but they cover long distances and are often difficult walking. EBMUD is working on the Coast to Crest Trail, which will go through some interesting country in this area, with access from various roads near the Mokelumne River, such as SR 49 at Electra and the Gwin Mine Road.

Campo Trail, near the intersection of Paloma Road and Campo Seco Road, will be a part of the Coast to Crest Trail and is now open past Lawry Flat to McAfee Gulch. It is a nice lower-foothills walk along a fire road, with vistas of rolling hills and open Oak woodlands, rock outcroppings, and some chaparral. The beginning of the trail has Meadowfoam and Prickleseed Buttercup in the moist areas and typical grassland plants such as Buttercups, Blue Dicks, Butter and Eggs, Miniature Lupine, pink Cranesbill, and Popcorn Flower.

The treasure of the trail is the old stage stop, the historic 140-year-old stone Wildermuth House, just 30 minutes from the trailhead. The house is beautifully nestled in front of a wonderful rock outcrop. Don't miss the clever stile built into the entry wall. The stone outbuilding was for storing hay. A pretty garden is maintained by the caretaker, Ken Williams, who pointed out the nearby spring and Indian grinding holes and identified some ancient trees in this landscape that can be confusing to a native plant enthusiast. They include Pecan, Cork Oak, Apricot, Plum, English Walnut, and Fig (which is fairly common at old homesites).

After leaving the stage stop, continue uphill along the fire road until you come to a tumbling creek (a suitable picnic spot). Then travel a little farther uphill, past some nice rock outcrops with Twining Brodiaea, Caterpillar Phacelia, and Blue Dicks, to Lawry Flat. Some rocks at the lower end of the meadow make this another possible picnic site. The meadow view is enhanced by white Douglas's Meadowfoam against the varying greens of the rushes and sedges along the watercourse through the center of the meadow. At the far end of Lawry Flat is a corral and beyond that chaparral. The botanical treasures in the chaparral are Frying Pans Poppy, Bush Poppy, and Fuzzy Indian Paintbrush. Take time to explore the chaparral since it is a new habitat. The pass is a good place to turn around, since it will take about 1½ hours to hike back out, depending on how much exploring is done along the way.

Directions: Turn east onto SR 26 in Stockton and drive east 30 miles to Valley Springs, then left onto Paloma Road, and left at Campo Seco Road. The trailhead is near the intersection of Campo Seco Road and Sandretto Road. An annual use permit is necessary ($10 at present) and you receive maps and information with the permit. It is available at the entry gates or the office, (209) 772-8204.

NEW HOGAN RESERVOIR is a wonderful birding spot and has good flower diversity. Stop by park headquarters and pick up the guide to the interpretive trail. Ask the rangers if their telescope on the back porch is focused on any eagle nests. There is a beautiful flowery road bank between park headquarters and the trailhead at the base of the dam. On the road bank there are Woolly Sunflower, Ball-headed Gilia, Caespitose Poppy, Whorled Lupine, Spider Lupine, Royal Delphinium, California Poppy, Rosy Clover, Grapes, and Elderberry shrubs.

River of Skulls Interpretive Trail is not quite a mile long and passes through several habitats. The flower displays and birding are both good around the lake toward Slate Creek. Along the road you may see: Nightshade, Blue Dicks, Skullcap, Whisker Brush, Purple Owl's-clover, Chinese Houses, Clematis, and Pearly Everlasting.

Directions: From SR 99 drive 35 miles east on SR 26 to Valley Springs, turn right on SR 26 and left onto New Hogan Road. Drive to the park headquarters and pick up a map and a trail guide to the River of Skulls Interpretive Trail, which is located right below the dam.

SOUTHWORTH ROAD Drive 2 miles east of Wallace on SR 12 and turn right (south) on Southworth Road. Watch for the lava cap at the junction with Ospital Road. There is *Lewisia rediviva* in the rocky area, as well as Tidy-tips, Clarkia, and at least three species of Brodiaea.

EAST OF JACKSON

DAFFODIL HILL A host of golden daffodils awaits you from mid to late March at Daffodil Hill. Go 13 miles east out of Sutter Creek on Shake Ridge Road to Daffodil Hill. Mary McLaughlin Lucot and Jessie McLaughlin honored their mother, Lizzie McLaughlin, by planting daffodils in her memory and dividing them every year. Mary Lucot Ryan has continued this tradition, and now 400,000 daffodils are tucked in pots and plots and wheelbarrows. Allow a couple of hours to wander and photograph and perhaps picnic if the weather has turned warm. An alternative route is to go south 3 miles down Rams Horn Grade to Volcano, where you can get a hot drink if the weather is still cool. From Volcano either go west to Sutter Creek on Sutter Creek Road (a beautiful road with pretty road banks and a creek beside the road) or south toward Pine Grove, 3 miles to SR 88, and stop on the way at Indian Grinding Stone State Park. (See *Sierra Heritage* magazine, March/April 1995, for an article on the history of Daffodil Hill.)

INDIAN GRINDING STONE STATE PARK is located half a mile south of Volcano and then left for a mile on the Pine Grove-Volcano Road, or 11 miles up SR 88 from Jackson to Pine Grove, where you turn left toward Volcano for a mile and a half. The park has a museum and Visitor Center, a campground, and several trails. It has several impressive structures like those one would see in a Miwok Indian village. Most impressive is the huge slab of granite with many grinding holes, or chaw'se, made by the Indians. The park has a few trails. A very informative guide to the South Nature Trail is available in the Visitor Center.

LAKE TABEAUD PICNIC AREA AND CLINTON ROAD Clinton Road leaves SR 49 just south of the SR 88 junction and meanders up to Tabeaud Road. Or take SR 88 about 8 miles east from Jackson, then turn right on Clinton Road. Continue on Clinton until it intersects with Tabeaud Road. Clinton Road has good displays of Yellow Pussy Ears, Strawflower, Clarkia, Hartweg's Iris, Buttercups, Brodiaea, and Paintbrush. Tabeaud Road has Trillium, Saxifrage, Mallow, Red Larkspur, Chinese Houses, and Phlox. As you enter the Lake Tabeaud gates, drive straight ahead and park. The flume is on your left. It is a pleasant 20-minute walk to the control gate for water entering the reservoir. You can also drive around the lake and get to the control gate. After enjoying the reservoir, continue uphill on Tabeaud Road for more flowers and pastoral views that will eventually lead to SR 88.

TIGER CREEK PICNIC AREA and reservoir is good fishing and flower chasing. The road down to the area is very pretty, especially if you see a horse in the "Meadowfoam pasture." There is a picnic site where the road meets the reservoir. Continue on to the PG&E Conference Center at the end of the lake. This was built in 1929 and is the only remaining employee recreation center in this area of many that were located at beautiful PG&E reservoirs. A short, pretty walk leads up the creek at the far end of the powerhouse. It takes about 20 minutes. The botanical treasures here are Bicolor Monkeyflower and Indian Pink. The trail gets narrow and full of Poison Oak once you pass the weir.

TRAIL PLANT LIST		ALONG THE ROAD
Agoseris grandiflora	Dandelion	**White**
Dichelostemma volubile	Twining Brodiaea	Elderberry, Deer Brush
Dodecatheon hendersonii	Shooting Star	Dogwood
Eriophyllum lanatum	Woolly Sunflower	California Mock Orange
Lithophragma affine	Woodland Star	Meadowfoam, Mariposa Lily
Lonicera hispidula	Honeysuckle	Watercress
Mimulus bicolor	Bicolor Monkeyflower	**Yellow**
Mimulus guttatus	Yellow Monkeyflower	Buttercups, Fiddleneck
Nemophila heterophylla	White Nemophila	Woolly Sunflower
Phacelia heterophylla	Varileaf Phacelia	**Pink to Rose**
Pityrogramma triangularis	Goldback Fern	Cow's Udder Clover
Rhamnus crocea var. *ilicifolia*	Holly-leaf Coffeeberry	**Red Maids, Milkweed**
Sanicula bipinnata	Poison Sanicle	**Blue**
Silene californica	Indian Pink	Sky Lupine, Penstemon
Thysanocarpus curvipes	Lacepod	Delphinium
Wyethia angustifolia	Mule Ears	

Directions: Drive up SR 88 from Jackson through Pioneer to Amador. Turn right in Amador on the PG&E Tiger Creek Road. Go 2 miles down through pretty country to Tiger Creek Afterbay Picnic Area. The powerhouse and trail are about a mile beyond the picnic area.

PIPI CAMPGROUND is 6.3 miles from SR 88 on Omo Ranch Road, then right on North South Road. Before the road starts downhill watch for Pussy-Ears in the flats, along with Mountain Misery. The Pipi Campground has wheelchair access along the river. Indian Rhubarb can be seen in the river, and walking through the campground you can find Mahonia, very large Trillium, Dogwood, Hazelnut, Coralroot, Gooseberries, and Apricot Monkeyflower.

SOUTH OF JACKSON

SR 49 has fabulous Poppy and Clarkia displays about 3 miles south of Jackson on the east side of the road. It is worth a stop at the large pullout. Some of the other flowers here are Purple Owl's-clover and Caterpillar Phacelia. Good photo stop.

ELECTRA ROAD is 6 miles south of Jackson on BLM land along the Mokelumne River. It has fabulous flower displays in the spring from late March to early June. On a beautiful fall-color weekend, Sierra Club kayakers may have a slalom competition, and spring is bound to bring more people for such activities as good fishing, swimming, kayaking, and picnicking. Try to go on a weekday, and get out and walk the road.

PLANT LIST: mid-March to late April

Achillea millefolium	Yarrow
Calochortus superbus	Mariposa Lily
Calycanthus occidentalis	Western Spice Bush
Collinsia heterophylla	Chinese Houses
Dichelostemma capitata	Blue Dicks
Dichelostemma volubile	Twining Brodiaea
Dudleya cymosa	Dudleya
Eriophyllum lanatum	Woolly Sunflower
Eschscholzia caespitosa	Caespitose Poppy
Eschscholzia lobbii	Frying Pans Poppy
Geranium molle	Soft Cranesbill
Gilia capitata	Ball-headed Gilia
Lupinus albifrons	Silver Bush Lupine
Lupinus benthamii	Spider Lupine
Mimulus bifidus	Sticky Monkey Flower
Mimulus guttatus	Yellow Monkeyflower
Montia perfoliata	Miner's Lettuce
Nemophila heterophylla	White Nemophila
Orthocarpus purpurascens	Purple Owl's-clover
Peltiphyllum peltatum	Indian Rhubarb
Phacelia cicutaria	Caterpillar Phacelia
Philadelphus lewisii ssp. *californicus*	California Mock Orange

Plagiobothrys nothofulvus	Popcorn Flower
Saxifraga californica	California Saxifrage
Streptanthus tortuosus	Jewel Flower
Styrax officinalis var. *redivivus*	Snowdrop Bush
Thysanocarpus curvipes	Lacepod
Trifolium hirtum	Rosy Clover
Verbascum blattaria	Moth Mullein

SOUTHEAST OF JACKSON

MURPHYS is a beautiful little town, east of SR 49, just off of SR 4. It is at a higher elevation (2,171 feet) than most of the southern mining towns. Flatlanders love to go up to Murphy's Hotel and the theater. Like Sutter Creek and many of the mining towns, it has beautiful gardens. There are some nice wineries a short way from town. Ironstone winery has beautiful gardens and some events. Stevenot Winery, almost 3 miles out of town, has a large patch of Baby Blue Eyes along the entry road to the winery. A sod roof covers the tasting room, which is situated in a lovely garden. Because of a fire several years ago on the ridge just north of the winery, you will see Bush Poppy in the area; its seeds germinate after intense heat.

SHEEP RANCH-AVERY ROAD, MURPHYS TO HATHAWAY PINES, is 9 miles by Sheep Ranch-Avery Road from the charming downtown of Murphys to Hathaway Pines, located on SR 4. There are more than just flowers along this road. Mercer Caverns, 1 mile out of town, has beautiful crystalline formations of stalagmites, stalactites, curtains, and other geologic formations within the many limestone caverns. After turning right onto the Avery-Sheep Ranch Road, it gets fairly steep and beautiful Gray's Lupine begins to appear along the road. The silver mats with blue spikes become more prevalent. The road takes on a parklike quality where Mountain Misery forms a solid groundcover under Ponderosa Pine. Ecologically it is difficult to figure out how this has happened. Are the shrub species in this forest being removed chemically, mechanically, or grazed for this open effect? Perhaps the owner is trying to keep fuel low for fire control. It really is unusual and beautiful.

CALAVERAS BIG TREES STATE PARK is located 4 miles above the town of Arnold on SR 4. This Giant Sequoia grove has some huge trees, as much as 24 feet in diameter and 325 feet tall, that may be 2,000 years old. Dogwood and Wild Azalea add to the beauty of the park. The park's North Grove Trail is right off the main parking lot and has a 1-mile gentle loop with numbered markers that correspond to a trail guide. Another trail in the park, particularly good for wildflowers, is the Lava Bluffs Trail. It is 5 miles down the parkway from the park entrance to the Lava Bluffs parking area. The trail is 2.2 miles long, with some up and down, lots of plant diversity, and interesting geologic formations. Some of the botanic trail treasures are Leopard Lily, Sierra Pea, Milkweed, Shelton's Violet, Gray's Lupine, Coral Root, and Indian Rhubarb.

The South Grove Trail is about 4.5 miles long and has the largest trees in the park. It is a 9-mile drive from the park entrance and blooms later than the Lava Bluffs Trail. A plant list can be obtained from the visitor center.

CAMP NINE ROAD is a florific old road built in the 1920s to access PG&E power stations at the river 7 miles down the road. This is one of the best flower roads in the gold country. It is a quiet road except for a cement plant a little way down the road. *Montia gypsophiloides* (Dwarf Miner's Lettuce), pale pink, collects like snow in the gutters and around big boulders. This plant and flowering Ash tree are the unusual botanical treasures of beautiful Camp Nine Road. There is a nice picnic area along a creek near the bridge that crosses the Stanislaus River.

PLANT LIST: mid-March to late April

White	Yellow	Pink to Red
Elderberry	Mountain Mahogany	Redbud tree
Flowering Ash tree	Smooth Cat's-ear	Shooting Stars
California Mock Orange	Tarweed	Chinese Houses
Deer Brush	Tidy-tips	Dwarf Miner's Lettuce
Clematis	Goldfields	Wavy-leaf Indian Paintbrush
Jewel Flower	Woolly Sunflower	Fuzzy Indian Paintbrush
Miner's Lettuce	Mule Ears	**Blue to Lavender**
Star Lily	Buttercups	Yerba Santa shrub
Whorled Lupine	Butter and Eggs	Silver Bush Lupine
Woodland Star	Yellow Monkeyflower	Spider Lupine
Fairy Lanterns	Foothill Lomatium	Sky Lupine
Valley Tassels	Wallflower	Miniature Lupine
Varileaf Phacelia	**Orange**	Penstemon
	Sticky Monkeyflower	Ithuriel's Spear
		Delphinium

Directions: Turn off SR 49 and go east on SR 4 about 5 miles to Vallecito, then right or south on Parrots Ferry Road for 1 mile and turn left onto Camp Nine Road (see Sonora map).

NATURAL BRIDGES TRAIL is a wonderful trail for children. Bring a bathing suit, lunch, water, and a flashlight. The short trail ends at an old homestead overlooking a cool pool in Coyote Creek. The trail is steep by the creek, but it has some steps to help. Shine your flashlight on the ceiling of the cave behind the pool and look for bats. A trail over the top of the cave goes up the creek to the other end of the cave. It is a very steep trail down to the cave on the far side. Don't become a spelunker unless the water is very low and you notice locals going through the cave! It can be dangerous if the water is flowing fast. Besides all this excitement, there are nice flowers and a trail guide. In case the box is empty, this list will help, though the guide goes into more details.

1. Blue Oak and *Brodiaea laxa*.
2. Toyon and small Lupines, Buttercups, Holly-leafed Coffeeberry, Golden Brodiaea, White Nemophila, Interior Live Oak.
3. Foothill Pine along with some Whisker Brush.
4. Gooseberry and Clematis vine.
5. Mountain Mahogany, Poison Oak followed by a small white Plectritis.
6. Red Bud tree.
7. Coffeeberry shrub.
8. Chamise, California Buckeye, Chinese Houses, and Valley Oaks.
9. Parry's Manzanita or *Arctostaphylos manzanita* (no burl). Look for the rock walls that formed a sluice in the creek to trap gold.
10. Goldcup Oak.
11. California Wild Grape.
12. California Bay, Bigleaf Maple with other riparian plants such as Maidenhair fern.
13. Black Oak with Shooting Stars.
14. Bigleaf Maple.
15. Ponderosa Pine and a Poison Oak look-a-like called Squaw Bush, but be careful, there is plenty of real Poison Oak all over the foothills. There is also Linanthus, Clarkia, and Foothill Poppy along with Gold-back Fern.
16. *Clematis lasiantha* and limestone rock. Don't miss the pink Twining Brodiaea. Oleander, Locust trees, Vinca, Lilacs, and Osage Orange were part of the homestead that was once in this idyllic location.

Directions: Natural Bridges Nature Trail is on Parrotts Ferry Road shortly after Moaning Cavern on the west side (the right, driving south) and about a half mile before the bridge.

Moaning Cavern is an interesting stop about a mile north of Natural Bridges. A long spiral staircase leads down into the caverns. There are picnic tables, cold drinks, and a nice 40-minute loop trail through chaparral. Along the trail there is a rocky outcropping with good plants and a canyon view.

SOUTHWEST OF JACKSON (SEE SONORA MAP)

MILTON ROAD FROM JENNY LIND TO SR 4 is about 12 miles. Milton Road (J14) is a right turn off SR 26 about 23 miles from SR 99. Milton Road, in the vicinity of Jenny Lind, has vernal pools with Downingia if your timing is right. There are good flower fields and little development along this road, perhaps because the soil is clay to hardpan to tiny gravelly rock, which bulbs seem to love and farmers find intolerable for crops. Early in the spring you'll see Blue Dicks, Ithuriel's Spear, White

Hyacinth Brodiaea, White Onion, or *Allium hyalinum*, and Popcorn Flower. As the soil begins to dry, Mariposa Lilies and *Brodiaea coronaria* appear. Several places on Milton Road have vernal pools with yellow Blennosperma, Goldfields, Tidy Tips, White Douglas's Meadowfoam, and White Navarretia. If you are lucky and most of the water is gone, there will be blue Downingia and bluish, thistlelike *Eryngium vaseyi*. Several lupines are in the tailings area: Spider Lupine or *Lupinus benthamii*, *Lupinus densiflorus*, and Sky Lupine, or *Lupinus nanus*. You may notice rosy purple right beside the road. Weedy *Erodium botrys*, or Cranesbill, along with another weedy member of the geranium family, *Geranium dissectum*, put on a pretty display.

ROCK CREEK ROAD PAST SALT SPRINGS RESERVOIR off Milton Road is a beautiful small road with lots of flowers at eye level on the road banks. On the shady banks you will find blue-lavender Fiesta Flower, the rosy Chinese Houses, and *Geranium molle*, white California Saxifrage, Shooting Stars, White Nemophila, Clematis, White Brodiaea, Lace Pod, Buckbrush, Maidenhair Fern, yellow Buttercups, and orange Sticky Monkeyflower. The Buckeye is spectacular when in bloom near the creek. As you near the top of the road near Salt Springs Reservoir, look for yellow Douglas's Viola, beautiful Royal Delphinium, or *Delphinium variegatum*, White Mariposa Lilies, and White Brodiaea. The reservoir area is wonderful bird watching for bald eagles and kingbirds after you have rounded the curve beyond the entry gate. The road ends at Copperopolis and SR 4.

TELEGRAPH ROAD OFF SR 4 FROM MILTON ROAD TO COPPEROPOLIS Along SR 4 watch for Meadowfoam, *Limnanthes striata*, in the gutters just as you begin to rise above the valley. Telegraph Road, about 6 miles up the hill from Milton Road, is a wonderful short road to walk. See if you can find at least three different species of Buttercups (pages 138, 182, 183) and yellow *Lomatium utriculatum*, pink Shooting Star, and Miner's Lettuce. Continue up SR 4 to Copperopolis. Stop for a snack at the store and wander around on the old road behind it to figure out what the yellow is along the creek, at the edge of the roads, under the Foothill Pines—it is everywhere! Most of the yellow flowers are beautiful Frying Pans Poppies, or *Eschscholzia lobbii*. Some of the yellow along the creek is Yellow Monkeyflower, or *Mimulus guttatus*. SR 4 has beautiful views in spring driving west from SR 49 down to the valley.

PLACERVILLE AREA

Best for Children: Goldbug Mine in Placerville, Phoenix Park, Bridal Veil Picnic Area, Coloma, Dave Moore Nature Area
Best for Botanists: Traverse Creek Botanical Interest Area, Phoenix Park, Pine Hill, Bridal Veil Nature Area
Best Displays: Phoenix Park, Nimbus Dam, south end of Meiss Road
Best Hikes: (all short) Straza Ranch, Coloma, Traverse Creek

HISTORY: Placerville began as Old Dry Diggings with the discovery of gold in 1848. Lawlessness accompanied the rapid influx of prospectors, and miners began to apply their own code of justice by hanging the perpetrators of the many robberies and murders being committed in the area. Thus Old Dry Diggings became Hangtown in 1849. By the mid 1850s placer mining had declined, but through the 1870s hydraulic and drift mining were extremely profitable. The town was always a thriving supply center and a destination point for overland travel. After their service in the U.S. Army during the Mexican War, members of the Mormon Battalion built Sutter's Mill and opened a trail from west to east over Carson Pass for their return home to Salt Lake City. This Carson-Mormon Emigrant Trail became the main overland route to the gold diggings after 1849. In 1859, after the Comstock Lode silver strike in Virginia City, a steady stream of horse-drawn vehicles moved over the newly constructed Placerville Road (later US 50).

When the El Dorado County seat was moved from Coloma to Hangtown in 1854, the town was incorporated as Placerville, a more respectable name. In the early 1860s Placerville was the western terminus of the short-lived Pony Express. Some of Placerville's early settlers became quite famous: J. M. Studebaker, a wagon and wheelbarrow maker, became an automobile manufacturer; Mark Hopkins and Collis Huntington, general store owners, became railroad tycoons; Philip Armour, a butcher, took his poke of gold and built a meat-packing empire.

Eight miles north of Placerville lies Coloma, where gold was first discovered. By the end of 1849 the settlement had grown to nearly 5,000. For a brief time, until the placer deposits played out, Coloma was the seat of El Dorado County (in a Spanish legend, *El Dorado* means "cloaked in gold"). Today the traveler can see ghosts of golden days in Coloma, now part of a 275-acre state park established in 1942.

PLACERVILLE (1,864-foot elevation) is located at the junction of highways 50 and 49 and is the last town of any size (pop. 8,444) before Lake Tahoe on US 50. Downtown Placerville has several historical buildings and ruins. The former Zeisz building pictured on page 37 is a little east of the courthouse, against the hill. Annual activities include the Miners Ball the last Saturday in March, and on the last Saturday in April,

Goldbug Mine

during apple-blossom time, the Western BBQ and Hoedown in Camino on "Apple Hill." Children are welcome.

GOLDBUG MINE in Placerville has mine tours, a nice creek and picnic area, a stamp mill, and a short trail where you will see lots of evidence of earth-moving during the mining days. Some of the special flowers are Baby Blue Eyes, Yellow Pussy Ears, White Globe Lily, Checker Mallow, and Wild Mock Orange. Notice the multitrunked trees; this probably occurred as the result of fire or of timber cutting for flumes or mines. For a mine tour, phone the Placerville Recreation Department, (916) 642-5232. See *Sierra Heritage* magazine, March 1994, for the history of the Goldbug Mine.

Directions: On US 50, go one signal light east of the SR 49 junction, turn left off US 50 on Bedford Avenue, and drive north one mile up the hill.

NORTH OF PLACERVILLE, GEORGETOWN DIVIDE

ROCK CREEK ROAD is the first road off SR 193, the road from Placerville to Georgetown, after crossing the American River. The first four miles of the road are just beautiful, with loads of flowers cascading down the road banks. The road is narrow and winding, but the several creeks that cross the road allow for adequate space to pull over. The road eventually runs into Mosquito Road, which gets you back to Placerville. The American River canyon down to Mosquito Bridge has a very steep road on both sides of the canyon, with hairpin turns and almost no parking at the river. It is not recommended (the best flower displays are within the first few miles of SR 193).

TRAVERSE CREEK SPECIAL BOTANICAL INTEREST AREA is a treasure trove for flower chasers because of the serpentine soil, moisture from seeps, Traverse Creek, and the very dry surroundings. It encompasses 220 acres that were used by Indians, as is shown by the bedrock mortars along Traverse Creek. The miners came along and removed the gravel beds to expose the serpentine bedrock. The pits and tailings that remain from mining in the 1920s are still visible in some places. In the 1940s a sawmill (possibly located on Bear Creek Road) removed many of the trees in the area. The Special Interest Area was created in 1989, thanks to the Forest Service and the Native Plant Society, to protect this unique area from further abuse. The El Dorado National Forest Interpretive Association (ENFIA) and an equestrian club have added their help. There are proposals to build three miles of trails, including a wheelchair path. Presently the area isn't very structured, so walk gently and be careful not to destroy any botanical gems.

Bitter Root is abundant just uphill from the creek crossing on the west side of the road. Walk through the shrubs to the rise of the hill, but be careful where you walk—the succulent Bitter Root (*Lewisia rediviva*) plants are everywhere. It needs sunshine and warmth to be showy, so check this site after the sun has been out for a while. Growing with the Bitter Root you will find Evening Snow (*Linanthus dichotomus*), Douglas's Violet, small magenta Mouse-ears, Monkeyflower or Chinless Mimulus (*Mimulus douglasii*), and a rare yellow subshrub, *Eriogonum tripodum*. In the woods look for Sierra Fawn Lily or *Erythronium multiscapoideum*, Trillium, and Brown Bells or *Fritillaria micrantha* (all early bloomers—late March) and Leopard Lily, a May bloomer.

The El Dorado National Forest office on Forni Road in Placerville has more information and complete plant lists, plus a volunteer group (ENFIA) to help protect and improve the Traverse Creek area. Call (530) 622-5061 and ask for the Forest Service botanist, Mike Taylor.

PLANT LIST

White	*Amelanchier pallida*	Service Berry
	Boykinia elata	Brook Foam
	Brodiaea hyacinthina	White Brodiaea
	Calochortus superbus	Mariposa Lily
	Ceanothus integerrimus	Deer Brush
	Chamaebatia foliolosa	Mountain Misery
	Chlorogalum pomeridianum	Soap Plant
	Clematis lasiantha	Virgin's Bower
	Collinsia tinctoria	White Chinese Houses
	Erigeron foliosus	Fleabane
	Fragaria californica	Wild Strawberry
	Linanthus dichotomous	Evening Snow
	Linanthus montanus	Mustang-Clover
	Lithophragma affine	Woodland Star
	Minuartia californica	Sandwort
	Nemophila heterophylla	White Nemophila
	Plagiobothrys nothofulvus	Popcorn Flower
	Prunus virginiana var. *demissa*	Western Choke Cherry
	Rubus leucodermis	Western Raspberry
	Scutellaria californica	Skullcap
	Zigadenus venenosus	Death Camas
Yellow	*Berberis aquifolium* var. *dictyota*	Oregon Grape
	Eythronium multiscapoideum	Fawn Lily
	Streptanthus tortuosus var. *tortuosus*	Mountain Jewel Flower
	Agoseris heterophylla	Woodland Agoseris or Dandelion
	Calochortus monophyllus	Yellow Star-Tulip, Yellow Pussy Ears
	Chaenactis glabriuscula	Yellow-flowered Chaenactis
	Eriogonum tripodum	Tripod Buckwheat
	Eriophyllum lanatum	Woolly Sunflower
	Grindelia camporum	Gum Weed
	Lasthenia californica	Goldfields
	Lomatium utriculatum	Foothill Lomatium
	Mimulus bicolor	Bicolor Monkeyflower
	Mimulus guttatus	Yellow Monkeyflower
	Orthocarpus erianthus	Butter and Eggs
	Potentilla glandulosa	Cinquefoil
	Ranunculus occidentalis	Western Buttercup
	Wyethia angustifolia	Mule Ears
Orange	*Eschscholzia californica*	California Poppy
	Lilium pardalinum	Leopard Lily
Pink to	*Allium membranaceum*	
Magenta	*Mimulus douglasii*	Purple Mouse-ears
	Mimulus kelloggii	Kellogg's Monkeyflower
	Mimulus torreyi	Torrey's Monkeyflower
	Trientalis latifolia	Star Flower
	Arctostaphylos viscida	Whiteleaf Manzanita
	Lewisia rediviva	Bitter Root
	Montia perfoliata	Miner's Lettuce
	Prunus subcordata	Sierra Plum

	Rhododendron occidentale	Azalea
	Allium sanbornii	
	Linanthus ciliatus	Whisker Brush
	Trifolium hirtum	Rosy Clover
	Plectritis ciliosa	Plectritis
	Geranium dissectum	Cranesbill
	Sidalcea hartwegii	Checker Mallow
	Trifolium tridentatum	Tomcat Clover
	Trifolium variegatum	White-tipped Clover
Red	*Calandrinia ciliata* var. *menziesii*	Red Maids
	Castilleja applegatei	Applegate's Paintbrush
	Silene californica	Indian Pink
	Aquilegia formosa	Columbine
Blue-	*Delphinium hansenii*	Hansen's Delphinium
Purple	*Delphinium patens*	Spreading Larkspur
	Delphinium variegatum	Royal Delphinium
	Gilia capitata	Capitate Gilia
	Hydrophyllum occidentale	Waterleaf
	Penstemon heterophyllus	Varied Leaf Penstemon
	Brodiaea laxa	Ithuriel's Spear
	Brodiaea multiflora	Wild Hyacinth
	Fritillaria micrantha	Brown Bells
	Sanicula bipinnatifida	Purple Sanicle
Greenish	*Osmorhiza chilensis*	Sweet Cicely
	Rhamnus californica var. *tomentella*	Coffeeberry
	Vitis californica	Wild Grape
	Cornus sessilis	Goldminer Dogwood
	Artemisia douglasiana	California Mugwort
	Quercus durata	Leather Oak
	Rhamnus crocea ssp. *ilicifolia*	Redberry, Buckthorn
Ferns	*Dryopteris arguta*	Wood Fern
	Pellaea mucronata	Bird's Foot Fern
	Pityrogramma triangularis	Goldback Fern

Directions: Drive 3 miles south of Georgetown on SR 193, turn east either onto Bear Creek Road or east on Meadowbrook Road (also off SR 193 a mile or so farther from Georgetown). Traverse Creek Botanical Area is at the junction of Meadowbrook and Bear Creek Roads. Bear Creek Road has serpentine outcropping with acres of *Mimulus bicolor* in April.

WEST OF PLACERVILLE, HIGHWAY 50 VICINITY

NIMBUS DAM OVERLOOK is just east of Sacramento. Exit US 50 at Hazel Avenue. Go left (if you are headed east on 50), cross the river, and at the top of the hill turn right on the small gated road along the bluffs overlooking the river. (See this area on your way to Phoenix Park, since you can't turn left coming from the other direction.) In April the flowers are everywhere: White Brodiaea (*Triteleia hyacinthina*), beautiful blue Royal Delphinium (*Delphinium variegatum*), small magenta Monkeyflower (*Mimulus tricolor*), and pink Clover (*Trifolium pratense*); yellow Mariposa Lily (*Calochortus luteus*) follows in late April. Park at the end of the road and follow the short loop trail, about 45 minutes, down to the river, passing three species of Brodiaea, as well as Fiddlenecks, on your way.

A popular bike and walking trail runs along the river. Turn left and follow the trail away from the river into the canyon; it will return you uphill to the parking lot. On the sides of the south-facing bluffs notice the huge colony of *Dudleya cymosa,* best seen with binoculars. In the shaded areas look for Goldback and Maidenhair ferns, and for Dutchman's Pipe (the black swallowtail butterfly is the clue that the Pipevine is nearby).

PHOENIX PARK VERNAL POOLS is a superb example of a vernal pool habitat and is easily accessible. Although surrounded by a residential area, it is protected and is a wonderful teaching area. Nancy Wymer (a botanist who has studied this area for years) and the California Native Plant Society often give guided tours. Plants typical of vernal pools are Blennosperma, Goldfields, Meadowfoam, Tidy-tips, White Brodiaea, Dwarf Brodiaea, and a beautiful pink Mallow, *Sidalcea calycosa.* With good timing Downingia may be in bloom; it is a pretty little blue lobelialike plant that grows in the center of the bull's-eye of flowers when the water has evaporated. Vernal pools have a base of hardpan soil, so the water doesn't percolate into the soil. When the rain ceases for the season, the pools gradually evaporate, leaving concentric rings of flowers with different water and soil requirements. In the first part of April you can see beautiful vernal pools where the Central Valley begins to rise to the foothills. SR 88 and SR 4 just barely above the Valley have lovely vernal pools. Study the Phoenix Park Vernal Pools and you will appreciate your next spring drive to the gold country or the mountains even more. For an extensive plant list from Nancy Wymer, phone (916) 726-9567.

Here are a few plants found in or near vernal pools (* = only in vernal pools).

Blennosperma nanum	
Brodiaea coronaria	
Brodiaea minor	Dwarf Brodiaea
*Downingia cuspidata**	
*Downingia bicornuta**	Double-horn Downingia
Downingia ornatissima	Folded Downingia (not at Phoenix Park)
*Eryngium vaseyi**	Vasey's Coyote Thistle
Lasthenia fremontii	Fremont's Goldfields
Limnanthes douglasii	Meadowfoam (not at Phoenix Park)
*Navarretia leucocephala**	White-head Navarretia
*Pogogyne zizyphoroides**	Sacramento Mesamint
*Psilocarpus brevissimus**	Dwarf Woolly-heads
*Sidalcea calycosa**	Checker-mallow
Trifolium depauperatum	Cow's Udder Clover
Trifolium variegatum	White-tipped Clover

Directions: Traveling east, exit US 50 at Hazel Avenue, turn left and cross the American River, continue on Hazel through three or four signals, turn right on Sunset, and go several blocks to Phoenix Park, on the right. An easy but full day would be Phoenix Park, Nimbus Dam Overlook, and Meiss Road, possibly continuing south into the Ione and Sutter Creek areas (Jackson chapter). Depending on the rainfall during the winter, these areas should be pretty from mid-March through April.

MEISS ROAD, with fields of flowers that would make good calendar photos, is located about 10 miles south of Carmichael, an eastern suburb of Sacramento. Some of the flowers to be enjoyed are Tidy-tips, Meadowfoam, White Brodiaea, Ithuriel's Spear, Lobb's Poppy, Popcorn Flower, Mallow, Johnny Tuck, and various species of Brodiaea. When the fields begin to dry, Farewell-to-Spring, *Brodiaea coronaria,* Vetch, Cream Cups, and Mariposa Lily come into bloom.

Directions: Take US 50 east of Sacramento to Sunrise (E2), south past Mather Air Force Base to Jackson Road, SR 16. Left on Jackson Road for 4 miles. Go past Meiss Road and turn right on Dillard Road. After a mile or so turn left on Meiss Road. The best wildflower displays seem to be toward the south end of Meiss Road. A nice loop is to continue on to Ione-Michigan Bar Road and turn right onto SR 104, which, after 24 miles, will bring you to SR 99.

PINE HILL ECOLOGICAL PRESERVE, El Dorado County, is reached by a stiff uphill walk along a quiet road. Several rare and endangered plants grow in this area, and perhaps you will see a flock of turkeys or some deer. There are good views at the top. The walk begins in an oak woodland with a north exposure. The plants, which are at eye level on the road bank, include Shooting Stars, Buttercups, Baby Blue Eyes, White Fairy Lanterns, Chinese Houses, Saxifrage, Hound's Tongue, Red Delphinium, Iris, Miner's Lettuce, and Mallows. Watch for Clematis clambering over the shrubs and a field of Baby Blue Eyes on the downhill side of the road. After passing a house on the right and a driveway or two on the left, start watching for Pine Hill Flannel Bush. As the road levels out toward the top of the hill, notice how the plants have changed because it is sunnier. This is a gabbro soil community that includes six rare plant species:

El Dorado Bedstraw	*Galium californicum* ssp. *sierrae*
Layne's Butterweed	*Senecio layneae*
Pine Hill Ceanothus	*Ceanothus roderickii*
Pine Hill Flannel Bush	*Fremontia decumbens*
El Dorado County Mule Ears	*Wyethia reticulata*
Red Hills Soaproot	*Chlorogalum grandiflorum*

There is also an unusual Redbud with red autumn foliage. On top of the hill beside the path, look for the rare Pine Hill Ceanothus, Pine Hill Flannel Bush, and El Dorado County Mule Ears.

PLANT LIST

Shrubs	*Berberis aquifolium* var. *dictyota*	Oregon Grape
	Ceanothus lemmonii	Lemmon's Ceanothus
	Haplopappus arborescens	Golden Fleece
	Helianthemum scoparium var. *vulgare*	Rock Rose
	Helianthemum suffrutescens	Bisbee Peak Rush-rose
	Lonicera interrupta	Chaparral Honeysuckle
	Lepechinia calycina	Pitcher Sage
	Solanum xanti var. *intermedium*	Nightshade
Herbs	*Allium peninsulare*	Wild Onion
	Allium sanbornii	Wild Onion
	Asclepias cordifolia	Milkweed
	Balsamorhiza deltoidea	Balsam Root
	Brodiaea bridgesii	Bridge's Brodiaea
	Brodiaea congesta	Ookow
	Brodiaea elegans	Harvest Brodiaea
	Brodiaea hyacinthina	White Brodiaea
	Brodiaea laxa	Ithuriel's Spear
	Brodiaea ixioides var. *scabra*	Golden Brodiaea
	Brodiaea multiflora	Wild Hyacinth
	Brodiaea pulchella	Blue Dicks
	Brodiaea volubilis	Twining Brodiaea
	Calochortus albus	Fairy Lanterns
	Calochortus luteus	Yellow Mariposa
	Calochortus monophyllus	Yellow Pussy Ears
	Calochortus superbus	Mariposa Lily
	Castilleja foliolosa	Woolly Paintbrush
	Castilleja subinclusa	Paintbrush
	Chlorogalum grandiflorum	Red Hills Soaproot
	Clarkia biloba	Two-lobed Clarkia
	Clarkia purpurea ssp. *quadrivulnera*	Winecup Clarkia
	Clarkia unguiculata	Elegant Clarkia
	Comandra pallida	Bastard Toad-flax
	Delphinium hansenii	Hansen's Delphinium
	Delphinium patens	Larkspur
	Helianthella californica var. *nevadensis*	Helianthella
	Iris hartwegii	Hartweg's Iris
	Iris macrosiphon	Ground Iris
	Lithophragma scabrella	Woodland Star
	Lupinus latifolius var. *columbianus*	
	Lupinus polyphyllus	
	Lupinus vallicola	
	Penstemon azureus	Azure Penstemon
	Penstemon lemmonii	
	Plectritis ciliosa	
	Plectritis macrocera	
	Polygala cornuta	Milkwort
	Sidalcea hartwegii	Hartweg's Mallow
	Sidalcea malvaeflora ssp. *asprella*	
	Swertia albicaulis	Whitestem Frasera

Wyethia angustifolia	Narrowleaf Mule Ears
Wyethia bolanderi	Bolander's Mule Ears
Wyethia reticulata	El Dorado County Mule Ears

A more complete plant list is available from the El Dorado National Forest office in Placerville. Call (530) 622-5061 and ask for the forest botanist.

Directions: Exit US 50 at Cameron Park Drive in Cameron Park. Go north 3 miles to Green Valley Road, turn right on Green Valley Road, and drive about 1.5 miles to Ulenkamp Road, then left 1.5 miles to Pine Hill. Stop at the large gate on the left, and park on either side of the gate. Walk through the pedestrian gate to the right of the main gate.

COLOMA, MARSHALL GOLD DISCOVERY STATE HISTORIC PARK is located along the South Fork of the American River on SR 49. Various activities are available in Coloma, such as the museum, docent tours, the river, rafting (it starts in Lotus just down the road), Chinese stores, Sutter's Sawmill, a mining exhibit, and the gold discovery site. A hike will take you past ancient flumes, an old spring house, a statue of James Marshall overlooking his gold discovery site, and of course wildflowers. This Monument trail, 1.5 miles, starts at the Gold Discovery Museum. As soon as you start up the trail, you'll see a bright magenta flower (related to Indian Pink) called *Lychnis coronaria* that jumped the fence out of a garden long ago and has naturalized, along with the blue-flowered Vinca. Watch for Indian Pink, a short, beautiful red carnation relative, on the banks of the trail. White Globe Lily and Iris are also along the trail. The hot sunny part of the trail has several varieties of Lupine, Clarkia, and Brodiaea. When you reach the vista point, notice the regrowth of the chaparral since a fire a few years ago on Murphy Mountain, across the canyon, just north of Coloma. In 1997 the hill was aflame with poppies but shrubs will soon shade out the flowers until the next fire.

Directions: In Placerville turn north on SR 49 at the stoplight. Coloma is 9 miles north on 49 (don't accidentally get on SR 193 to Georgetown) along a slow, pretty, winding road with Globe Lilies, Milkweed, Broom, Woolly Sunflower, Rosy Clover, Mule Ears, and Golden Brodiaea.

DAVE MOORE NATURE AREA is designed for the physically impaired. The Clark Trail is a 15-minute walk to the American River. The treasures of this trail are the river access, the beautiful rock walls, and the Fairy Lanterns. Picnic tables are scattered here and there along the trail. This area is only about two miles from Coloma, where gold was first discovered in 1848; keep this in mind as you view the unnatural terrain, full of humps and ditches and piles of rocks that were rearranged by the miners in their quest for gold. Some of the flowers to be found here are Baby Blue Eyes, Five Spot Nemophila, magenta Kellogg's Monkeyflower, Yellow Monkeyflower, Golden Brodiaea, and Blue Dicks.

43

Directions: Follow the directions for Coloma, then continue about two miles farther on SR 49. Or look at your mileage when you cross the American River and continue north on SR 49 for one mile. The entrance to the Dave Moore Nature Area has a large rock entryway. Park outside along the road if the gate is closed; this adds only about 200 more yards of walking.

STRAZA RANCH, a recent acquisition of 450 acres, is now being operated by BLM and the American River Conservancy. The marvelous quality of this property is the freedom to roam and explore without trails or signs. The boundaries are obvious—SR 49, Hastings Creek, the American River, and Greenwood Creek—so you are not liable to wander onto private land. If you feel lost, go to the top of a hill and look or listen for the highway.

The land has been grazed for 100 years, so there are many non-native plants here. (The non-native species often arrive in feed; disturbed areas are easily invaded by non-native plants.) Tunica, a bright pink Carnation relative, is everywhere. A couple of beautiful natives that have survived the grazing are Baby Blue Eyes, or *Nemophila menziesii,* and Five Spot Nemophila. On the wooded, rocky hillsides that border the river the natives are healthy. Of course there is Poison Oak, but there are also Fairy Lanterns, Dutchman's Pipe, and Clarkia. California Poppies and Silver Bush Lupine, whose combined colors are splendid, grow in the rocks and sand along the river. Other plants include Verbena, Oregon Ash, Bunchgrasses, and several species of Willows. Notice the debris from the New Year's 1997 storm high in the shrubs and trees along the river.

Watch for Indian grinding holes in the bedrock along the river. It is wonderful to be able to wander here without restrictions. It would be wise to sight on a hill near the highway or to orient yourself to the highway with a topographic map before leaving your car. Bear left as you enter the center gate and you will get to the river, or follow one of the old farm roads. Pick up a walking stick to tap ahead of you when walking cross-country if you cannot see the ground. Rattlers sometimes seek the shade of the bunch grasses and lupine near the river, and a tapping stick is handy.

Directions: Drive about 3 miles north of Coloma on SR 49. You'll see a road bank of Poppies across from the main gate to the Straza Ranch. The entrance doesn't have any welcome sign yet, so read the directions carefully. The three gates to the property are located begining at road marker #2700; the Poppies are at marker #2743, and the northernmost gate is just before Lilyama Road. At present it is necessary to squeeze through or climb over the gate. How many times have you rolled under a barbed-wire fence? It's OK this time!

MURPHY MOUNTAIN ROAD is a quiet, steep, narrow, 3.5-mile road just east of Coloma, with lovely wildflowers and an occasional bobcat. It ends at Marshall Road, where there are some picturesque ruins. Garden Valley is not far from the Traverse Creek Serpentine Area and is worth the visit. The bridge across the American River to Murphy Road is just before Coloma on the Placerville side of the state park. Some of the plants along the road are Valley Tassels, Fiddleneck, Golden Brodiaea, Ithuriel's Spear, Blue Dicks, Chamise, Yerba Santa, Yarrow, Fairy Lanterns, Nightshade, Clematis, and Chinese Houses.

SALMON FALLS, FOLSOM LAKE STATE RECREATION AREA, is the takeout area for rafters on the South Fork of the American River. Some of the attractive shrubs adjacent to the parking lot are Pitcher Sage, Snowdrop Bush, Deer Brush, Hollyleaf Redberry, and blue Ceanothus. Wild Clematis is very showy clambering over the shrubs. The Sweetwater Trail is fairly shady and a good trail for viewing shrubs that are suitable for landscape use in their native setting. A 45-minute walk will take you through several habitats (chaparral, riparian, oak woodland) to a grassland habitat on a point with a view of Folsom Lake.

Besides the chaparral shrubs at the parking lot, along the trail you can find Toyon or Christmas Berry, and Manzanita. Sonoma Sage and Pennyroyal, perennials for landscape use, are found growing in the chaparral habitat. Some of the ferns along this trail are Bracken Fern, Goldback Fern, Wood Fern, and California Polypody Fern. The showy bulbs of the area are Golden Brodiaea, Blue Dicks, pink Twining Brodiaea, and white Fairy Lanterns. The showy annuals at the point are Butter and Eggs, Tunica, and Lupine. Two unusual plants along the trail are a non-native blue and yellow Forget-Me-Not, or *Myosotis versicolor,* that has naturalized in El Dorado County and *Lotus grandiflora,* a large showy yellow lotus.

Directions: Turn off US 50 at El Dorado Hills Road, which becomes Salmon Falls Road. The trailhead is at the parking lot on the lake side of the road, at the bridge over the American River where it becomes Folsom Lake.

SOUTHEAST OF PLACERVILLE

HAPPY VALLEY CUTOFF ROAD is a pretty 2-mile loop road that must have been the "old road." You can stop and photograph in peace and quiet. The river is in a steep canyon spanned by a delicate bridge. Some of the shrubs along the road are Chamise, Manzanita, California Mock Orange, Storax, Buck Brush, Deer Brush, Toyon, Golden Bush, and Yerba Santa. Some of the wildflowers are Shooting Stars, Yellow Pussy Ears, Indian Pinks, Kellogg's Monkeyflower, White Nemophila, and Miner's Lettuce. On the road banks near the "no trespassing bridge" there are Sedum and Heuchera. This same spot is beautiful to photograph in the fall, with Bigleaf Maples, the creek in the sunshine, and dark Douglas Fir in the background.

Directions: Happy Valley Cutoff Road is a right turn off of Mt. Aukum Road about an eighth of a mile north of Somerset. If you miss the turnoff, cross the river, drive a little way up the hill, and turn right on Happy Valley Cutoff at the other end, off of Mt. Aukum Road. After checking out Happy Valley Cutoff, drive up Mt. Aukum Road (E16) to Jenkinson Reservoir and the Sly Park picnic area (short pretty hikes), about 15 miles, for a pretty drive through vineyards and open country. Continue on through a residential area that is dotted with Dogwood blossoms in late April or early May, to return to US 50 at Pollock Pines.

SLY PARK RECREATION AREA AT JENKINSON LAKE has two delightful nature trails. Maidu Nature Trail, along the main road, is a short loop trail along a creek that tumbles downhill through a Douglas Fir forest. The treasures of this trail are Trillium, which blooms in April, and Dogwood, which should be beautiful in late April and early May. Be sure to look for trout in the creek. They are there. An educational bulletin board lists most of the plants of the area. The fall color should be good about the time the apples on "Apple Hill" are ripe. The Freedom Trail is located at the end of the Stonebreaker Campground parking lot 2.3 miles from the gatehouse. It has a warmer exposure and therefore a few plants that are not found at the Maidu Trail. They are Sugar Pine, Brown Bells, or *Fritillaria micrantha,* and Deer Brush. Near the creek entry to Jenkinson Lake, look for Leopard Lily and Indian Rhubarb.

Directions: Exit US 50 at Sly Park Road in Pollock Pines, about 8 miles east of Placerville. Drive down Sly Park Road about 4 miles to Jenkinson Lake. Alternative directions from SR 49 are given in the Happy Valley Cutoff writeup. There is a day-use fee for this area, which is managed by El Dorado Irrigation District in cooperation with the U.S. Bureau of Reclamation; camping, fishing, biking, swimming, water-skiing, and equestrian trails are also available.

BRIDAL VEIL PICNIC AREA is 19 miles east of Placerville along the American River. This is part of the El Dorado National Forest, and there is a use charge. It is a marvelous rest stop for a family on the way to the mountains. The river is gentle here for children, the tables have nice views, and there is a nature trail. Before leaving the parking lot, check out the most exciting plant in the area, *Clintonia uniflora,* or Queen's Cup, a short white Lily, located at the back of the parking lot under the willows, near where the lot becomes the road up the hill.

Follow the nature trail numbered posts and see if you can find all these plants.

1. Trailblazer, Ginger, Currant, Hazelnut, Bigleaf Maple, Sweet Cicely, Wild Rose, Bracken Fern, Fairy Bells, Blue Oak, Dogwood, Bedstraw, and False Solomon's Seal.
2. Douglas Fir, Trailblazer, Bracken Fern, Bedstraw, Bigleaf Maple, Goldminer Dogwood, Enchanter's Nightshade, Miner's Lettuce, and False Solomon's Seal.
3. Pacific Dogwood, Hazelnut, Bigleaf Maple, Trailblazer, and Columbine.
4. Yew Tree, Rattlesnake Plantain, Trillium, and Prunella.

The eastern end of the park along the river banks has Leopard Lilies, Queen's Cup Lilies, White-veined Wintergreen, Foxglove, and *Geum*. Some of the plants along the western-most picnic sites are Indian Rhubarb, Enchanter's Nightshade, Azalea, Hazelnut, Bigleaf Maple, Cedar, Ponderosa Pine, and Douglas Fir.

PEA VINE AND TELEPHONE RIDGE This area has good flowers into late June. The elevation here is 4,700 feet with a diverse flora and some rare plants such as *Calochortus clavatus* ssp. *avius* and *Phacelia stebbinsii*. Take US 50 about 20 miles east of Placerville, just east of Riverton, after the highway has crossed the American River, turn north (left) onto Ice House Road, then west (left) on Pea Vine Road. Since the Cleveland Forest fire of September 1992 many plants seem to have enjoyed the sunlight and heavy rainfall of the last few years. ENFIA and the Native Plant Society often lead walks in this area. It is at a higher altitude than anything else in this book, but do explore here. The El Dorado National Forest Interpretive Association (ENFIA), a volunteer organization, 3070 Camino Heights Drive, Camino, CA 94709, phone (530) 644-6048, can let you know about its walks in the area.

AUBURN AREA

Best for Children: Griffith Quarry Park, Limestone Quarry Trails
Best for Botanists: Ponderosa Way, Drum Powerhouse Road, Mosquito Ridge Road, Clark Tunnel Road
Best Displays: Clark Tunnel Road, Yankee Jims Road, Ponderosa Way, Lake Clementine Road
Best Hikes: Stevens Trail, Cool to Limestone Quarry Parking Lot (near river), Codfish Falls

HISTORY: In May 1848, Claude Chana, a French immigrant, and a band of Native Americans discovered gold in Auburn Ravine. The news traveled quickly, and camps sprang up everywhere. Auburn was known first as Wood's Dry Diggings, then North Fork Dry Diggings, then Rich Dry Diggings. The town became the Sutter County seat in 1850, at which time it was renamed Auburn, for a contingent of miners from Auburn, New York. Auburn continued as the seat for Placer County when it was carved out of Sutter and Yuba counties in 1853. After fire destroyed the town in 1855, it was relocated farther up the ravine and rebuilt in brick and stone with iron doors and shutters. Some of these buildings can be seen today in Auburn's Old Town.

The Auburn area is the gateway to the Northern Mines area. The town sits on a ridge that divides the Bear and American river drainages and overlooks the North Fork of the American River. The Central Pacific Railroad ran up this divide through Dutch Flat and over Donner Summit. Theodore Judah, an engineer, conceived and founded the Central Pacific in 1861, with the financial backing of the "Big Four": Charles Crocker, who supervised the construction, which began on January 8, 1863; Mark Hopkins, the treasurer of the project; Collis P. Huntington, the company's lobbyist and purchasing agent in Washington and New York; and Leland Stanford, the president and public symbol of the Big Four.

Between 1864 and 1866, a major wagon road from Dutch Flat to Donner Lake was constructed to transport materials for the workers on the new railroad. Dutch Flat, settled by German merchants who found gold in the gravels in 1851, was also a major staging station for miners on their way to the rich silver mines in Virginia City. (The "Dutch" was probably a distortion of the German *Deutsch*.) Crocker eventually hired 15,000 Chinese to work on the road and the railroad, and many of them lived in and around Dutch Flat. Today, the many ailanthus trees the Chinese planted and the unusual hillside contours left from the hydraulic mining are evidence of the area's Gold Rush history.

AUBURN is a bustling town of about 11,000, at an elevation of 1,125 feet, often putting it above the Sacramento Valley winter fog. It is the county seat for Placer County. Like many foothill towns, it is close to beautiful outdoor recreation and is growing fast.

Auburn State Recreation Area contains about 30,000 acres and has within its boundaries more than 30 miles on the North and Middle Forks of the American River. It basically incorporates the river canyons that would have been flooded if the proposed Auburn Dam had been built. This chapter would have to be drastically reduced if the dam were ever built. The Auburn Recreation Area office, (530) 885-4527, is located on SR 49 about a mile south of town on the uphill side of the road. The area

has many wonderful trails for hiking, mountain-biking, and horseback riding, plus river and reservoir access for swimming, fishing, rafting, boating, camping, and picnicking. Dogs are allowed on leash only. A good general map of the North and Middle Forks of the American River by Don E. Robinson is available at Pioneer Mining, 943 Lincoln Avenue, Auburn, (530) 885-1801.

LAKE CLEMENTINE ROAD is about 2 miles from Auburn off Foresthill Road. It is a florific 2.5-mile paved road—narrow, but empty in spring—down to the lake. The dam here was completed in 1939. When the lake is full, as it can be at wildflower time, the noise of crashing water spilling over the dam to the rocks below fills the canyon. It is a sight to see! Lake Clementine is 3.5 miles long, in a steep narrow canyon. The showy plants along this pretty road are Indian Pinks, Spider Lupine, Clarkia, Milkweed, Tarweed, Sedum, Twining Brodiaea, Golden Brodiaea, Iris, and Delphinium, to name just a few. Two beautiful native shrubs that are prolific in the canyon are Snowdrop Bush and California Mock Orange. There are parking and a marina at the lake. It would be a wonderful place to canoe on a weekday.

Directions: Exit I-80 at Foresthill Road. Drive about 2 miles toward Foresthill; after crossing the high bridge (Auburn Dam would have flooded this area), notice Old Foresthill Road turning off to the right, and just after that Clementine Road turns off to the left.

AMERICAN RIVER CANYON is reached by turning off I-80 and going south on SR 49 for about a mile. (A beautiful alternative route to the canyon, which avoids the town, is to take the Foresthill Road exit from I-80, and about half a mile after the bridge turn right on Old Foresthill Road. It has good views of the canyon and a quarry.) You can get a map of the many trails in the American River Canyon in the Recreation Area Office. If you take the SR 49 route, after about a quarter of a mile or less, at the first pullout in the canyon on the right, you'll see a trail gate that leads to an interesting part of the Wendell Robie Trail. Follow this gentle trail west into the canyon for about 40 minutes, and eventually you come on a view of the site where the Auburn Dam construction was halted.

The **Wendell Robie Trail** continues just across from the Auburn Recreation Headquarters about half a mile down SR 49 on the river side of the road. This trail has flumes, old bridges, waterfalls, mileage markers, and access to beaches along the American River. A few of the showier flowers are Indian Pinks, Iris, Shooting Stars, Clematis, and Snowdrop Bush. For a nice downhill walk, arrange a shuttle, leaving one car at the park headquarters and one at the confluence of the North and Middle Forks of the American River, where SR 49 crosses the river. A parking area for river access is located on the north side of the river at the confluence. You are likely to see pretty displays of spring flowers on the hot road banks here.

Limestone Quarry Area Trails give several hiking or biking choices. Two of them may involve a shuttle. The Limestone Quarry parking lot is located on SR 49 a little way uphill on the south side of the river. A very enjoyable trail, with lots of flowers and nice river views, runs along the old railroad bed used by the quarry (which was started in the 1880s), past several streams, to an area that looks like a former loading dock. From here the choice is to walk farther along the river, through a disturbed area, to where the trail comes down from Cool, or to hike uphill from the loading dock in a series of switchbacks.

The uphill choice soon brings you past an inviting valley of limestone cliffs, rocks, and at least two caves (not many flowers in this area) and ends at the top of American River Canyon, on the south side overlooking the quarry, beside SR 49. Some special plants are found on these upper switchbacks: *Meconella californica*, a Poppy relative (look at the seed pod that reminds you of a Poppy, not the white flower), and Naked Broom-rape, or *Orobanche uniflora*. As you near the top of the ravine you'll see a power installation with a gravel road that heads toward the highway; but don't take it, stay left and follow the dirt trail. When the quarry is in view, watch for a trail through the Silver Bush Lupines over to the highway, where hopefully you may have left a shuttle car. There is a small pullout on SR 49 just at the top of the American River Canyon.

After reading the next paragraph about the Cool to Limestone Quarry hike, you will see that a loop is possible, with minimal walking on the highway, by walking up just beyond the quarry entry to the trail from Cool to the river. Do not park by the cyclone fence near the quarry entry, as this makes visibility difficult for traffic coming out of the quarry. Parking is not allowed in the Spreckels quarry lot. The trail crosses the road just south of the quarry entry. Allow about 2½ hours from the Limestone Quarry Parking Lot to your shuttle car at the top of American River Canyon.

Cool to Limestone Quarry Parking Lot (near the river) is a delight because of the different habitats encountered as you descend past the Spreckels Limestone Quarry into the river confluence area. You may wish to leave a shuttle car in the Auburn Recreation Area's Limestone Quarry Parking Lot down near the river. The trail begins near SR 49, in the parking lot behind the Cool Firehouse, and skirts halfway around a pasture. While walking on the part nearest SR 49, watch for Frying Pans Poppies, or *Eschscholzia lobbii*, and Five Spot Nemophila. At the far side of the pasture, turn north (right) into an open Oak woodland. The treasures here are a red-stemmed lavender lupine (*Lupinus latifolia* var. *columbianus*), Mule Ears, Foothill Lomatium, and a beautiful brick watering trough dedicated to Paige Harper. He was very active with the Western States Trail Foundation and worked hard on these trails we are enjoying. Observe the old stones lining the spring at the back of the trough.

The trail crosses SR 49 just south of the quarry parking lot. It is a bit noisy for a while, but the beauty of the flowers along this part of the trail makes up for that. White Fairy Lanterns, Indian Pinks, Fawn Lily, and Yellow Pussy Ears adorn this part of the trail. The trail follows a quarry road for a little while, but watch for it to turn right off this road. Soon it crosses a creek, where a sign tells you that it is three-quarters of a mile to Western States Trail. Across the ravine, the Old Foresthill Road (beautiful flower displays) climbs out of the ravine, and you may spot the OHV road that goes down to the river from there. Once down on the old railroad bed, you have one slight rise near some old structures, and then it is about 40 minutes to the parking lot near the river. Allow about 3½ hours.

Directions: Leave a shuttle car in the Auburn Recreation Area's Limestone Quarry Parking Lot on SR 49, near the American River, and drive the other car to Cool, 4 miles up the hill. If you have only one car, hike the suggested loop or just walk along the river, where the plants are beautiful.

EAST OF AUBURN OFF I-80

WEIMAR EXIT, PONDEROSA WAY, is a 10-mile, well-graded dirt road from I-80 to Auburn-Foresthill Road. It has a few high spots, so drive carefully and slowly. Allow an hour because of flower stops. This area is popular with gold seekers, rafters, fishermen, and naturalists. The BLM and the Auburn Recreation Area manage the land in the canyon of the

51

North Fork of the American River along Ponderosa Way, though some of it is private land, such as that around Codfish Falls. There is a wonderful swimming hole under the bridge 5 miles down from I-80, though at wildflower time the water is too cold.

Some of the flowers along the southwest exposure on the road down to the bridge from I-80 are Foothill Poppy, Blue Dicks, Silver Bush Lupine, Lace Pod, Yerba Santa, Coreopsis, Phacelia, Lomatium, Popcorn Flower, Miner's Lettuce, Delphinium, Woolly Sunflower, Hound's Tongue, and mosslike Selaginella. You can take a beautiful hike downriver to Codfish Falls on the I-80 side of the bridge.

The northern exposure from the bridge up to the Auburn-Foresthill Road has banks of California Saxifrage and Sedum right near the bridge. Along the road up to Foresthill are Buttercups, Honeysuckle, Shooting Stars, and Alum Root. The trees and shrubs along the way are Redbud, Douglas Fir, Foothill Pine, Ponderosa Pine, Canyon Live Oak, Black Oak, Madrone, Bay, Toyon, California Mock Orange, and Deer Brush. A nice stopping place is the creek crossing near the top of the Foresthill side of the canyon, at an old dam with a metal railing that has become a trellis for grapevines. Get out of the car and you will see interesting plants at this site: Trillium, Giant Chain Fern, and Yew trees. Between the little dam and Foresthill Road, watch for Iris, Soap Plant, Klamathweed, Cat-tails, Mountain Misery, and Elderberry. Turn right on Auburn-Foresthill Road to return to Auburn.

Directions to Ponderosa Way: Exit I-80 at Weimar Cross Road, stay on the south side of the freeway, turn right, and the frontage road quickly becomes Ponderosa Way. About 2 miles down Ponderosa is your last chance for cold drinks, at Ponderosaland. If you choose, instead, to drive from the Foresthill end of Ponderosa Way, exit I-80 in Auburn at the Foresthill exit and drive about 10 miles, just past Everybody's Inn Bar. Watch for a left turn onto NF Ponderosa Way Road. If you come to Spring Garden Road, you have passed the turnoff.

Codfish Falls Trail at the Ponderosa Way Bridge starts on the sandy beach and follows the river downstream on a narrow trail above the river. Hiking boots are needed. Many of the plants that are listed in the Ponderosa Way paragraph are also along this trail. The treasures of this trail are Evening Snow, or *Linanthus dichotomus* (which blooms late in the day), Cream Cups, and the small magenta Kellogg's Monkeyflower. It takes about an hour to walk to Codfish Falls from Ponderosa Bridge. The last twenty minutes along Codfish Creek is on private land belonging to the Placer Land Trust and Nature Center, (530) 878-6053. Many organizations, such as the California Native Plant Society and the Nevada County Land Trust, use this trail.

Directions: See Ponderosa Way directions. The bridge is about 5 miles from I-80.

YANKEE JIMS ROAD is a 15-mile road between Foresthill and I-80. Plan on 3 hours to drive it, with flower stops, or most of the day if hiking the Indian Creek Trail (2 miles round trip), or swimming, watching kayackers, or gold panning at the North Fork of the American River. Bring water, a picnic, bathing suit, camera, and a gold pan. Yankee Jims Road is a wonderful road with views and lots of plant diversity. The road is mostly one lane and dirt, but is safe and has adequate pullouts. In late spring, after it gets warm, a weekday is best, to avoid the weekend traffic to the popular swimming hole on the North Fork, which is 4 miles down the canyon from I-80. Usually traffic is very light on the American River to Foresthill part of the road.

In Foresthill **check your mileage** on Gold Street; the road is level for a while, with small blue peas (*Lathyrus nevadensis* var. *nevadensis*) along with Hartweg's pale yellow Iris, Indian Paintbrush, Lupine on the road banks, and Dogwood in the forest in late April. The road gets steeper—use low gear to make it easier to stop if a treasure is spotted along the roadside. The **5-mile corner** has a shady pullout beside a pretty creek. Look for Waterfall Buttercup on the banks, along with Bleeding Hearts, as well as Elk Clover, Fringe Cups, California Mock Orange, Sedum, Hazelnut, Boykinia, and Bigleaf Maple. Don't miss Devil's Falls. The Alum Root, or *Heuchera micrantha,* and Sedum are thick on the shady banks on the left bank of the road.

At **7 miles** cross the rickety-rattley old suspension bridge over the North Fork and enter a totally different habitat with all new flowers. Watch for Snowdrop Bush, Clarkia, Poppies, Lupines, and Indian Paintbrush. Near the top of the canyon in early spring watch for pink Indian Rhubarb bobbing back and forth in the flow of the stream. Across the road from the houses, on the steep shady banks, in early spring there are delicate white flowers of Isopyrum, pinkish Milkmaids, and Trillium just before Canyon Way or Placer Hills Road.

Directions: Yankee Jims Road is just off eastbound I-80 at Canyon Way. Go right downhill, turn left on Yankee Jims Road toward Foresthill, and go 4 miles to the bridge. A preferable alternative route from Foresthill does not have the morning sun in your eyes, so miles have been measured from Foresthill to I-80. Foresthill is 15 miles from Auburn on a good fast highway. In Foresthill turn left on Gold Street. **Check your mileage at Gold Street. There are some good stops along Yankee Jims Road, and the mileage is measured from this turnoff.**

Indian Creek Trail is a 2-mile walk on a well-worn trail high above the American River that ends where Indian Creek meets the North Fork of the river. It is necessary to ford Shirttail Creek (wait until mid-April or later, when the creek is not so full, or take off your boots—and sometimes your pants as well) to get over to the old outhouses where the Indian Creek Trail begins. Wear long pants as a protection against Poison Oak, and bring Wash and Wipes. Some of the special flowers on this trail that are white are Skull Cap, Fairy Lanterns, and Water Buttercup. Yellow specials are Frying Pans Poppy, Golden Brodiaea, and Tauschia. Others are pink Clarkia and red Indian Pinks, and aromatic lavender Pennyroyal. The short walk up to Indian Creek ends at a small pool and waterfall. *Sierra Heritage* magazine, March 1991, has an article about Indian Creek called "A Walk on the Wild Side," written by Katie Lynch, with Robert Elder, wildflower guide.

Directions: See the Yankee Jims Road directions above. The trail is a little way up Yankee Jims Road from the river, on the Foresthill side of the bridge. The fastest route to Indian Creek trailhead is from I-80.

STEVENS TRAIL, located near Colfax, is a fabulous 4.5-mile trail to Stevens Bridge site and Secret Ravine. It is a little less than 4 miles to the river. You will find good views and wonderful spring flowers, with some unusual plants such as *Lotus argophyllus*, Waterfall Buttercup or *Ranunculus hystriculus* (a mid-March bloomer), and Indian Pink. The first 45 minutes of the trail are strenuous, but after that it is gentle all the way down to the North Fork of the American River. It will take a serious flower chaser about three hours to get to the river. Bring water, food, bathing suit, camera, and gold pan. The trail has several pretty creek crossings, with their associated riparian plants within the forest, though most of the unusual and prettier plant displays occur when you emerge from the trees. This part of the trail may be easy but it can get hot. If fatigue sets in or the day is too hot, try to make it to the creek with the cascade of Waterfall Buttercups just below the trail and the ancient, beautifully stacked stone foundation that supports the trail. This is where, if you listen carefully, you can almost hear the mule-train packs scraping the sides of the trail as they carried supplies to the miners in Iowa Hill.

Truman Allen Stevens, who ran a ranch in Iowa Hill and a livery stable in Colfax, built this trail in 1859 and charged a toll for the use of it and the bridge. For more history, see the July 1993 *Sierra Heritage* magazine article "Preserving the Stevens Trail," by Jim Mayer. The return trip could be hot, due to the southwest exposure, but there are several creeks where you can wet your scarf, shirt, or hat to keep cool.

Trail: The first part of the trail is a little obscured by jeep roads and mine tailings in a few places. Watch for the trail markers on steel rails in the first mile. Whenever there is a break in the trees, within the first mile, look up and notice the steep rock walls of the Cape Horn railroad bed, built by Chinese laborers who hung in baskets while they drilled holes and blasted out a ledge to support the railroad bed. Keep this wall off your left shoulder and watch for the rail trail markers on your way down (remember these intersections for your return trip), so you will not stray onto one of the private jeep roads.

Directions: Take the Colfax exit off of I-80 east and go east a short way on the frontage road past the Colfax Cemetery, on your right in the pines on the hill. The road ends at the trailhead parking lot, near the freeway.

DRUM POWERHOUSE ROAD runs for about 6 florific miles to Bear River Powerhouse, with many different plant communities, including serpentine soil associates. Just past the homes, keep your eyes open for Yellow Pussy Ears on the right side of the road. The showiest plant along the road is Bleeding Heart. Dogbane (*Apocynum androsimaefolium*) and *Nemophila heterophylla* are also found on the road banks. In the hotter areas look for Yellow Bush Poppy. Heuchera, Sedum, Gooseberries, Tarweed, and Wallflower can be seen on the uphill banks. Look for pink-tinted Meadow Foam in moist ditches. Fragrant Deer Brush is the predominant white shrub along the road.

PLANT LIST BY COLOR

White	Yellow	Pink
Deer Brush	Bush Poppy	Currant
Buckbrush	Woolly Sunflower	Gooseberry
Sierra Plum	Pine Violet	Wild Rose
California Mock Orange	Klamathweed	Dogbane
Thimbleberry	Monkeyflower	Bleeding Heart
Mountain Misery	Sedum	Collomia
Blackberry	Wallflower	Chinese Houses
Hawkweed	Bear Buckwheat	Milkweed
Morning Glory	Tarweed	Alum Root
White Chinese Houses	Honeysuckle	Meadowfoam
Sweet Cicely	**Orange**	Star Flower
Jewel Flower	California Poppy	**Blue**
White Chrysanthemum	Leopard Lily	Yerba Santa
Skullcap	Sticky Monkeyflower	Wild Hyacinth
Keckiella	**Red**	Brewer's Phacelia
Yarrow	Columbine	Pennyroyal
Fleabane	Indian Pink	Penstemon
White Nemophila	Indian Paintbrush	Lupine
	Dudleya (coral)	Draperia
		Ball-headed Gilia

Directions: Leave I-80 at the Alta exit, the first one after Dutch Flat. Go under the freeway. Don't go into Alta, but bear left. Notice the beautiful old brown shingle homes on Lake Alta. Take the second road to your right toward Dutch Flat. Cross over the flume and railroad tracks, and turn right on Drum Powerhouse Road. The road passes through a residential area and then becomes a narrow paved road. One of several pleasant alternative routes back to I-80 is to drive east through Alta, past the store and school, passing through Dogwoods and ancient apple trees, to Baxters and I-80.

The best alternative is a right turn (downhill) at Drum Powerhouse Road that leads to the beautiful little mining town of Dutch Flat, at an elevation of 3,200 feet. It is worth the time to go into the store for some cold drinks and to walk around the main block of the town to see the church, schoolhouse, and some pretty gardens. In the summer the blackberry picking along the creek through town is wonderful. Notice the quartz-rock house just down from the store; our young family lived there for two summers. Continue on the little road up the hill 2 miles to I-80.

FORESTHILL AREA SOUTHEAST OF AUBURN

MOSQUITO RIDGE ROAD blooms from late March to late May. It is 6 miles to Oxbow Reservoir on a narrow paved road. Mosquito Ridge Road is a beautiful road for flowers, canyon and Sierra views, geology, mines, picnicking, and swimming on the Middle Fork of the American River, where it enters Oxbow Reservoir. The bad news is the truck traffic; be careful to pull off anytime you can. You may spot something at every pullout, you will be safer, and truck drivers won't get angry with the naturalists. Signal! There seem to be more pullout spots going down into the canyon than on the way up. Two of the good shrubs here are *Philadelphus* and Snowdrop Bush. Several of the more unusual plants are *Streptanthus polygaloides* (rare), *Lotus argophyllus*, or Silverleaf Lotus, *Brodiaea bridgesii*, and *Erigeron foliosus*, or Fleabane Daisy. The showy plants are *Mimulus bifidus* or Apricot Monkeyflower, *Gilia capitata*, *Clarkia biloba*, *Clarkia rhomboidea*, and *Collinsia tinctoria*, or White Chinese Houses. Several of these, including the rare plant, are within walking distance of the Ralston picnic area at Oxbow Reservoir.

WEST OF AUBURN

GRIFFITH QUARRY PARK is a place where children will enjoy escaping from the car to follow the paths in this small park. The history and flowers will please the adults. The museum is open Saturday and Sunday from noon until 4 p.m. (916-663-1837). Enjoy a picnic in the welcome shade cast by Interior Live Oaks, Blue Oaks, Buckeyes, Walnut trees, and Digger Pines. Large granite boulders are a reminder that the mountains are near. The park has 3 miles of trails including a short walk to view the large pit where the granite was quarried for the California State Capitol and the San Francisco Mint. Cottonwoods grow near the water. The large shrubs in the area are Toyon, Buckbrush, or *Ceanothus cuneatus*, Coffeeberry, and of course Poison Oak. The treasure plant for this location is Twining Brodiaea. Blue, waxy-appearing Harvest Brodiaea is also found here along with another bulb with wavy leaves called Soap Plant. Some of the showy wildflowers in the park are Spider Lupine, Miniature Lupine, Indian Paintbrush, Delphinium, Pearly Everlasting, Winecup Clarkia, and Poppies.

Directions: Take the Penryn exit off I-80 and go north almost 1 mile; turn right on Taylor Boulevard (old SR 40) about a mile to the park.

CLARK TUNNEL ROAD is very near Griffith Park. Go straight across Taylor Boulevard from the Griffith Park driveway onto English Colony Road, which goes through historic Penryn and past ancient Palm trees. Turn right onto the 4.5 mile Clark Tunnel Road. There are yellow non-native Bermuda Buttercups, pretty gardens, and homes for about a mile, then Woolly Sunflowers, blue Ball-headed Gilia, and Spider Lupine decorate the road banks. The dandelionlike seed heads on the right side of the road are Blow Wives. After about 2 miles, the road becomes dirt and the rocky fields are beautiful with Royal Delphinium, White Brodiaea, White-tipped Clover, Bird's Eye Gilia, and Goldfields. The black swallowtail or pipe vine butterfly is so prevalent that one worries about their demise on the front of the car.

The treasure plant in the rocky fields is white Glass Lily, or *Triteleia lilacina*. Look carefully at the flower center to see the small crystal bubbles at the base of each petal. As the road descends, Dutchman's Pipe is everywhere along the oak-shaded road. The butterflies go up on the ridge to enjoy the flowers and sun, and return to this area to lay their eggs. The bulbs are beautiful along this part of the road: there are Twining Brodiaea, Golden Brodiaea, Ithuriel's Spear, Onions, and Fairy Lanterns. Clark Tunnel Road ends at SR 193 halfway between Lincoln and Auburn. Either direction is pretty. If you are meandering and have a good detailed map, then downhill toward Lincoln and Camp Far West would be pleasant. If you need to get someplace soon, uphill to I-80 is more efficient.

CAMP FAR WEST ROAD, located 8 miles north of Lincoln on SR 65, is a beautiful flower road, good also for cyclists. It has rolling hills, pretty streams, a reservoir (private), and good birdwatching, with a nice loop trip returning to SR 65 at Wheatland on Spenceville Road. Some of the flowers along the road are White Brodiaea, Wild Hyacinth, Ithuriel's Spear, Golden Brodiaea, Purple Owl's-clover, Tidy-tips, Goldfields, and Meadowfoam. Access to the Spenceville Wildlife Area (see pages 61-62) is at the northern end of the reservoir on Long Ravine Road.

GRASS VALLEY AND NEVADA CITY AREA

Best for Children: *Empire Mine, Bridgeport, Rock Creek Nature Area, Bowman Lake Road, Independence Trail*

Best for Botanists: *Hell's Half Acre, McCourtney Road, Bridgeport, Canyon Creek Trail, Skillman Flat*

Best Displays: *Bridgeport, Hell's Half Acre*

Best Hikes: *Humbug Trail, Canyon Creek Trail, Edwards Crossing to Purdon Crossing Trail, Indian Valley to Goodyears Bar*

HISTORY: In September 1849 several prospectors arrived from Boston and built four cabins on the southern slope of a ravine at the lower end of Grass Valley. This little settlement, called Boston Ravine, grew as more newcomers came to work the placers of Wolf Creek and other streams, flats, and gulches. Miners also occupied tents and log cabins at the nearby settlement of Deer Creek Dry Diggings, where they dug "coyote" holes (shallow man-sized tunnels such as coyotes dig) to reach the gold-rich gravels of a prehistoric river system. By 1851, when Nevada County was carved out of part of Yuba County, the Dry Diggings had become Nevada City, and the town became the third largest in California.

When placer mining began to decline at Grass Valley, George McKnight stumbled over a large quartz rock with glints of gold. The spot became known as Gold Hill, and his discovery hastened the development of Grass Valley. Since a significant investment in equipment was necessary to wrest gold from quartz veins, small claims were consolidated to form large mining companies. Thus Grass Valley became a "company town" and the owners hired hard-rock miners from Cornwall, England, famous for their experience in England's tin and copper mines. At one time 85 percent of the Grass Valley workers were Cornish miners.

In 1853 Edward E. Matteson invented a new technique of "hydraulic" mining that literally changed the contours of the foothills (see page xvii), and in 1878 Lester Pelton designed a more efficient waterwheel. The South Yuba Canal Company developed the largest network of water flumes and ditches in California to supply water for hydraulic mining, and these ditches and Pelton's wheel provided the foundation for Pacific Gas and Electric Company's vast hydroelectric system.

The Empire Mine, the Idaho-Maryland Mine, the Eureka Mine, and others made Grass Valley and Nevada City the richest and most famous gold mining district in California, producing more than $400 million in gold from 1850 until 1956, when the Empire Mine closed due to high operating costs. At the end, the Empire had 367 miles of underground tunnels, with an incline depth of more than 2 miles and a vertical drop of more than 5,000 feet. The ruins of the North Star Mine's 60-stamp mill are a ghostly reminder of the process used to crush gold-rich ore. The Sawyer decision of

1884 finally put an end to hydraulic mining, which had dumped debris into the rivers and was ruining farmlands in the Sacramento Valley.

Downieville, north of Nevada City, was named for Major William Downie, a Scotsman who brought a diverse party in 1849 to The Forks, a junction of the North Fork of the Yuba River and a smaller tributary stream also named for Downie. His group, made up of a dozen black sailors, an Indian, a Kanaka (Hawaiian), and other prospectors, fanned out along the Downie and other tributaries, making rich strikes on gravel bars and flats. By 1851 news of the rich placer diggings had spread and the population around Downieville increased to 5,000. The remoteness of the area, the richness of the diggings, and the need for local government spurred the citizens to petition the state government to create a new county to be called Sierra County. The petition was granted on April 16, 1852, and Downieville became the county seat.

Prior to Downie's arrival, gold had been discovered by the prospecting Goodyear brothers in the gravels several miles downstream from The Forks at the junction of the Yuba and Goodyears Creek, which they named Goodyears Bar. For a while, the diggings there yielded rich returns, but the miners wanted more. In 1851 they diverted the Yuba River into flumes (ditches) stretching the entire four miles from Downieville to Goodyears Bar, in order to mine the river's bedrock. However, winter floods washed the flumes away.

Sierra City began as a trading center on an old stage road from Downieville. The small town lies next to the rushing Yuba River at the base of the jagged, towering peaks of the Sierra Buttes, which rise to 8,500 feet. Philo A. Haven and Joseph Zumwalt arrived in this Yuba River wilderness in the spring of 1850, probably the first white men to explore the area. Quartz gold was discovered here in 1850, reputedly by a man named Murphy. By 1852 the Sierra Buttes were riddled with hundreds of shafts and tunnels. Mules and sleds were used to transport equipment up the rugged Buttes. Tremendous perseverance and ingenuity were required to wrest gold from the Sierra Buttes. The grand order of E Clampus Vitus, a convivial fraternal organization, began here in 1857. This organization has placed many historic plaques along SR 49 to inform travelers about the gold country's past.

GRASS VALLEY, with a population of 9,393, is at a delightful elevation of 2,420 feet, just high enough above the Sacramento Valley to be out of the extreme summer heat and yet usually below the snow elevation. This bustling town has historical buildings next to newer structures. The Nevada County Fairgrounds are beautiful and almost always have something going on. The Chamber of Commerce, 248 Mill Street, (530) 273-4667, has more information to enhance your visit.

EMPIRE MINE STATE HISTORIC PARK, GRASS VALLEY, is located at 10791 Empire Street, just off SR 49 as you enter Grass Valley coming from Auburn. It is a convenient meeting place for groups heading out to enjoy this wonderful part of the gold country. There are very interesting docent tours of the mining activities, and of Bourn Cottage and the beautiful gardens. A 2-mile loop hike of the Hardrock Trail is fun for children, history buffs, and engineers. The visitor center has a plant list for the Hardrock Trail. Scarlet Fritillary, Hartweg's Iris, and Yellow Pussy Ears are the treasures of the trail. Gardeners will appreciate the beautiful grounds and rose garden behind the Bourn Cottage. Filoli, south of San Francisco, was the primary residence of Mr. Bourn. Reservations are sometimes required for the tour of Bourn Cottage, (530) 273-8522. A plant list is available at the park office.

HELL'S HALF ACRE may soon be partially developed, but it is included here because the California Native Plant Society (with the help of concerned citizens) has been able to protect part of this unique habitat. It is one of the best wildflower sites in the foothills because of the plant diversity in a relatively small space. How does ripe fruit remain on Sierra Plum so close to town? Butter and Eggs turn the grasslands yellow. The Lily family is well represented with two species of Onions, *Allium sanbornii* and *Allium amplectens,* as well as several species of Fritillary and several Brodiaea: Blue Dicks, Golden Brodiaea, White Brodiaea, *Brodiaea purdyi,* and Harvest Brodiaea. Tiny magenta *Mimulus tricolor* is a treat. The property consists of about 300 acres of chaparral, grassland, vernal pools, and volcanic soil at an altitude of 2,600 feet.

Directions: Take SR 49 to downtown Grass Valley, then take Main Street west out of town. The road becomes Rough and Ready. Hell's Half Acre is at the junction of Rough and Ready Highway and Ridge Road.

McCOURTNEY ROAD has easy access to some unusual plants and pretty wildflower fields. This area is developing into large homesites, so some of the flower fields are disappearing. Take the Fairgrounds exit (a fabulous, clean, Pine-strewn fairground with constant events) off SR 20 just off SR 49. This is a busy road, so be aware of traffic behind you and pull off the road for flowers. Along McCourtney Road early in spring Clematis climbs over some of the shrubs in the chaparral; blue Lemmon's Ceanothus and yellow Bolander's Wyethia can also be spotted from the car. The side roads near the Grass Valley dump have unusual plants on the gabbro soil and are relatively safe from development.

On the Grass Valley side of the dump is a stand of McNab Cypress, often found on serpentine soil, but here the soil is gabbro. In the vicinity of the Cypress look for Fawn Lily in early March, followed by Bolander's Wyethia. This same area has rare Stebbins Morning-glory, *Fremontia decumbens,* and Swertia blooming in late April and early May.

Wolf Mountain Road, on the far side of the dump, has lots of beautiful flowering native plants: Chaparral Pea Shrub, Red Bud tree, Ash Paint-brush (*Castilleja pruinosa*), Pentstemon, Pennyroyal. In early spring Fawn Lily (*Erythronium multiscapoideum*), Milkweed (*Asclepias cordifolia*), and Balsam Root (*Balsamorhiza deltoidea*) are a few of the plants along this quiet road.

At the end of the road, take the left branch of the Y to the top of the hill and pull into the west-facing parking area. Under the trees in the parking area, look for Twining Brodiaea and Checkers, or *Sidalcea malvaeflora*. Walk southwest through the trees to the open rocky field; if you look carefully you will find *Odontostomum hartwegii,* and also a large patch of low Oregon Grape (*Berberis aquifolium* var. *repens*). You'll have a beautiful view of the Sacramento Valley, Sutter Buttes, and, on a clear day, Mount Diablo and the Coast Range. Local nature lovers call this spot Sunset Rocks.

WEST OF GRASS VALLEY

BRIDGEPORT STATE PARK is a great area for hikers, historians, engineers, children, and flower chasers. Dogs must be on a leash. Flowers begin to bloom in mid-March because of the low elevation and slope exposure. The 225-foot bridge, built in 1862 by David Wood, is the longest single-span covered bridge in the United States. It was built on the Virginia Turnpike and Toll Road that carried traffic and ore from Virginia City to the port at Marysville. The Nevada County Historical Society *Bulletin* of January 1996 has an extensive article about the covered bridge. The Yuba River has sandy coves with swimming holes, and picnic tables at several locations overlooking the river. The best wildflower trail is the **Buttermilk Bend Trail**, which begins across the road from the visitor center and bridge, at the parking lot on the north side of the river. The trail is about 2.5 miles round trip and is fairly level. See the plant list at the end of this chapter, or ask for a list at the visitor center.

Point Defiance Trail is a pleasant 1-mile shady walk to Lake Engle-bright, with constant views of the Yuba River. The highlights of the trail are Hartweg's Iris, Blue Dicks, and Dutchman's Pipe, as well as access to sandy beaches and good fishing. Get a boating friend to pick you up at Point Defiance on Lake Englebright so you don't have to retrace your steps.

Directions: Take SR 20 west from Grass Valley, toward Marysville, to Penn Valley. Turn right on Pleasant Valley Road, past Lake Wildwood (which was once part of the 27-mile Excelsior Mining Ditch to Smart-ville), and drive 8 miles to Bridgeport. As the road narrows and dips downhill toward the river, the banks on the left side of the road have beautiful yellow Pussy Ears, Brodiaea, Clarkia, and Chinese Houses.

SPENCEVILLE WILDLIFE AREA, operated by the California Department of Fish and Game, consists of 11,213 acres of grasslands,

chaparral, oak woodlands, and creeks at a 600-foot to 1,000-foot elevation. This is cattle country, so dogs need to be controlled. Bloom time
starts in mid to late March. A nice loop hike to **Shingle Falls**, about 2.5
miles through oak woodland and foothill pines, will take you to a rocky,
flowery overlook. The temptation is to follow the creek up to the falls, but
there is an easier high trail. Cross the old bridge and walk up the road past
the former copper mines and fig tree. Instead of going down to the creek,
follow the fire road up the hill until you come to an iron gate on the trail
on your right. Go through the gate and the cattle guard. At the fire road
junction, angle upward through the trees, where you follow a small "ghost
of a ditch" that contours the hill. In this area you will find Golden
Brodiaea, yellow Mariposa Lily, two species of blue Brodiaea, several
Clovers, Fiddleneck, Caespitose Poppy, Woolly Sunflower, Lupines, and
Fleabane. At Shingle Falls, enjoy an early spring picnic sitting among the
rocks surrounded by Caespitose or Foothill Poppy. Later in spring a
beautiful hill of flowers, mostly Clarkia, blooms across Dry Creek. Then
meander back down the dirt road, which does leave the creek, or cut over
to the creek below the falls. Observe the Indian grinding holes and, if you
are adventuresome, follow the creek, by means of some rock hopping and
scrambling, back to the site of the copper mines and the cars. The May
1989 *Sierra Heritage* magazine has a historical article on Spenceville.

 Directions: Take SR 20 west out of Grass Valley about 15 miles until
you come to the State Forestry Station near the intersection of Hammonton Road, Smartville Road, and SR 20. Go south (Hammonton Road
turns off in 0.9 mile) on Smartville Road for about 5 miles to Waldo Road.
Go left on Waldo Road and in 2 miles cross Waldo Bridge, built in 1920;
there (deep swimming holes in Dry Creek here) turn left, and go 2.5 miles
to the site of Spenceville. Continue to the end of the road to the parking
area for the Shingle Falls hike. A beautiful alternative is to take SR 65, near
Lincoln, turn off on Camp Far West Road, go around the dam onto Long
Ravine Road, and take a right at the Spenceville townsite (see Auburn map).

NORTH OF GRASS VALLEY

NEVADA CITY, with an elevation of 2,840 feet, is slightly higher than
Grass Valley. The downtown area is situated in a valley. The town with its
white church spires is very picturesque against fall foliage. The downtown
area is charming, with good bookstores, antique stores, restaurants, and a
nature store in wonderful old buildings. Shopping malls, with the usual
fast-food stops, are situated away from downtown. More information
regarding this charming town is available from the Nevada City Chamber
of Commerce, 132 Main Street, (530) 265-2692.

HIGHWAY 49 north of Nevada City is a beautiful road to Downieville
and Sierra City. It is difficult to pull off the road to see the flowers, but

there are a few pullouts that do have good plant material. The **Independence Trail** 5.5 miles northwest of Nevada City is described below. The South Fork of the Yuba River, on the south side of the bridge, has a nice parking lot with *Mimulus bifidus* on the rocks, picnic tables just across the old concrete bridge, and great swimming holes after the flowers have gone to seed. Watch for Tyler-Foote Crossing Road and Birchville Road. Birchville Road winds its way down to French Corral and Bridgeport. Tyler-Foote Crossing Road leads to Malakoff Diggings.

The second river crossing is the Middle Fork of the Yuba River, where there is an easy pullout with good swimming at Oregon Creek. Oregon Creek Campground is on the east side of SR 49; the Oregon Creek Covered Bridge, built in 1860, still remains. Shortly after the Middle Fork crossing, Ridge Road turns off to Alleghany, where you can visit a working gold mine at the Original Sixteen to One Mine—reservations required, (530) 287-3264. The North Fork of the Yuba River crossing has a beautiful swimming hole one mile downstream from the bridge, at Shenanigan Flat. A wonderful hike with unusual flowers and floral displays (starting at the banks by the parking lot) is on the Canyon Creek Trail through Shenanigan Flat (described later).

Still on SR 49, after the Fiddle Creek Campground at Sierra Co. road marker 5.00, there is a good pullout with sunny cliffs of Lupine, Jewel Flower, Blue Witch, Apricot Monkeyflower, Dudleya, Clover, Wallflower, Mountain Misery, two species of Brodiaea, and Poppies. Indian Valley Campground has a bridge across the North Fork of the Yuba that leads to a 7-mile hike to the Mountain House Road by Goodyears Bar. Between Downieville and Sierra City watch for the good river views, as well as Indian Paintbrush and Lupine hanging from the red rocky road banks.

INDEPENDENCE TRAIL on SR 49, 5.5 miles northwest of Nevada City, has parking space against the rock wall in a turnout. The trail follows the Excelsior Canal and Flume System that was built in 1856 to carry water from here to Smartville, 25 miles downstream. As you walk where the water once flowed, you are nose to nose with many flowers such as White Fairy Lantern, Hartweg's Iris, Indian Pink, Sierra Nevada Pea, pink Phlox, and Delphinium. This trail blooms from April to mid or late May. Dogs need to be leashed. See the Yuba River plant list at the end of the chapter. The 2.5-mile **east trail**, on the parking pullout side of the road, leads to large mossy rocks covered with Sedum, past a ferny creek where Spicebush grows, and over a cliff-hanging bridge with river views. The **west trail** (2.5 miles) across the road from the parking lot (walk through the underpass) leads to a roofed overlook. Beyond the overlook about a half mile is a marvelous trestle with a switchback ramp leading down to the creek. This wonderful trail is wheelchair accessible except right after a rain, when it is liable to be wet and muddy. The trail is the result of John Olmsted's hard work with many volunteers from Sequoya Challenge, Boy Scout troops, local citizens, Sierra Club, and California State Parks and Recreation, who all cooperated in building and maintaining the trail. The Sequoya Challenge phone number is (530) 265-9398.

NORTH FORK OF THE YUBA RIVER

CANYON CREEK TRAIL THROUGH SHENANIGAN FLAT at SR 49 along the river. The 7-mile trail takes about 4 hours round trip to the confluence of the North Fork of the Yuba River and Canyon Creek and back. The trail parallels the North Fork on the north side. The historic road to Shenanigan Flat is well traveled by placer miners who live at the Flat, and by those going to one of the better swimming holes in the Yuba River at Shenanigan Flat. This is one of the best wildflower hikes in the Northern Mines area.

The treasure of the trail is Scarlet Fritillary, not just one or two plants, but scattered here and there along the trail as far as Cherokee Creek Bridge. Due to seeps on the hillside, the display of wildflowers in the first half mile is wonderful. A few of the flowers found at this location are *Delphinium gracilentum,* Kellogg's and Yellow Monkeyflowers, Butter-cups, Blue Dicks, Oregon Saxifrage, White Nemophila, and Meadowfoam. Bleeding Heart and blotched-leaf *Hydrophyllum capitatum* are also along these banks. Two shrubs that are not common in the gold country appear along this trail. They are Mountain Pink Currant, or *Ribes nevadense,* and Oregon Boxwood, or *Paxistima myrsinites,* which resembles Huckleberry.

After Shenanigan Flat the road continues as far as a slide, nicely repaired by today's miners. The ghosts of this trail are those who planted the Lilac bushes and built the rock walls, as well as the Indians who ground their meal by the river. The trail is easy and fairly level from the parking area to Cherokee Bridge. The rocks under the bridge make a good picnic spot to sit and watch the water ouzels race up and down the creek in April. The pink flowers of Indian Rhubarb bob back and forth at your feet.

Beyond the Cherokee Creek Bridge, the trail to the Canyon Creek confluence is up and down and has steep dropoffs that are not good for children or those with a fear of heights. An alternative is to walk up Cherokee Creek, on the Shenanigan Flat side of the bridge, to a pretty waterfall 15 minutes up a primitive trail. A short way up the trail toward the Canyon Creek confluence, you will notice the little used trail to Brandy City that dates back to the 1850s. A pretty mossy creek crossing the trail is a good opportunity to dampen a scarf or shirt if the day is hot. There are a few Indian grinding holes at the confluence. During the spring runoff, the tumbling Yuba River and, almost as large, Canyon Creek are a thrill.

Directions: Canyon Creek Trail is about 29 miles from Nevada City, on SR 49. It is located at the north end of the bridge over the North Fork of the Yuba River. Turn left and park in the parking area just downstream. Be considerate of the miners; don't block the access gate, and leave seemingly abandoned gold pans, tools, and equipment alone.

INDIAN VALLEY TO GOODYEARS BAR This 7-mile trail has great plant diversity because of several different habitats, including serpentine soil, rock outcroppings, Oak woodland, Pine forests, and riparian. *Swertia albicaulis,* rare *Streptanthus polygaloides,* and *Campanula praenanthoides* are found associated with the serpentine soil near the Goodyears Bar end of the trail. Hiking in from either end of the trail and retracing your steps, rather than doing the whole trail, is a way to see the best of the plants if you have only one car. Otherwise, with two cars, do a shuttle and start at Goodyears Bar.

The lower end of the trail at Indian Valley is perhaps more picturesque, but the plant material at Goodyears Bar is more unusual and is within a mile or so of the trailhead in the serpentine outcrops. The trail at Indian Valley Campground starts at a "magic" bridge that crosses the North Yuba River. As soon as the bridge is crossed, the ghosts of miners are everywhere. You can almost hear them pitching the rocks out of the way as they wear their fingernails to a nubbin scrabbling for gold. In the Douglas Fir forest, the ghosts are all around in the tailing piles and mining holes. The understory plants are Dogwoods, Hazelnut, Currants, Mock Orange, Wild Roses, and Deer Brush. Beneath them are Indian Pink, white Hawkweed, Starflowers, Bleeding Heart, Columbine, False Solomon Seal, and White-veined Wintergreen (*Pyrola picta* var. *aphylla*).

A lovely creek crossing about a mile up the trail is a nice picnic spot to stop and admire the Indian Rhubarb, Elk Clover, and Boykinia, and watch the dipper birds (water ouzels) enjoying the waterfalls. After the bridge, the trail climbs up through the forest, where you might see white California Skullcap and a little blue bell-shaped flower called *Campanula praenanthoides.* Then, bingo! You are out of the forest and into a whole new habitat with some really good flower displays. *Clarkia biloba* and *Clarkia rhombifolia,* Woolly Sunflower, Wallflower, Azalea Monkeyflower, or *Mimulus bifidus,* Rock Ferns, Jewel Flower, and Ball-headed Gilia are found in this rocky open area. This is a good place to turn around if you have only one car. It takes about an hour and a half to hike out to Indian Valley from these beautiful rocky gardens.

Directions: Take SR 49 a few miles above North Fork Bridge, which is 29 miles from Nevada City, and watch for Indian Valley Campground. It is best to have two cars, so one can be left at Indian Valley Campground. Drive about 5 miles to the town of Goodyears Bar, just across the river from SR 49. Go through the pretty garden town and about half a mile beyond to a spot where the road is wider for parking. The trail starts on the wet bank on the uphill side of the road.

DOWNIEVILLE is the county seat for Sierra County and has a population of 325; it seems higher than its 2,865 feet of elevation. It is a charming little mountain town that shares the narrow valley with the North Fork of the Yuba River. Be sure to walk around the town. You'll see beautiful dry rock walls, pretty little terraced gardens, wooden sidewalks, and a very good museum at 330 Main Street.

SIERRA CITY has a population of 225, which grows in the summer, and its elevation is 4,287 feet. The tiny town is nestled under the towering Sierra Buttes. It has some nice bed-and-breakfasts and motels. In the summer the locals and the tourists (hikers, miners, fishermen) do most of their major shopping in Graeagle (15 miles away on the east side of the Sierra Crest). The summer jazz concerts at the Kentucky Mine Museum are a must, as is the 20-minute drive up to Bassetts, Sardine Lake, and Lakes Basin Recreation Area. (See Toni Fauver's book, *Wildflower Walking in Lakes Basin*, available at Bassetts.) In the mid-1980s Sierra Buttes swarmed with mining engineers core drilling for gold on the western slopes of the Buttes.

LOVES FALLS TRAIL FROM SR 49 OR SIERRA PLUM CAMPGROUND

Loves Falls is 15 minutes from SR 49 on the PCT (Pacific Crest Trail, which runs the length of the Sierra). The falls are in a gorge that creates a cascade of waterfalls. The plants, as well, are exciting and different, as one might expect from a higher elevation. Due to the increased altitude, the blooming time is May and June. The botanic treasures of this walk are Sierra Gooseberry, False Solomon's Seal (*Smilacina racemosa*), Shelton's Violet, Fremont's Garrya, and Washingtonia Lily (found in Manzanita shrubs on the slope above the road to Wild Plum Campground). *Wildflower Walking in Lakes Basin* has pictures of plants from this elevation and higher. A beautiful bridge arches over the gorge. Notice Mother Nature's super landscape job in the rocks. The rather heavy magenta *Penstemon newberryi* and delicate pale pink Alum Root (*Heuchera micrantha*) are combined against the backdrop of this massive metavolcanic rock and the beautifully engineered bridge.

Loves Falls is 1.5 miles from the bridge at Wild Plum Campground. The trail is gentle until after you have crossed Haypress Creek, where you meet the PCT. Be sure to look up at the Sierra Buttes towering over you. The best way to hike this trail is to start from the campground so you have the Buttes views and the best falls and rock garden views. Park a car at the PCT trailhead on the north side of SR 49 if you need to save time. However, you can cheat and do a quickie into the falls from SR 49, or do the more honorable hike up from the campground and return.

Directions: Turn onto Wild Plum Road (a road sign indicates the campground) at the east end of Sierra City, just after the Yuba River Inn

Motel. The trailhead for Loves Falls is one mile or so, just before the bridge and a little beyond the parking area and picnic tables. The alternative 15-minute walk is found by parking at the PCT and SR 49, a little way uphill from the Kentucky Mine Museum (which has docent tours and is one of the highlights of the entire gold country, according to one author).

NORTH BLOOMFIELD ROAD NORTH OF NEVADA CITY

Edwards
Crossing

PURDON CROSSING-EDWARDS CROSSING (late March to June) This winding 4-mile trail above the river, with a difference of several hundred feet between the two bridges, has good plant diversity because of the different exposures, the elevation change, and various soils and habitats. It has Black Oak forests, riparian habitats, and wonderful rock outcrops. The trail treasure plant is the rare *Lewisia cantelovii,* most easily seen by walking about a mile in from Edwards Crossing. Fawn Lily, another treasure, is at either end of the trail—but remember that it is a mid-March bloomer. Some of the other early plants along the trail are Isopyrum, Dutchman's Pipe, Violet, Fritillary, Milkmaids, Sedum, and Bleeding Heart.

Purdon Crossing has a safe, sandy swimming hole about 20 minutes up the trail close to the river. The half-truss Purdon Bridge, built in 1895, is the only one of its kind in California. Edwards Crossing Bridge, built in 1904, has a 114-foot span with three hinged metal arches. In 1853 the first bridge was erected here along the early toll road to North Bloomfield. There was great excitement at Edwards Crossing one day in 1866 when a Wells Fargo stage was held up by three men at 4:15 a.m. and robbed of $7,900. Use the South Yuba River plant list (pages 71-73).

Directions: To **Purdon Crossing**: at the intersection of SR 20 and SR 49, turn onto SR 49 to Downieville for a few blocks to North Bloomfield Road. Turn right onto North Bloomfield Road and go about half a mile uphill to the T, where you **turn left** on the Lake Vera-Purdon Road and continue for 5.5 miles to the river. As you near the river, the road becomes steeper, with nasty potholes, big rocks, and blind curves, so take it easy. The parking lot is to the right of the bridge and just upstream a way. The entry to it looks like a driveway.

To go to **Edwards Crossing**, get onto North Bloomfield Road as directed for Purdon Crossing. At the T **continue right** on North Bloomfield Road for 7 miles to the river at Edwards Crossing. The best way to do this hike is to have a car at either end so you can do a shuttle (a long shuttle), or arrange with friends to hike in opposite directions and trade keys when you meet on the trail. If you have only one car, take the Edwards Crossing part of the hike; the views, the treasure flowers, and the road are better here, although the Leopard Lilies at Purdon Crossing are terrific and the river access is better.

HUMBUG TRAIL is an exciting 6-mile round trip, with a 1,000-foot descent to the Yuba River along cascading Humbug Creek. The ghosts of the Gold Rush miners are evident in many places along the trail—mines, cabin flats, ditches, and tailing piles. Some of the vertical mine shafts have orange polluted-looking water emerging from them, caused by algae. A picnic table is situated in a beautiful creekside location about 20 minutes down the trail. A few of the special flowers along the trail are Bleeding Heart, a ground cover of Miner's Lettuce, Rattkesnake Plantain (*Goodyera*), Sedum, yellow Rayless Arnica (smell the leaves), Elk Clover, and red Indian Pinks. The showy shrubs and trees are California Mock Orange, Currant, Deer Brush, Dogwood, and Redbud. (See the South Yuba River plant list on pages 71-73).

Halfway down, the trail gets steep, with views of cascading Humbug Creek and water-formed channels and pools in the rock. At the confluence of Humbug Creek and the Yuba River is a plateau with picnic tables and a nice camping site. Notice the 60-foot gravel banks at your feet. These were the result of hydraulic mining near where you parked. These banks resemble the Ancestral Yuba River sediment that is so visible on Highway 80 between Gold Run and Dutch Flat. The South Yuba Trail now extends in both directions up and down river. For further history of the Humbug Trail, see *California Explorer* magazine, December 1994, "A Winter Hike Through Mining History" by Hank Meals.

Directions: Follow the directions to Edwards Crossing and continue 6.7 miles, following the signs to Malakoff Diggins State Historic Park, the site of what was once a very large and very rich hydraulic mining operation.

Visit the museum and pick up your $5 parking permit. From the museum, drive 2.5 miles west toward Edwards Crossing. The trail is well signed on the downhill side of the road below the big Malakoff gravel pit or pond. No dogs or bikes are allowed.

HIGHWAY 20 EAST OF NEVADA CITY

ROCK CREEK NATURE AREA is a nice place to visit on a hot May day or when the fall color is out. The loop trail is not quite a mile long and has numbered posts with interesting natural history information put out by Tahoe National Forest. A plaque near the beginning of the trail tells about a mill that used to be here. One of the botanical treasures of this location is *Linnaea borealis* (Twinflower).

1. Trailblazer plant, Goldminer's Dogwood, Hazelnut, Fringe Cups, Cedars, Yew Tree, Sweet Cicely, Starflower, Bigleaf Maple
2. Bleeding Heart, White Alder, Madrone
3. *Cornus sessilis* or Goldminer's Dogwood, Honeysuckle, Gooseberry, Wild Raspberry, Lobed Violet
4. At this post there are twined Bigleaf Maples
5. Yew Tree, Black Oak, White Fir, Douglas Fir, Iris, Rattlesnake Plantain, Poison Oak, Snowberry
6. Incense Cedar
7. Hazelnut
8. Creekside: Pipsisiwa, Elk Clover
9. Yew Tree
10. Madrone
11. Lichens and Mosses
12. The Yew and Maple are competing for sunlight
13. Douglas Fir
14. White Fir
15. Old cabin site
16. Bracken Fern
18. Ponderosa Pine
19. Meadow staging area
20. Sugar Pine
21. Greenleaf Manzanita
22. Mountain Misery
23. Black Oak
25. Wild Rose

Directions: Drive about 6 miles east of Nevada City on SR 20. Just after the Lone Grave on SR 20 is a sign for the Conservation Camp. Turn left on Washington Ridge Road for 1 mile, then left on Rock Creek Road. Go 1 mile down Rock Creek Road to the peaceful forest glade at Rock Creek Nature Trail. Continue on this road back up to SR 20.

SKILLMAN FLAT has some wonderful botanical treasures in late April and May. There are Twin Flower, or *Linnaea borealis,* Phantom Orchid, or *Cephalanthera austiniae,* and *Goodyera oblongifolia,* or Rattlesnake Plantain, to name just a few. It is shocking that this has become a group horse camp, with all these delicate plants that could be trampled. Park outside the gates to the campground. The treasures are all within a stone's throw of the entry road. The Twinflower can be found growing in the moist ditch on the little dirt road that continues past the campground gate. The Phantom Orchid is found by locating a path across the little road from the Twinflower and following the path into the woods; as soon as you come to a slight clearing, if the season is right, they should be there. There are also Azalea, Hartweg's Iris, Washington Lily, White-veined Wintergreen, and Rattlesnake Plantain. Wander through this whole campground and down to the creek looking for the plants listed. Skillman Flat, along the Pioneer Trail, was the site of an old lumber mill from the mining days.

Directions: Drive 13 to 15 miles east of Nevada City on SR 20, and shortly after the Washington Road watch for the Skillman Campground road on the right. It is hard to see because it is on a curve and below the level of the highway.

OMEGA ROAD is a little way beyond Skillman Flat. Make a left turn and drive a few hundred yards down the hill. Stop when you see a small ridge or nose on the left side of the dirt road. Climb up on the bank, and there you will find Bear-grass, *Xerophyllum tenax*. This plant is fairly rare in the foothills.

OMEGA REST STOP has a dry, gravelly habitat that permits some unusual foothill plants to survive here. A new nature walk is being installed along the ridge. It would be great if they would put a boardwalk on the hill below the parking lot. Don't try walking down the hill; it is very unstable, with gravel on top of solid rock, and walking there would ruin the vegetation. Some of the plants you can see just over the edge are *Allium tribracteatum,* Steer's Head (it follows the snow melt), Gay Penstemon (*Penstemon laetus*), and Balsam Root. The Alpha and Omega Diggings was one of the larger hydraulic mining operations in the area.

Directions: Omega Rest Stop is a mile or two up SR 20 from Skillman Campground on the left (north) side of the road.

2.8 miles after Omega Rest Stop, continuing east on SR 20, is a stop only for botanists or enthusiasts. This is a difficult place to find but there is *Gaultheria ovatifolium,* or Oregon Spicy Wintergreen, in thick mats in the moist areas on the north side of the road.

BEAR VALLEY ON SR 20 has beautiful meadow flowers in May and June. The PG&E Discovery Trail on Bowman Lake Road comes very near the east side of the meadow in Bear Valley.

BOWMAN LAKE ROAD Just after Bear Valley, as the road starts up the grade toward I-80, look up at the cliffs: pioneer wagons were lowered from these cliffs into Bear Valley. Turn left onto Bowman Lake Road; it is a fairyland of white Dogwood blossoms in late April to mid-May. PG&E has a nature area adjacent to Bear River called the Discovery Trail that has plants in bloom into June. It is just under a mile long and easy walking. It has a wealth of plants adjacent to the parking lot and across the street under the power poles. A few of the botanical treasures are Brown's Peony and Bleeding Heart. *Hesperochiron pumilus,* a small basal-leafed plant with white flowers nestled into the leaves, is also found at the rocky edges of this meadow. Bear River, with pools here and there along the trail, and the boardwalk through a beautiful Corn Lily meadow are the main attractions of this walk. Numbered posts mark points of interest.

Continue driving slowly on Bowman Lake Road, downhill toward the river. The leaky flume along this road has created a perfect habitat for wet growers such as *Boykinia elata,* several Orchids, Ferns, and Yellow Monkeyflower. Cross the bridge, park, and walk upriver to Morning Glory Pool, a fabulous swimming hole. In May you might see a very spiny, hardy yellow rose blooming, left from a long-ago garden. Just beyond the bridge after the corner there are lots of interesting plants on the road bank. Leave the car and explore on foot. Just to the west of the road on the curve is a path. Follow that out onto the granite, and you will find Onions, Brodiaea, and Death Camas. Walk or drive on up the road to find Varied Leaf Penstemon, Apricot Monkeyflower, Bear Buckwheat, Sulphur Buckwheat, Woolly Sunflower, Dudleya, Sierra Gooseberry, Newberry's Penstemon, Pussy Paws, Wallflower, and Yerba Santa.

YUBA RIVER PLANT LIST

White		
	Achillea millefolium	Yarrow
	Aesculus californica	Buckeye
	Aristolochia californica	Dutchman's Pipe
	Boykinia elata	Brook Foam
	Brodiaea hyacinthina	White Brodiaea
	Calochortus albus	Fairy Lantern
	Calochortus superbus	Mariposa Lily
	Calystegia occidentalis	Morning-glory
	Ceanothus integerrimus	Deer Brush
	Chamaebatia foliolosa	Mountain Misery
	Cornus nuttallii	Mountain Dogwood
	Fragaria californica	Wild Strawberry
	Goodyera oblongifolia	Rattlesnake-plantain
	Heuchera micrantha	Alum Root
	Hieracium albiflorum	Hawkweed
	Linanthus bicolor	Bicolor Linanthus
	Lithospermum californicum	Puccoon
	Nemophila heterophylla	White Nemophila

	Phacelia cicutaria	Caterpillar Phacelia
	Plagiobothrys nothofulvus	Popcorn Flower
	Rhododendron occidentale	Azalea
	Rhus diversiloba	Poison Oak
	Rubus leucodermis	Western Raspberry
	Rubus parviflorus	Thimbleberry
	Sambucus caerulea	Blue Elderberry
	Saxifraga californica	California Saxifrage
	Scutellaria californica	Skullcap
	Thysanocarpus curvipes	Lacepod, Fringepod
Yellow	*Agoseris grandiflora*	Mountain Dandelion
	Amsinckia intermedia	Fiddleneck
	Brodiaea ixiodes var. *scabra*	Golden Brodiaea
	Calochortus monophyllus	Yellow Star-Tulip
	Centaurea solstitialis	Star Thistle
	Dudleya cymosa	Live-Forever
	Eriophyllum lanatum	Woolly Sunflower
	Erythronium multiscapoideum	Fawn Lily
	Grindelia camporum	Gum Weed
	Iris hartwegii	Hartweg's Iris
	Lathyrus sulphureus	Sulphur Pea
	Lomatium utriculatum	Foothill Lomatium
	Lonicera hispidula var. *vacillans*	Honeysuckle
	Lotus argophyllus	Silverleaf Lotus
	Mimulus bifidus	Sticky Monkeyflower
	Ranunculus occidentalis	Western Buttercup
	Sanicula bipinnata	Poison Sanicle
	Sanicula crassicaulis	Pacific Snakeroot
	Sedum spathulifolium	Stonecrop
	Verbascum thapsus	Common Mullein
	Viola lobata	Pine Violet
	Viola sheltonii	Shelton's Violet
Orange	*Eschscholzia caespitosa*	Caespitose, Tufted Poppy
	Eschscholzia californica	California Poppy
	Lilium pardalinum	Leopard Lily
Pink to Red	*Apocynum androsaemifolium*	Dogbane
	Aquilegia formosa	Columbine
	Arctostaphylos viscida	Whiteleaf Manzanita
	Asclepias cordifolia	Milkweed
	Brodiaea volubilis	Twining Brodiaea
	Calandrinia ciliata var. *menziesii*	Red Maids
	Cercis occidentalis	Redbud
	Clarkia biloba	Clarkia, Farewell to Spring
	Dicentra formosa	Bleeding Heart
	Dodecatheon hendersonii	Shooting Star
	Erodium botrys	Filaree, Storksbill
	Fritillaria recurva	Scarlet Fritillary
	Geranium dissectum	Cranesbill
	Geranium molle	Soft Cranesbill
	Lathyrus latifolia	Perennial Sweet Pea

	Lupinus stiversii	Harlequin Lupine
	Mimulus kelloggii	Kellogg's Monkeyflower
	Montia perfoliata	Miner's Lettuce
	Peltaphyllum peltatum	Indian Rhubarb
	Plectritis ciliosa	Plectritis
	Pyrola picta	White-veined Wintergreen
	Rosa gymnocarpa	Rose
	Silene californica	Indian Pink
	Symphoricarpos albus	Snowberry
	Trientalis latifolia	Star Flower
	Trifolium tridentatum	Tom-Cat Clover
Blue-	*Brodiaea laxa*	Ithuriel's Spear
Purple	*Ceanothus prostratus*	Mahala Mat, Squaw Carpet
	Cynoglossum grande	Hound's Tongue
	Delphinium patens	Spreading Larkspur
	Eriodictyon californicum	Yerba Santa
	Fritillaria micrantha	Brown Bells
	Gilia capitata	Capitate Gilia
	Gilia tricolor	Bird's Eye Gilia
	Iris macrosiphon	Ground Iris
	Lathyrus nevadensis var. *nevadensis*	Sierra Nevada Pea
	Lupinus albifrons	Silver Bush Lupine
	Lupinus benthamii	Spider Lupine
	Lupinus bicolor	Miniature Lupine
	Lupinus nanus	Sky Lupine
	Nemophila menziesii	Baby Blue Eyes
	Salvia sonomensis	Sonoma Sage
	Sanicula bipinnatafida	Purple Sanicle
	Trillium chloropetalum	Wake Robin
	Vicia sativa	Spring Vetch
Greenish	*Acer macrophyllum*	Bigleaf Maple
	Alnus rhombifolia	White Alder
	Pellaea mucronata	Bird's Foot Fern
	Pityrogramma triangularis	Goldback Fern
	Populus fremonti	Fremont's Cottonwood
	Rhamnus californica var. *tomentella*	Coffeeberry
	Rhamnus crocea ssp. *ilicifolia*	Redberry
	Vitis californica	Wild Grape

OROVILLE AREA

Best for Children: Table Mountain, Oroville Dam Visitor Center, Caribou Road

Best for Botanists: Table Mountain, Honey Run Road, Caribou Road

Best Displays: Table Mountain, Palermo Road, Upper Bidwell Park

Best Hike: Dan Beebe Trail below the dam spillway

HISTORY: On July 4, 1848, General John Bidwell discovered gold on the Middle Fork of the Feather River—called *Rio de Las Plumas* when California belonged to Mexico. Bidwell was the leader of the Bidwell-Bartleson party of 1841, the first overland company of Americans to settle in California. The first miners to follow Bidwell formed a mining camp in 1849 at the confluence of the North and Middle Forks of the Feather River and called it Bidwell's Bar. The camp became one of scores of flourishing mining camps along the Feather River in the 1850s. Oroville was founded in 1850 as Ophir City, a biblical reference meaning a land rich in gold. It was renamed Oroville when it became the Butte County seat in 1856. Louise Clappe ("Dame Shirley") in her book, *The Shirley Letters,* provides engaging insights into life along the Feather River in 1851-52, especially at Rich's Bar and Indian Bar, two rough mining camps. Today, Bidwell's Bar and some of the larger tailings lie buried under water, the result of the damming of the Feather River to create Lake Oroville.

In 1849 Bidwell left his gold strike on the Feather River to return to his 22,000-acre Rancho Chico, which he had bought from the original Mexican grantees. His interests were now in agriculture and horticulture, and he farmed for the rest of his life. The land for the town of Chico was carved from his Rancho Chico in 1860.

After the surface placers played out, Oroville became a trading center for the mining towns along Table Mountain and the camps up the forks of the Feather River. From the 1850s to the 1870s, hydraulic mining was the chief mining activity in the Oroville area. The town of Cherokee, to the north of Oroville on the north side of Table Mountain, was named by white settlers in 1849 for the Cherokee Indians who mined there. The area was so rich that claims were limited to a space ten feet square. By 1876 all of the claims and the mining activities were consolidated into one company, which became one of the largest hydraulic gold mines in the world. Many Chinese were hired to work the mines, and Oroville's Chinatown grew to a reported 10,000 people, second only to that in San Francisco.

Ditches, old flumes, canals, deeply scarred hills, and enormous piles of gravel can still be seen as evidence of hydraulic mining. Cherokee is also the site of the first diamond discovery in the gold-bearing gravels in California. The Cherokee Diamond Mine has produced more that 400 diamonds, the largest being a little more than two carats.

OROVILLE is barely above the Sacramento Valley, at an altitude of 178 feet. It is a busy town, with a population of 4,000. Business is supported by the nearby small communities and by tourism, agriculture, water, power, and lumber. It is located near creeks, dams, the Feather River Canyon, and Sutter Buttes, so it has wonderful outdoor activities such as birdwatching, hiking, bicycling, hunting, fishing, horseback riding, camping, and gold panning.

THERMALITO FOREBAY Exit SR 70 on Garden Drive (after Grand Avenue exit) just north of Oroville, and go west under the freeway and into the Lake Oroville State Recreation Area. This is a handy meeting spot if you are going with friends to Table Mountain and the Paradise area for the day. The picnic area and restrooms are convenient, and the flower fields are beautiful. Walking north toward the hills, cross a ditch, and look for Tidy-tips, Brodiaea, Onions, Mallows, Purple Owl's-clover, Lupine, Monkeyflower, Clover, and Popcorn Flower.

CHEROKEE ROAD TO TABLE MOUNTAIN Take the Garden Drive exit (the northernmost SR 70 exit for Oroville) east until it intersects Table Mountain Boulevard. Turn left (north) on Cherokee Road. Just as the road starts up the hill, look at the fields above the road; they are often blue with Ithuriel's Spear (*Brodiaea laxa*) and *Brodiaea multiflora*. This is a narrow road, so stopping can be hazardous. You might pull off to the right on Burma Road so you can stop and look closely at the flowers.

At the turnoff for Burma Road there is a beautiful Virgin's Bower vine, or *Clematis lasiantha*. Along this dirt side road you can find Fiddleneck, Clarkia, *Lupinus bicolor, Calochortus albus*, Buck Brush, and *Nemophila heterophylla*. Back on the main road banks there is succulent Dudleya, Globe Lily, Broomrape, Shooting Stars, Delphinium, Saxifrage, and *Eriophyllum lanatum*. Yellow Mariposa lily and Clarkia bloom as the grass begins to dry. The Clematis is usually quite showy, whether in flower or seed. As you approach Table Mountain and the road gets steeper, look to the right at the volcanic cliffs. If the rainfall has come at the right time in the right amount and if your timing is perfect, the Caespitose Poppies will look like red-hot lava flowing off the tableland. In an El Niño year, you'll see waterfalls instead of Poppies.

Try to picture the ancient molten basalt filling up a canyon as water does, cooling, and then the canyon walls eroding, leaving the Miocene age basaltic Table Mountain. It is not as flat as it appears from Cherokee Road. It is undulating, with little rills filled with white Meadowfoam, Yellow Monkeyflowers, Clovers, Lupine, and Purple Owl's-clover. On the valley side of the tableland are spectacular cliffs and waterfalls (possibly now a no-trespassing area). Along the road there are vernal pools, with Meadowfoam, Downingia, *Blennosperma nana*, and Tidy-tips. Table Mountain was

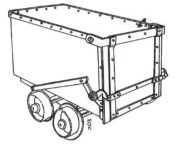

was off limits for a few years because of littering, fence snipping, and cattle being teased by people and dogs, but "rites of spring" have resumed now, with kite fliers, picnickers, birdwatchers, and botanists all sharing the tableland with the cattle.

This is probably the number-one flower display in the northern Sierra foothills. The first week in April is usually the peak wildflower season. Fragrant Sky Lupine borders the rock outcroppings clear across the tableland. Parking and public access to the 3,000 acres are located near the cattle chutes at the eastern end of the tableland. We are very lucky that the Division of Fish and Game and the landholders were able to work out an agreement so this beautiful land can be enjoyed by all. Keep dogs under control, don't litter, and don't trespass beyond the public boundary.

Continue on Cherokee Road, through the mining town of Cherokee. Notice the effects of hydraulic mining in the distance when passing through the little town. Don't miss the old wooden outbuilding absolutely covered by "Fortune's Double Yellow" peach-colored Rose. It is also in the trees across the street.

PLANT LIST

(For a flora of Table Mountain see James E. Jokhurst in the bibliography.)

White	*Allium amplectens*	Paper Onion
	Arenaria californica	Sandwort
	Calochortus albus	White Fairy Lantern
	Limnanthes douglasii v. rosea	Meadowfoam
	Linanthus ciliatus	Whisker Brush
	Marah fabaceus var. *agrestis*	Wild Cucumber
	Micropus californicus	Cotton Batting Plant
	Navarretia leucocephala	White-head Navarretia
	Odontostomum hartwegii	
	Phacelia cicutaria	Caterpillar Phacelia
	Plagiobothrys nothofulvus	Popcorn Flower
	Streptanthus tortuosus var. *suffrutescens*	Jewel Flower
	Thysanocarpus curvipes	Lace Pod
	Triteleia hyacinthina	White Brodiaea
	Triteleia lilacina	Glass Brodiaea
Blue	*Brodiaea elegans*	Harvest Brodiaea
	Brodiaea minor	Dwarf Brodiaea
	Delphinium patens	Zigzag Delphinium

	Dichelostemma capitatum	Blue Dicks
	Downingia cuspidata	Toothed Downingia
	Gilia capitata	Ball-headed Gilia
	Gilia tricolor	Bird's Eye Gilia
	Lupinus bicolor	Miniature Lupine
	Lupinus nanus	Sky Lupine
	Triteleia laxa	Ithuriel's Spear
Yellow	*Agoseris heterophylla*	Woodland Agoseris
	Calochortus luteus	Golden Mariposa Lily
	Hypochoeris glabra	Smooth Cat's-ear
	Lasthenia californica	Goldfields
	Layia fremontii	Fremont's Tidy-tips
	Lomatium utriculatum	Hog Fennel
	Mimulus guttatus	Monkeyflower
	Parvisedum pumilum	Golden Rock Fringe
	Ranunculus canus	Foothill Buttercup
	Ranunculus muricatus	Prickleseed Buttercup
	Sanicula bipinnata	Poison Sanicle
	Triteleia ixioides	Golden Brodiaea
	Viola douglasii	Douglas's Violet
	Viola pedunculata	Johnny-Jump-Up
Yellow-orange	*Amsinckia intermedia*	Fiddleneck
	Dudleya cymosa	Live Forever
	Eschscholzia caespitosa	Tufted Poppy
	Eschscholzia lobbii	Lobb's Poppy
Pink, Rose, Magenta	*Calandrinia ciliata* var. *menziesii*	Red Maids
	Lewisia rediviva	Bitter Root
	Mimulus douglasii	Purple Mouse-ears
	Mimulus kelloggii	Kellogg's Monkeyflower
	Mimulus tricolor	Tricolor Monkeyflower
	Orthocarpus purpurascens	Purple Owl's-clover
	Trifolium depauperatum	Udder Clover
	Trifolium tridentatum	Tomcat Clover
	Trifolium variegatum	White-tipped Clover

PALERMO ROAD and SR 70, south of Oroville, have fields of flowers. It is nice to be able to stop and figure out what the flowers are, so turn east onto Palermo Road. The first road is Powerhouse Road. There is a wealth of flowers at this intersection. A few of the noticeable flowers are several blue Brodiaea, Tidy-tips, Goldfields, Mallows, and Purple Owl's-clover. This is private land, so enjoy it by walking along the road or by driving Powerhouse Road into Oroville.

OROVILLE DAM VISITOR CENTER AND CHAPARRAL TRAIL The visitor center is located at 917 Kelly Ridge Road, off SR 162 or the Olive Highway. Be sure to stop at the visitor center for a map. The trails in the park are sometimes confusing, because multiuse trails, hiking trails, and equestrian trails intersect. Pick up the Chaparral Trail booklet and enjoy the self-guided 30-minute loop trail out of the visitor center parking lot. Dogs are not allowed on the trails in Lake Oroville State Recreation Area.

DAN BEEBE TRAIL BELOW THE DAM SPILLWAY This portion of the multiuse trail along the Feather River passes two ponds, is level, and has nice river and spillway views. Watch for bald eagles fishing along this section of the river. The flowers are particularly good along the multiuse trail below the spillway in the Glen Pond area. There are White Fairy Lantern, Clematis, and Dutchman's Pipe, Iris, Caespitose Poppies, blue Delphinium, Miniature and Spider Lupines, red Indian Pinks and Indian Paintbrush, yellow Woolly Sunflower, Pussy Ears, and Buttercups.

Trail: Be sure to get a trail map from the visitor center. The multiuse part of the trail takes off at the horse crossing sign on Oroville Dam Road East, between Glen Drive and Canyon Drive. A pleasant hike is the walk along the multiuse trail as far as Long Bar Pond. Turn into that area and picnic in the meadow, returning the way you came. A more strenuous 3-4 hour hike is down to the multiuse trail, then downriver past the two ponds. Turn left at Long Bar Pond, where you join the Dan Beebe Trail over Sycamore Hill, returning to a trail that is halfway up the access trail (under the power lines) and up to the car. Power towers over the access trail between the river and the road, as well as the spillway, can be used as reference points to get back to your car in case you get lured onto side trails.

Directions: The trailhead is located on Oroville Dam Road East just below the dam at the horse crossing sign. From the visitor center, turn west toward the dam on Royal Oaks Drive, which turns into Oroville Dam Road East.

LAKE OROVILLE, LOAFER CREEK TRAIL Drive in the entry gate, and be sure to pick up a map, since the trails are confusing. Fortunately trail signs mark most intersections. Park opposite the campfire circle, cross the street, and walk down the road past the campfire area and some employee housing, where you will find a trailhead sign. No dogs are allowed on this trail because horses use these trails also. Where the Loafer Creek Trail intersects the horse trail at the creek, we like to follow the creek, which is also the horse trail, where there is Fawn Lily early in the year. Both trails come out of the woods within view of Saddle Dam. The trail then runs along a ridge and past a horse camp, after which you are on a larger trail, just above a fire road for a little way. Some of the flowers in this area are Delphinium, Shooting Stars, Indian Paintbrush, and Silver Bush Lupine.

Directions: Take Olive Highway or SR 162 to Loafer Creek campground, which is a left turn after (east of) the Forbestown Road.

NORTH OF OROVILLE

UPPER BIDWELL PARK, just east of downtown Chico, off SR 99, is the largest municipal park west of the Mississippi. Take Wildwood Avenue into Upper Park Road; follow the road northeast to the day camp parking area. Yaqui Trail is parallel to the road and creek. Big Chico Creek looks like wonderful swimming. The showy flowers here are several species of Brodiaea, Lupines, and Clarkia, as well as Chinese Houses, Buttercups, Monkeyflowers, Royal Delphinium, Bird's Eye Gilia, Tidy-tips, Redbud, and much more. As you walk along the rocks above the creek, the lilting, falling song of the canyon wren fills the air. There is limitless hiking in this beautiful park. Since Bidwell Park is north of the area covered by this book, serious flower followers should buy *Checklist of Vascular Plants of Upper Bidwell Park* by Vern Oswald and a map, available at Big Creek Nature Center, 228 Main Street, in Chico.

VINA PLAINS, a Nature Conservancy property, is located on SR 99 about 15 miles north of Chico, just after the Butte-Tehama County line. The entry gate is across from Haille Road. It has beautiful vernal pools and fields in late March and early April. Be sure to phone first for a reservation: (415) 777-0487.

HONEY RUN ROAD AND COVERED BRIDGE There are lots of good plants along this road, but be sure to park completely off the road if you stop. Some of the special plants along the lower part of the road, before the covered bridge, are Dutchman's Pipe, Spicebush, and Wild Grapes on the creek side of the road. Across the street on the road banks, often in Poison Oak, are such beauties as pink Twining Brodiaea, white Globe Lily or Fairy Lanterns, Milkweed, red Indian Pink, Clematis, and pale yellow Hartweg's Iris. The covered bridge is a wonderful picnic spot if a wildflower class has to seek refuge during an infrequent spring downpour. Butte Canyon residents say that Honey Run Bridge, built in 1887 and since repaired many times by local concerned citizens, is the only tri-span bridge in the United States. Stay to the right after the bridge, on the road up to Paradise, which was once the access to the mining towns on the ridge. It is fairly narrow, with lots of wildflowers. Before the road starts to climb, watch for Indian Pink and Iris. Take advantage of the turnouts and get out and walk. You will see Tarweed, red Delphinium, Shooting Stars, California Mock Orange, Redbud, Wallflower, Death Camas, yellow Pussy Ears (*Calochortus monophyllus*), Saxifrage, Lupine, and undoubtedly more flowers than are listed.

Directions: Drive north of Oroville and SR 70. Exit SR 70 onto SR 99. Drive about 8 miles on SR 99 to the Skyway exit to Paradise. Honey Run Road is a left turn in half a mile off SR 99. Honey Run Covered Bridge is 5 miles up Honey Run Road.

MAGALIA SERPENTINE is located 5 miles above Paradise. Turn off Skyway at Coutolenc Road and park at any wide spot. There are some shrubs of yellow Bush Poppy just after the junction. Get out of the car and look under the McNab Cypress trees, in late March or early April, and you will see blankets of pale yellow Fawn Lilies (*Erythronium multiscapoideum*). In the same locale are *Senecio lewisrosei, Fritillaria phalanthera,* large True's Manzanita, Hartweg's Iris, Milkwort (*Polygala cornuta*), and yellow Pussy Ears. The late Tom Howell, formerly associated with the California Academy of Sciences, recorded 140 different plants at this location. Check these out and then do the Feather River Flume Intake Hike right across Coutulenc Road. Or hop back in the car and continue up Skyway to DeSabla Reservoir, to look for the magnificent Red Bud and Indian Warrior, rust colored instead of magenta. The Butte Creek walk is just beyond DeSabla Reservoir

FEATHER RIVER FLUME INTAKE HIKE is about 1 mile, through a serpentine soil habitat, down to the North Fork of the Feather River. This is the water intake for a flume that purportedly continues 15 or 20 miles down the canyon. These flumes were built over 100 years ago so that short wooden logging boats could be floated on them. Unfortunately, there are "NO TRESPASSING" signs where the flume starts. Park on Coutolenc Road just off Skyway. The trail starts at a dirt road half a block from Skyway, and the flume begins about a mile down into the canyon. Some of the botanical treasures are Pussy Ears or *Calochortus coeruleus,* Fawn Lily, Bunchgrass, Spicebush, California Sunflower, and blue Varied Leaf Penstemon, or *Penstemon heterophyllus.* Rare *Senecio lewisrosei* is also on this trail.

BUTTE CREEK BLM TRAIL is found by driving a quarter of a mile beyond the DeSabla Reservoir. Turn left on Powellton and then very soon left onto Doe Mill Road. Look for Indian Rhubarb in the creek at the intersection of Doe Mill and Powellton. Drive down until the road crosses Butte Creek. The trail, originally built by gold miners, follows the creek downstream for 1.5 miles (if it has been repaired) through a gorge with wonderful scenery. There is great species diversity because the habitat varies from forest to chaparral. Butte Creek is sparkling clear and in view from the trail all the time. The trail is fairly narrow. Shortly after the steps, the trail was eroded by the 1997 New Year's floods (because of the gravelly surface, we almost had a horrible accident here) so don't try to go farther unless the trail has been repaired. A delightful picnic area, with a trail down to the creek, is located just below the entry kiosk. Some of the plants you will enjoy are Fawn Lily, or *Erythronium multiscapoideum, Aspidotis densa, Polypody californica,* and rare *Mimulus glaucescens.* Two northern California natives, Vine Maple, or *Acer circinatum,* and *Smilax californica,* are not often seen this far south.

80

EAST OF OROVILLE

FEATHER RIVER HIGHWAY, SR 70, is a spectacular drive, with bowers of flowers in late April and May along the road, rugged granite domes, water everywhere, great fishing along Caribou Road, beautiful campgrounds, a railroad buff's delight, and a place to return to year after year. SR 70 turns east toward the mountains 7 miles north of Oroville. It is a two-lane road, with some passing spots, lots of pulloff places, and, unfortunately, fast-moving lumber trucks. Plan on spending a full day driving the 70 miles to Quincy, because there is so much to see! Caribou Road, 46 miles up the canyon, has a small restaurant and store at the junction with SR 70. Nice campgrounds (Queen Lily Campground is the prettiest) are a little way up Caribou Road, or drive on to Quincy or Graeagle to spend the night in a motel or lodge.

So that you don't miss the many treasure plants along the Feather River, whenever there is a habitat change with a convenient pullout, stop and see what you can find. Remember, the logging trucks can't stop, so watch out for them as you approach the turnouts. (Pull over often so you never have anyone behind you; that way you can go 45 mph and spot flowers worth stopping for.)

Shady Rest Stop is a left turn near massive granite walls. Mock Orange is near the restrooms. Cross the highway and walk several hundred yards to the end of the small road. Look for beautiful Snowdrop shrubs, Redbud trees, Apricot Monkeyflower, Nightshade, fragrant Pennyroyal, Delphinium, Draperia, Wallflower, and a PG&E water tunnel and waterfall at the end of the road.

Caribou Road is a left turn soon after Belden. This is a quiet road where it is easy to see the flowers from the car. It will be worth your time to get out at a few special stops and see some unusual or very beautiful plants. The large rocks on the right just after the store have *Lewisia cantelovii,* Sedum, Alum Root, and Red Delphinium in drifts. The swampy area a mile up the road on the right has Rush Lily, or *Schoenolirion album,* that the author has never seen anywhere else. The azaleas in this area are beautiful, as are the Leopard Lilies and Chokecherry shrubs. Queen Lily Campground is perfect on Mother's Day. It is possible to see apple blossoms set off by the dark, high, sometimes still snowcapped peaks in the background while you are still in your sleeping bag. Mother's Day is especially wonderful here if, while Mom is fishing for breakfast, a loving teenage daughter drops a bouquet of wildflowers on the end of her fishing line in front of her mother's nose. This prompts an immediate walk to find Azalea, Balsamroot, Pennyroyal, Delphinium, Milkmaids, Wild Ginger, Dogwood, Red Larkspur, Wild Rose, Penstemon, Lupine, and Monkeyflower.

Just beyond Queen Lily Campground, where the bridge crosses the river, is a large mossy rock covered with Sedum and Saxifrage. Stand on the bridge for a while and watch the water ouzels (dipper birds) dipping up and down on the rocks before they dive into the stream. A mile or so beyond the campground, a creek bubbles off the bank to your left. Some treasures grow here near the Azaleas. Across the road, in mid to late May, Leopard Lilies abound. Continue driving up the road until you find a convenient turn-around. Several of the pullouts are river access spots where Fish and Game has modified the river bank to make better breeding locales for the fish. Once the road climbs above the river, it becomes steep and narrow, and leads eventually to beautiful wildflower-laden meadows. But you had better have plenty of gas, a good detail map, and the whole day to explore.

PLANT LIST FEATHER RIVER CANYON
mid-April to late May   (* = Caribou Road)

White	Yellow	Pink
Deer Brush	Woolly Sunflower	Red Bud Tree
California Mock Orange	Wallflower	Dogbane
Snowdrop Bush	Balsam Root *	Cantelow's Lewisia *
Elderberry	Buttercup	Western Azalea *
Choke Cherry	Sedum	Pussy Paws
Thimbleberry	Mule Ears	Bleeding Heart
Alum Root	Dandelion	Phlox
Draperia	Hartweg's Iris	Wild Rose
Waterfall Buttercup	Harlequin Lupine	Chinese Houses
Morning Glory	**Apricot to Orange**	Star Flower
Keckiella	Apricot Monkeyflower	Spice Bush
Hawkweed	Poppy	**Red**
White Rush Lily *	Leopard Lily	Indian Paintbrush
Lady Slipper Orchid *	**Blue**	Red Larkspur
Dogwood	Minature Lupine	
	Ball-headed Gilia	
	Delphinium	
	Pennyroyal	
	Penstemon	

   SR 70 above Caribou Road is not as rich floristically, with the exception of Butterfly Valley, which is a right turn just after Keddie at the school bus shed. Then follow the signs to Butterfly Valley botanical area where there are bogs of Ledum, Azalea, Pitcher Plant, and Drosera. There is a book on Butterfly Valley by Walter Knight and a recent update by Jim Battagin. Although Butterfly Valley is outside the range of our book, it is absolutely worth a visit in late May or June.

BUCKEYE   BUCKEYE
Aesculus californica   Hippocastanaceae
Height: TO 40 FT.   Tree/deciduous   ❀ WHITE ❀
Habitat: SLOPES, DRY
Elevation: BELOW 4,000 FT.
Locale: EL PORTAL EAST OF MARIPOSA

This plant is not a good garden plant, because of summer leaf loss, even though it is interesting all year. In early spring the emerging leaves are beautiful in flower arrangements. In mid-April the tree is covered with huge spires of white-pink flowers that are poisonous to honeybees. By midsummer the buckeye balls are developing and are very noticeable because the tree is losing its leaves through estivation (summer dormancy to prevent water loss through the leaves). In winter the silvery bark and a few remaining Buckeyes with their split husks are all that remain. The Indians would crush the seed and put it in a pool to stun fish.

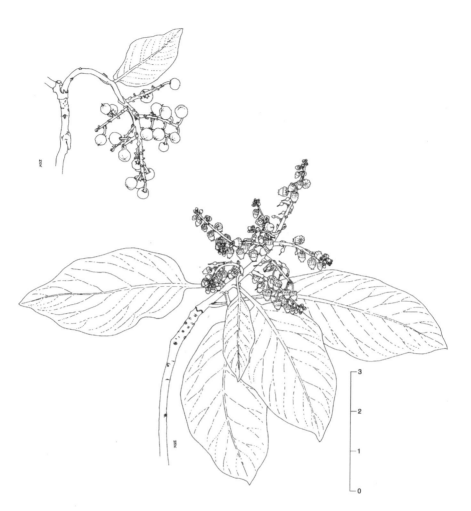

MADRONE   HEATH
Arbutus menziesii   Ericaceae
Height: 20-80 FT.   Tree/evergreen   ❀ WHITE ❀
Habitat: FOREST
Elevation: BELOW 5,000 FT.
Locale: SR 49 NEVADA CITY TO DOWNIEVILLE

Nature has planned well for the distribution of Madrone seeds. In October, when the beautiful orange-red berries ripen, the band-tailed pigeons migrate into the foothills and feast on the fruit, then deposit the seeds. Red Madrone bark is similar to Manzanita bark and the flowers of both are urn-shaped; the Madrone leaves look like those of Rhododendron. All three of these plants are in the Heath family.

CALIFORNIA BAY
Umbellularia californica

LAUREL
Lauraceae

Height: TO 90 FT.   Tree/evergreen   ❀ WHITE-CREAM ❀
Habitat: CANYONS
Elevation: BELOW 5,000 FT.
Locale: COMMON

Spice Islands Company now sells California Bay leaves in supermarkets. Bay wreaths with a few heads of garlic make a nice aromatic Christmas gift. The Bay tree is the climax species of lower elevations. This means Bay can grow from seed in its own shade or the shade of other trees. The amount of sunlight is the limiting factor for many plants, but not Bay.

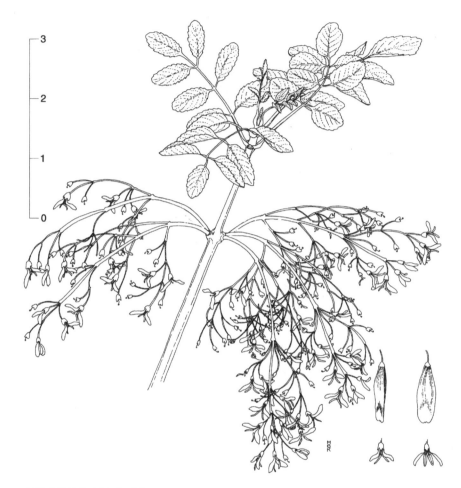

FLOWERING ASH
Fraxinus dipetala

Height: 7-30 FT.   Tree/deciduous

Habitat: SLOPES, DRY

Elevation: BELOW 3,500 FT.

Locale: CAMP NINE RD. CALAVERAS CO.

OLIVE
Oleaceae
❀ WHITE ❀

Flowering Ash is a delicately beautiful tree, whether in flower or seed. It should be in cultivation; the main requirement is good drainage. It seems to occur primarily on north-facing slopes, though the Camp Nine Road location is an exception.

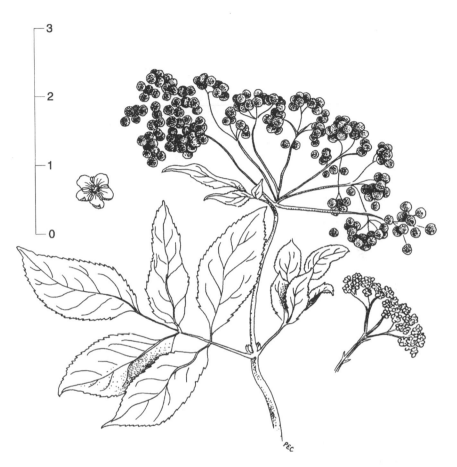

BLUE ELDERBERRY

Sambucus caerulea; Sambucus mexicana

Height: 6-24 FT.   Shrub, Tree/deciduous

Habitat: SLOPES, OPEN

Elevation: BELOW 10,000 FT.

Locale: CAMP NINE RD. CALAVERAS CO.

HONEYSUCKLE
Caprifoliaceae
❀ WHITE ❀

This beautiful small tree (or large shrub) has large white heads of flowers, followed by dark blue berry clusters in late summer. Europeans make fritters by dipping the flowers in batter and frying them. The berries are good as a spicy wine or jelly but are bitter when raw. Don't eat raw or red Elderberries. They can be toxic. There are coastal and montane species of Red Elderberry.

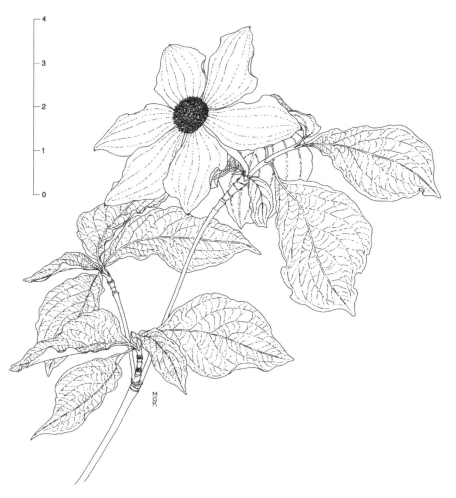

MOUNTAIN DOGWOOD
Cornus nuttallii

Height: 12-75 FT.   Tree/deciduous

Habitat: FORESTS

Elevation: BELOW 6,000 FT.

Locale: TWAIN HARTE NEAR THE LAKE

DOGWOOD
Cornaceae
❀ WHITE ❀

Large flowers that light up the forest are not the only beauty to come from Mountain Dogwood; red fall color is another advantage of this delicate tree. Unfortunately, it is difficult to cultivate. Jim Roof, who laid the foundation for Tilden Botanical Garden in Berkeley, planted about thirty plants but only a few of them survived. *Cornus sessilis,* Goldminer Dogwood, is easily mistaken for Mountain Dogwood when it is not in bloom. It has a more shrublike form, slightly smaller very shiny leaves, and insignificant flowers. The fruits start green and age to purple-black.

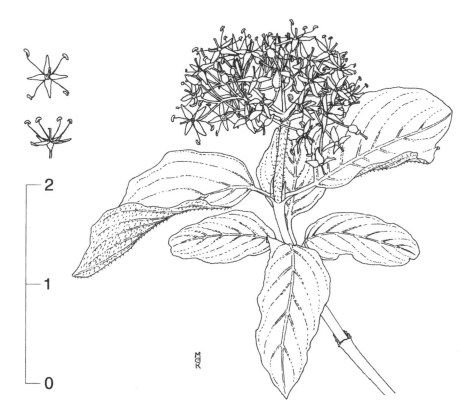

AMERICAN DOGWOOD, CREEK DOGWOOD, RED-TWIG DOGWOOD

DOGWOOD
Cornaceae

Cornus stolonifera; Cornus sericea ssp. *sericea*

Height: 5-12 FT.   Shrub/deciduous   ❀ WHITE ❀

Habitat: MOIST

Elevation: BELOW 8,000 FT.

Locale: DISCOVERY PARK, BOWMAN LAKE RD. OFF SR 20

This Dogwood shrub has beautiful red-purple bark, flower clusters like Pyracantha, and white fruit. Cut an artistic reddish branch in winter, when it is deciduous, and put it in a simple crystal or glass bottle; it will send out roots that twine in the container and in spring it will sprout leaves, but it does not seem to transfer well to soil.

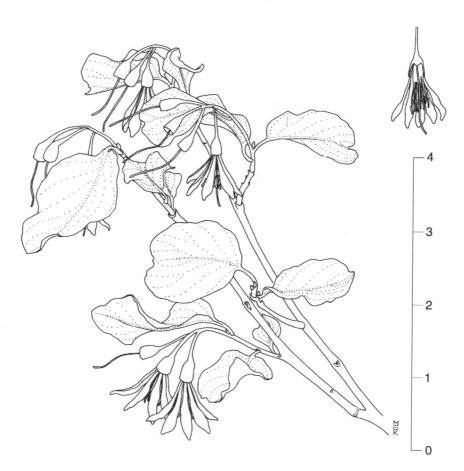

SNOWDROP BUSH
Styrax officinalis var. *californica*
Styrax officinalis var. *redivivus*
Height: 3-12 FT.   Shrub/deciduous
Habitat: ROCKY, DRY
Elevation: BELOW 3,000 FT.
Locale: FEATHER RIVER HWY.

STORAX
Styracaceae

❀ WHITE ❀

Snowdrop Bush is one of our most beautiful native shrubs for use in a drought-tolerant garden. It usually blooms in May. Jim Roof, who started Tilden Botanical Garden in Berkeley many years ago, had this recipe for germination of Styrax seed: put the large (almost a half inch) seeds into a coffee can with moist manure, cover the can, and leave until spring. The acid in the manure breaks the dormancy by etching the waxy seed coat, thus enabling the seed to absorb moisture and initiate growth.

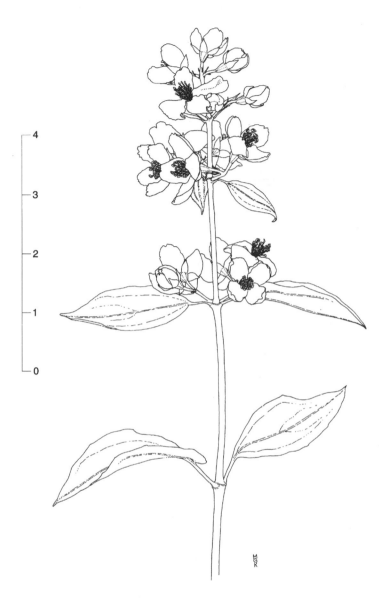

CALIFORNIA MOCK ORANGE
Philadelphus lewisii
Height: 3-10 FT. Shrub/deciduous
Habitat: SLOPES, ROCKY
Elevation: 1,000-4,500 FT.
Locale: MOSQUITO RIDGE RD.

MOCK ORANGE
Philadelphaceae
❀ WHITE ❀

Philadelphus is a wonderful drought-tolerant landscape shrub. The white flowers are spectacular on Mosquito Ridge Road against the evergreen Pines and Douglas Fir. It usually blooms in late April or early May.

91

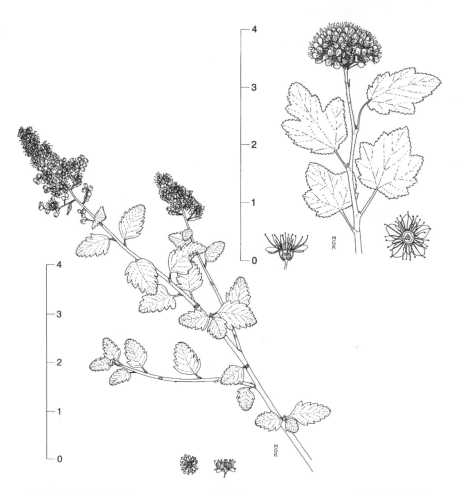

CREAM BUSH	ROSE	NINEBARK
Holodiscus	Rosaceae	*Physocarpus*
discolor	❀ WHITE ❀	*capitatus*

Height: 4-18 FT. Shrub/decidous   TO 6 FT.

Habitat: FORESTS, ROCKY   MOIST

Elevation: BELOW 4,000 FT.   BELOW 4,500 FT.

Locale: EDWARDS CROSSING   CANYON CREEK HIKE OUT OF GRASS VALLEY

Cream Bush, or Ocean Spray as it is called in the Coast Range, is a great landscape plant under oak trees. It tolerates dry shade and blooms beautifully, in cascades of white to very pale pinkish clusters of small flowers. *Physocarpus capitatus* or Ninebark is another attractive plant for use under Oaks. As long as it is in shade it does not need summer water (in the San Francisco Bay area) though its native habitat is listed as moist. The follicles sometimes have a reddish cast. See the Appendix for a list of nurseries that specialize in native plants.

3

2

1

0

M
G
K

MOUNTAIN MISERY   ROSE
Chamaebatia foliolosa   Roseaceae
Height: 8-24 IN.   Shrub/evergreen   ❀ WHITE ❀
Habitat: FOREST, OPEN
Elevation: ABOVE 2,000 FT.
Locale: COMMON, ESPECIALLY BEAUTIFUL ON SHEEP RANCH RD.
        BETWEEN MURPHYS AND SR 4

The aroma, the Strawberrylike flower, and the woody, ferny foliage covering large spaces in the open forest make it easy to identify Mountain
Misery. The genus name, from Greek *chamae*, low, and *batos*, bramble, is
descriptive of the plant. The common name is also descriptive: the plant is
difficult to walk through, it has a strong aroma, and it leaves a stain on
clothes after contact. Sheep Ranch Road has acres of Mountain Misery
under huge trees. It looks like a park and makes one wonder if it is
maintained to keep out shrubby species of plants.

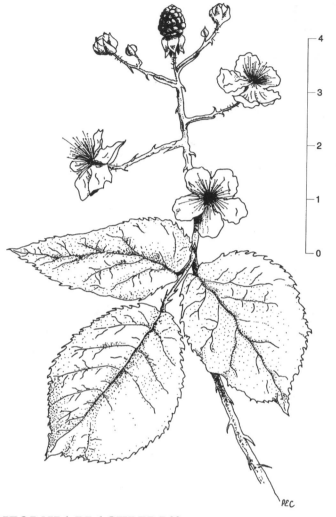

CALIFORNIA BLACKBERRY

ROSE

Rubus vitifolius; Rubus ursinus

Rosaceae

Height: LONG ARCHED STEM   Vine

❀ WHITE ❀

Habitat: FORESTS, MOIST

Elevation: BELOW 4,000 FT.

Locale: NATURAL BRIDGES ON PARROTTS FERRY RD.

Blackberry is very common throughout California. Most often it is the Himalayan Blackberry that takes over disturbed areas. It has a white underside to the leaves. The native California Blackberry is green on the underside of the leaves. In the summer it is fun to take a one by six inch plank, about four feet long, and plop it into a Blackberry patch, then walk onto the board and stand there with berries all around ready to be scooped off into your pail or popped into your mouth.

WESTERN RASPBERRY   ROSE   **THIMBLEBERRY**
Rubus   Rosaceae   *Rubus*
leucodermis   ❀ WHITE ❀   *parviflorus*
Height: TO 7 FT.   Shrub/weak-stemmed   Woody   1-7 FT.
Habitat: SLOPES, CANYONS   FORESTS
Elevation: BELOW 7,000 FT.   BELOW 8,000 FT.
Locale: PRESTON TRAIL   SOUTH FORK YUBA RIVER CANYON

Rubus leucodermis has delicious little black Raspberries. They have the
same shape as domestic Raspberries. The stems have a whitish bloom on
them, hence the species name, *leuco*, referring to white, and *dermis*, skin.
Rubus parviflorus, or Thimbleberry, is another tasty berry, a bright red
Raspberry lookalike with large Maple-looking leaves and shredded bark. It
is a wonderful landscape plant, though it might be considered invasive.
The flower is generally white; a pink form has been found in Squaw Valley
and the nurseries carry a lavender form as well as the white form.

95

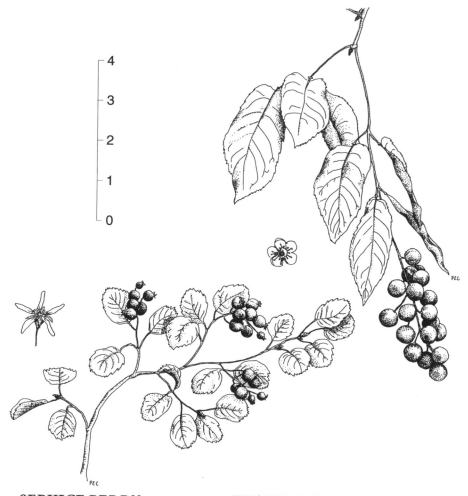

SERVICE BERRY *Amelanchier pallida* *Amelanchier utahensis*

ROSE
Rosaceae
❀ WHITE ❀
Shrub/deciduous

WESTERN CHOKE CHERRY
Prunus virginiana
var. *demissa*

SERVICE BERRY
Amelanchier pallida
Amelanchier utahensis
Height: 3-12 FT.
Habitat: FORESTS
Elevation: 2,500-9,000 FT.
Locale: BOWMAN LAKE RD. OFF SR 20

WESTERN CHOKE CHERRY
Prunus virginiana
var. *demissa*
4-17 FT.
SLOPES, DAMP
BELOW 8,000 FT.
CARIBOU RD.

Service Berry, *Amelanchier pallida*, has apple-green rounded serrated leaves. The common name supposedly originated in Scotland, where it blooms in early spring when the ground has thawed and the burial services can take place. A rather gruesome story for a lovely, delicate shrub. Choke Cherry, or *Prunus virginiana* var. *demissa*, has a very different growth habit from other native members of the *Prunus* genus. It has pendant racemes of flowers, then fruits. The fruit is dark colored, late season, and good for jelly.

96

SIERRA PLUM   ROSE
Prunus subcordata   Rosaceae
Height: 6-10 FT.   Shrub/deciduous   ❀ WHITE/PINK ❀
Habitat: SLOPES, ROCKY
Elevation: BELOW 6,000 FT.
Locale: HELL'S HALF ACRE

This is a very stiff-appearing shrub whose plums are sought for jelly. Be sure to distinguish Sierra Plum from Bitter Cherry. The fruit is almost an inch in diameter; the Bitter Cherry, *Prunus emarginata*, is half that size, and the growth habit is much different.

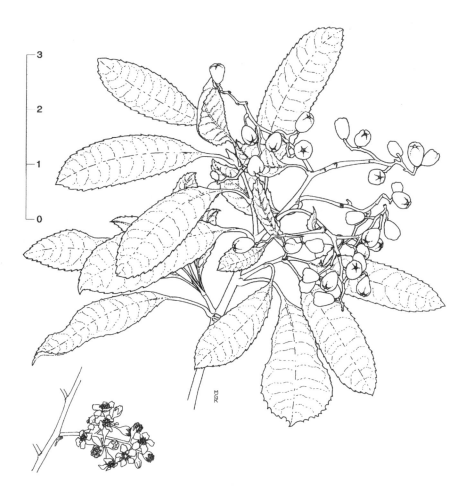

TOYON, CHRISTMAS BERRY   ROSE
Heteromeles arbutifolia   Rosaceae
Height: 7-34 FT.   Shrub/evergreen   ❀ WHITE ❀
Habitat: SLOPES, CANYONS
Elevation: BELOW 4,000 Ft.
Locale: PINE HILL PRESERVE

The highway department uses this attractive evergreen, drought-tolerant shrub for erosion control and screening. The white flower clusters in late spring and the red berry clusters in November and December make Toyon a good landscape plant. The species name refers to foliage like *Arbutus*, the Madrone tree.

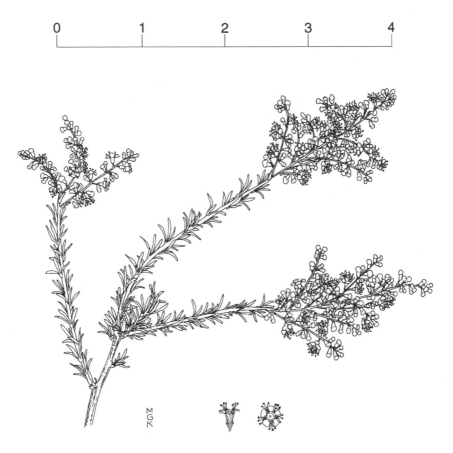

CHAMISE ROSE

Adenostoma fasciculatum Rosaceae

Height: 2-10 FT.   Shrub/evergreen   ❀ WHITE ❀

Habitat: CHAPARRAL

Elevation: BELOW 5,000 FT.

Locale: SALMON FALLS RD. NEAR FOLSOM LAKE NORTHWEST OF
      PLACERVILLE

This prominent member of the chaparral plant community turns the hills
green in March, creamy white for a few weeks in late April, and brownish
in summer. The leaves are small and needle-shaped, bound in fascicles or
bundles like Pine needles, hence the species name. Chamise is adapted to
fire and the crown sprouts after a fire.

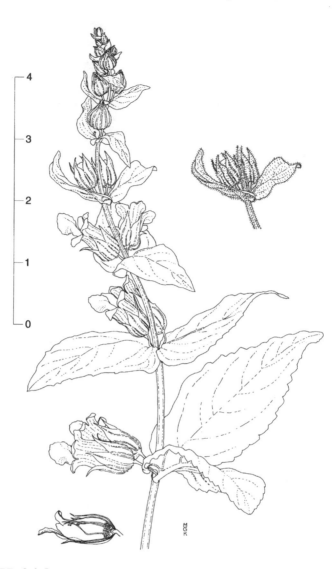

PITCHER SAGE   MINT
Lepechinia calycina   Lamiaceae
Height: 12-60 IN.   Shrub/deciduous   ❀ WHITE ❀
Habitat: CHAPARRAL
Elevation: BELOW 3,000 FT.
Locale: SALMON FALLS PARKING LOT, FOLSOM LAKE

This robust aromatic shrub is closely related to Sage (Salvia) and has a five-lobed flower, one lobe being the larger lower lip. The species name *calycina* is from Greek meaning cuplike, referring to the shape of the white to slightly blue flowers. After flowering, the large inflated green calyxes are quite conspicuous.

BUCK BRUSH	BUCKTHORN	**DEER BRUSH**
Ceanothus	Rhamnaceae	*Ceanothus*
cuneatus	❀ WHITE ❀	*integerrimus*
Height: 3-7 FT.	Shrub/evergreen	3-12 FT.
Habitat: SLOPES, DRY		SLOPES, DRY
Elevation: BELOW 6,000 FT.		1,000-5,000 FT.

Locale: McCOURTNEY RD. NEAR GRASS VALLEY　　I-80 COLFAX-DUTCH FLAT

Buck Brush is found blooming in late March throughout the Sierra foot-hills. The white flower clusters perfume the air. The shrub is stiff, with spurlike branches and small dark green leaves that usually have a notch at the tip of the leaf. Deer Brush, *Ceanothus integerrimus*, is a graceful, fragrant shrub with small Lilac-shaped flowers that bloom in April and May. Deer Brush softens rocky, gray shale or red dirt road banks as it drips and cascades over narrow back roads. It is especially beautiful on old SR 40 between Colfax and Gold Run.

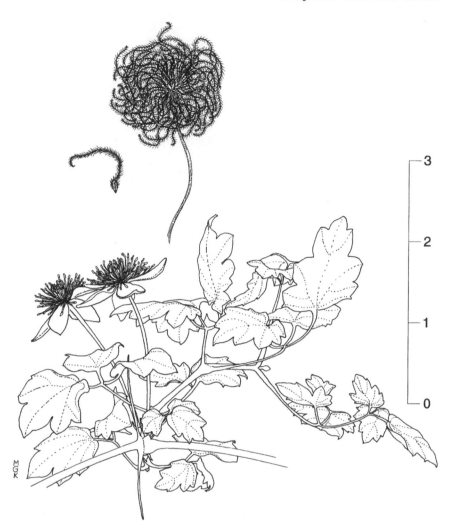

VIRGIN'S BOWER
Clematis lasiantha
Height: 12-16 FT.   Perennial
Habitat: CANYONS
Elevation: BELOW 6,000 FT.
Locale: CHEROKEE RD. NEAR TABLE MOUNTAIN JUST
          NORTH OF OROVILLE

BUTTERCUP
Ranunculaceae
❀ WHITE ❀

Clematis is an attractive vine for garden use. Like the cultivated members of this genus, the plant needs its base in shade and preferably a shrub it can climb on. It is covered with creamy white blossoms in April. The flower display is followed by showy, shiny seed heads that reflect the sunlight off each silvery hair. Priest Grade, a steep short-cut on SR 120, has beautiful Clematis that is very evident since a fire several years ago.

POISON OAK	SUMAC	SKUNK BUSH,
Rhus diversiloba	Anacardiaceae	*SQUAW BUSH*
Toxicodendron diversilobum		*Rhus trilobata*

❀ WHITISH ❀   ❀ YELLOW-GREEN ❀

Height: 4 IN.-105 FT.   Shrub, Vine/deciduous   TO 6 FT.

Habitat: CANYONS   CANYONS

Elevation: BELOW 3,500 FT.   BELOW 3,000 FT.

Locale: EVERYWHERE AT LOWER ELEVATIONS; LIMESTONE QUARRY TRAIL
            WORSE ON NORTH SLOPES   ALONG AMERICAN RIVER

Poison Oak is not exactly everywhere; it prefers the shadier canyons or an overstory of Black Oak, where it may grow only ankle-high hidden by Mountain Misery, and that's when it is dangerous. Poison Oak toxin bonds to the skin within minutes, so when you are hit by a branch pull out a Wash and Wipe or alcohol swab right away. *Rhus trilobata*, Skunk Bush or Squaw Bush, looks like Poison Oak but is not toxic. Poison Oak flowers are in the axils of the leaves, whereas Squaw Bush has terminal flowers. The berries on Poison Oak are white, and those on Squaw Bush are red.

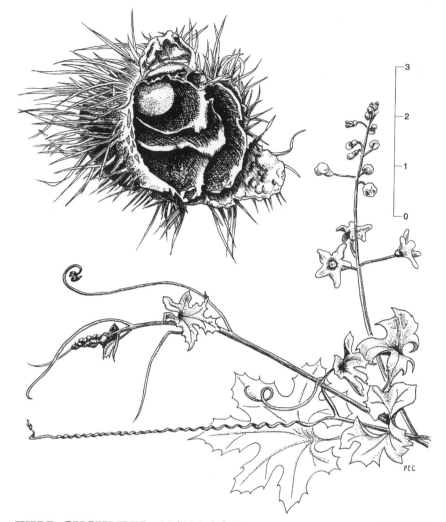

WILD CUCUMBER, MANROOT
Marah horridus
Height: 3-12 FT.   Perennial
Habitat: SLOPES, DRY
Elevation: BELOW 2,500 FT.
Locale: BRICEBURG

GOURD
Cucurbitaceae
❀ WHITE ❀

Manroot is so named because of the huge underground tuber about one foot across. The stems sprawl across the ground, with pretty racemes of small white flowers sticking up above the leaves and stems. These are the male or staminate flowers; the female flowers are sensibly located in the axils of the leaves near the stem, where the large (two inches or more) heavy oblong spiny fruit will have the support of the stem. *Marah*, from the Latin, means bitter, applying to all parts of the plant. It is not edible.

104

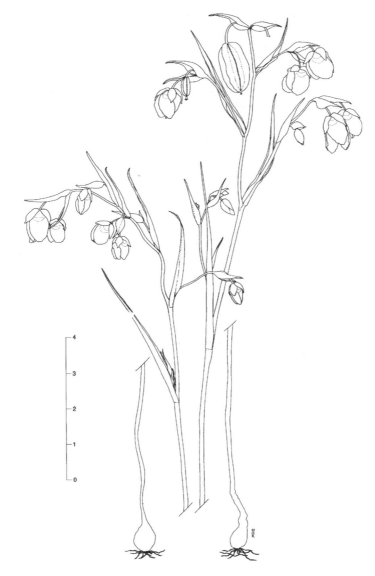

FAIRY LANTERN　　　　　　　　　　　　　　　　LILY
Calochortus albus　　　　　　　　　　　　　　　　Liliaceae
Height: 8-28 IN.　　　　　　　Bulb　　　　❀ WHITE ❀
Habitat: SLOPES, SHADE, ROAD BANKS
Elevation: BELOW 5,000 FT.
Locale: HONEY RUN RD. NEAR PARADISE

The genus *Calochortus* is from the Greek *kalos*, meaning beautiful, and *chortos*, grass. The species name refers to the white color. This showy Lily is easily seen by car on shaded road banks in the foothills. Another common name, though not so fanciful, is Globe Lily.

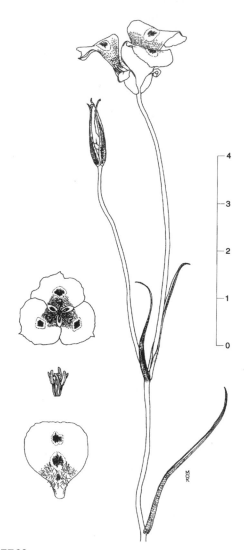

MARIPOSA LILY
                                        LILY
Calochortus venustus
                                   Liliaceae
Height: TO 12 IN.   Bulb   ❀ WHITE ❀
Habitat: SLOPES, DRY, ROAD BANKS
Elevation: BELOW 5,000 FT.
Locale: McCOURTNEY RD. 7.5 MI. FROM GRASS VALLEY FAIRGROUNDS
Calochortus venustus or Mariposa Tulip has recurved sepal tips, a rectangular yellow spot at the petal base with a rose spot in the center and often a yellow-bordered darker one above that. *Calochortus superbus* or Superb Mariposa Lily has an upside-down V at the petal base with a yellow-bordered purple spot above it and can be up to 24 inches tall. Both of these species bloom in May.

BEAVERTAIL-GRASS
Calochortus coeruleus

LILY
Liliaceae

Height: TO 8 IN.   Bulb   ❀ **WHITE/PALE VIOLET** ❀

Habitat: SLOPES, ROCKY, WOODLANDS

Elevation: BELOW 7,500 FT.

Locale: COUTOLENC RD. NEAR MAGALIA ABOVE PARADISE

Calochortus coeruleus has a hairy petal surface, except at the petal tip. The flowers are generally white with a slight blue cast. It has blunt-tipped anthers with a tiny projection at the tip. *Calochortus elegans*, a similar species, has pointed antlers and a thin spearlike projection from the tip of the anthers. It generally grows at a higher elevation in Northern California and Oregon.

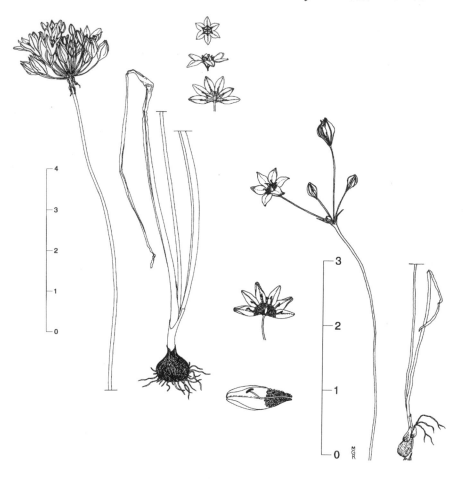

WHITE BRODIAEA	LILY	GLASS LILY

WHITE BRODIAEA
Brodiaea hyacinthina
Triteleia hyacinthina
Height: 4-16 IN.
Habitat: GRASSLAND
Elevation: BELOW 5,500 FT.
Locale: CAMP FAR WEST RD. NORTH
          OF LINCOLN

LILY
Liliaceae
❀ WHITE ❀
Bulb

GLASS LILY
Triteleia
lilacina
TO 20 IN.
VOLCANIC GRASSLANDS
100-500 FT.
CLARK TUNNEL RD. OUT
OF PENRYN

White Brodiaea is beautiful blowing in a field of shiny waving grass. The umbels of the flowers are about two inches across. The difference between the genus *Triteleia* and *Brodiaea* is that *Triteleia* has six anthers and *Brodiaea* only three. Brodiaea is used as a common name for *Dichelostemma* and *Triteleia*. Glass Lily, or *Triteleia lilacina*, is smaller than White Brodiaea and has tiny glasslike bubbles (on fresh flowers) at the base of each petal. Brodiaea has an edible bulb (survival use only) that tastes like a water chestnut.

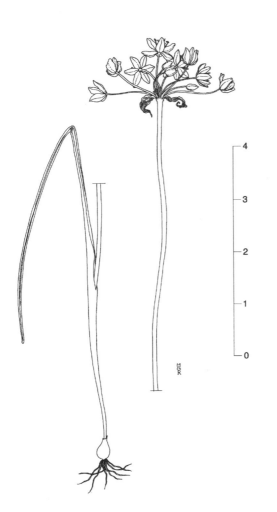

GLASS ONION	LILY	PAPER FLOWERED ONION
Allium hyalinum	Liliaceae	*Allium amplectens*
Height: 6-12 IN.	❀WHITE/PINK❀	TO 2 FT.
Habitat: GRASSLAND	Bulb	GRASSLAND
Elevation: 500-5,000 FT.		500-5,000 FT.
Locale: TABLE MOUNTAIN		PALERMO RD. SOUTH OF OROVILLE

The rounded petals of the graceful Glass Onion are shiny. The flowerhead is an open umbel of 6 to 15 flowers which vary from white to pale pink. The flowers of *Allium amplectens* are papery. The umbel of flowers is almost globose. The ovary of this Onion has six lateral crests.

109

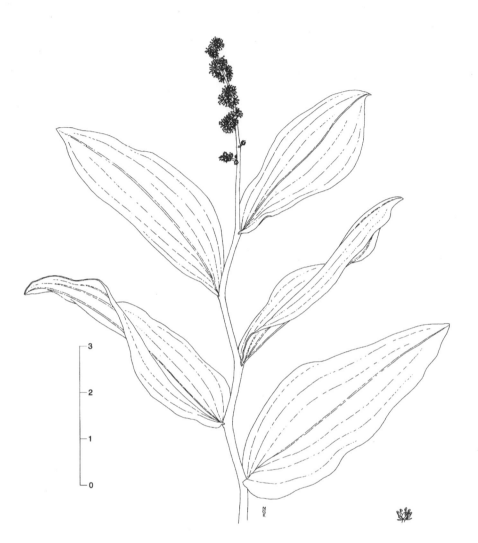

FALSE SOLOMON'S SEAL   LILY
Smilacina racemosa   Liliaceae
Height: 12-20 IN.   Perennial   ❀ WHITE ❀
Habitat: FOREST, DAMP
Elevation: BELOW 6,000 FT.
Locale: BOWMAN LAKE RD.

Smilacina racemosa has a panicle of white flowers at the tip of the stem and is a heavier-appearing plant than *Smilacina stellata*, which has narrower leaves and delicate starlike flowers. *Smilacina stellata* is nice used in a woodland garden with Ferns and *Heuchera*.

FAIRYBELL   LILY
Disporum hookeri   Liliaceae
Height: 1-3 FT.   Perennial   ❀ WHITE ❀
Habitat: FOREST, SHADE
Elevation: BELOW 5,000 FT.
Locale: DISCOVERY PARK, BOWMAN LAKE RD. OFF SR 20

Fairybell is similar to False Solomon's Seal, except that the small white flowers hang below the stem. Also, Fairybell is branched and False Solomon's Seal is not. The red fruits, like the flowers, hang below the leaves.

111

WHITE RUSH LILY   LILY
Schoenolirion album; Hastingsia alba   Liliaceae
Height: 25-40 IN.   Bulb   ❀ WHITE ❀
Habitat: WET
Elevation: 1,500-8,000 FT.
Locale: CARIBOU RD.

Schoenolirion, derived from the Greek *schoinos*, a rush, and *lirion*, lily, grows in large colonies in wet areas along Caribou Road. Mother's Day and a bit after is often prime time in this area, where Leopard Lily, or *Lilium pardalinum*, White Rush Lily, and Western Azalea are often in bloom together.

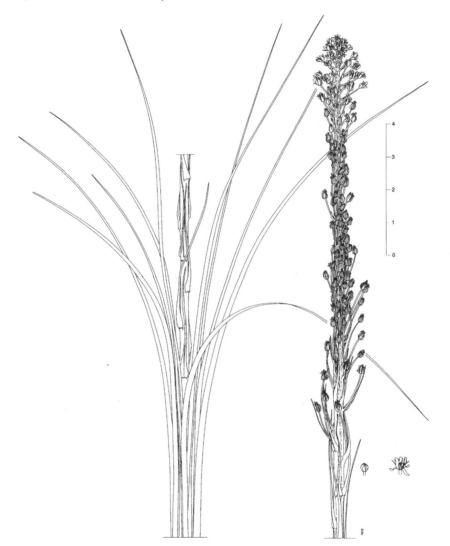

BEAR-GRASS   LILY
Xerophyllum tenax   Liliaceae
Height: 12-24 IN.   Perennial   ❀ WHITE ❀
Habitat: SLOPES, DRY
Elevation: BELOW 6,000 FT.
Locale: OMEGA RD.

The genus name is derived from the Greek *xerophyllum*, meaning dry leaf, a reference to the tough persistent leaves. These grassy leaves are sold at the San Francisco flower market for use in flower arrangements. Let us hope they come from out of state because Bear-grass is not too prevalent here, but is more plentiful in Washington. The flowers are spectacular and seem to bloom better following a fire.

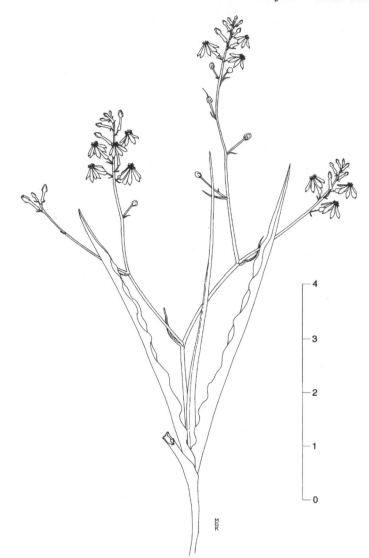

ODONTOSTOMUM   LILY
Odontostomum bartwegii   Liliaceae
Height: 5-16 IN.   Corm   ❀ WHITE/CREAM ❀
Habitat: GRASSLAND, ROCKY
Elevation: BELOW 2,000 FT.
Locale: WOLF RD. OFF McCOURTNEY RD.

The genus name *Odontostomum* is from the Greek *odous*, tooth, and *stoma*, mouth, referring to the staminodia. There are six stamens that alternate with staminodia. The flower is tubular, with six reflexed or swept-back tepals. This Lily has basal linear leaves that sheath the stem. It is the only member of this genus.

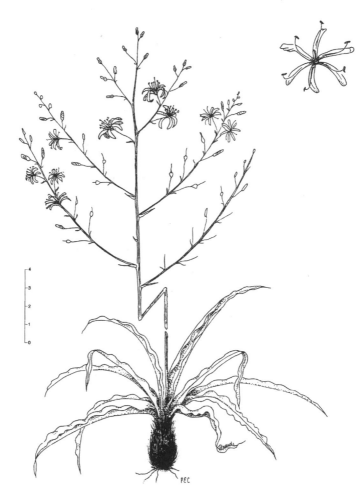

SOAP PLANT   LILY
Chlorogalum pomeridianum   Liliaceae
Height: 23-60 IN.   Bulb   ❀ WHITE ❀
Habitat: SLOPES, DRY
Elevation: BELOW 4,000 FT.
Locale: BRIDGEPORT NORTHWEST OF GRASS VALLEY

Soap Plant blooms after most of the wildflowers have finished, and it is also a night bloomer, pollinated by moths, so it can easily be overlooked on spring hikes. The two-foot-long rippled leaves or the exposed large hairy bulb, which looks like a recently buried brown furry animal along a trail, are more likely to be seen than the flowers. Indians used the bulb, crushed and tossed in a pool, to stun fish. The fibrous bulb covering was used as a brush. A soapy lather can be produced from the bulb, hence the common name. The bulb is toxic unless it has been baked for many hours.

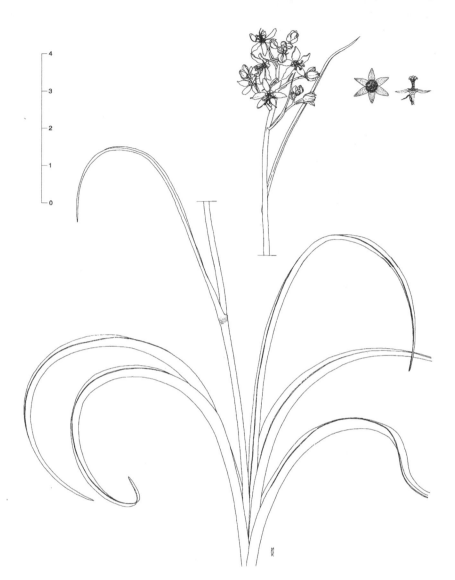

STAR LILY   LILY
Zigadenus fremontii   Liliaceae
Height: 20-24 IN.   Bulb   ❀ **WHITE** ❀
Habitat: GRASSY
Elevation: BELOW 3,500 FT.
Locale: OMO RANCH RD. OFF SR 88

Star Lily is usually an early bloomer and quite showy and much larger than
Death Camas, *Zigadenus venenosus* var. *venenosus*, which is poisonous and
is often found in the same moist or grassy habitat where *Camassia* grows.
Camassia bulbs were a much desired food for the Indians.

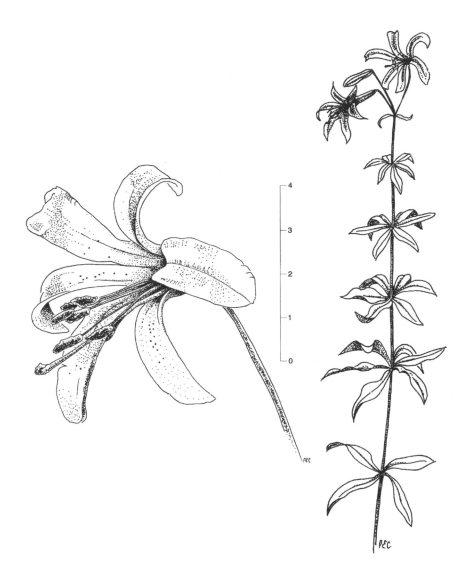

WASHINGTON LILY
Lilium washingtonianum
Height: 24-72 IN. Bulb

LILY
Liliaceae
❀ WHITE ❀

Habitat: SLOPES, BUSHY
Elevation: 3,800 FT.
Locale: WILD PLUM CAMPGROUND NEAR SIERRA CITY

Washington Lily, named in honor of Martha Washington, is similar in appearance to the Easter Lily. This fragrant Lily is most often found poking out of brush, frequently Manzanita. These tough shrubs offer the plants protection from deer browsing.

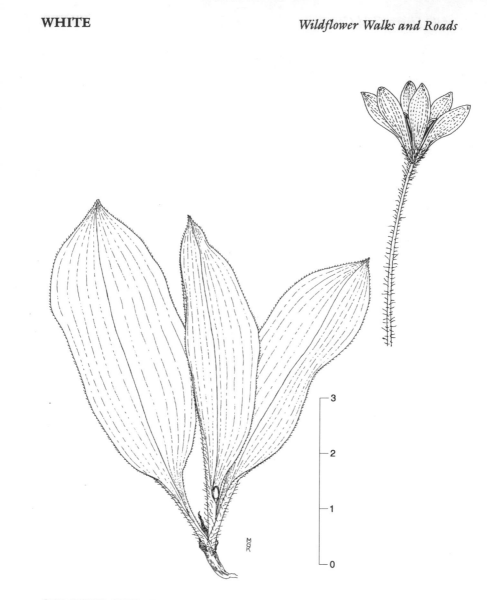

QUEEN'S CUP, BRIDE'S BONNET

Clintonia uniflora

Height: 5-7 IN.   Perennial/rhizome

Habitat: FOREST, SHADE

Elevation: 3,500 FT.

Locale: BRIDAL VEIL PARK 18 MI. EAST OF PLACERVILLE

LILY
Liliaceae
❀ WHITE ❀

What a thrill to see this lovely Lily in the Sierra foothills when it is usually thought of as a plant of the northwest. It is nestled under shrubs at the edge of the parking lot at Bridal Veil Picnic Area along the American River. The white 1-inch flower blooms in late April. It is similar in size to *Erythronium*.

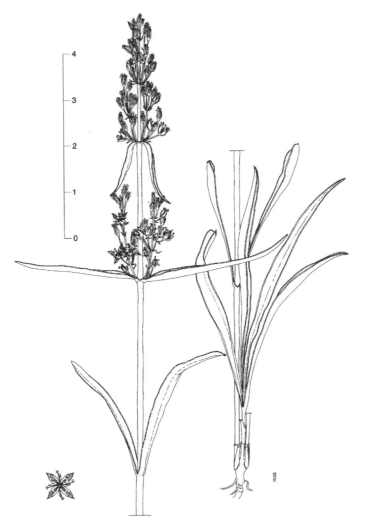

SWERTIA   GENTIAN
Swertia albicaulis var. *nitida*   Gentianaceae
Height: 12-24 IN.   Perennial ❀ **WHITE WITH BLUE CAST** ❀
Habitat: SLOPES, DRY
Elevation: 500-7,000 FT.
Locale: LAST SMALL ROAD TO LEFT OFF McCOURTNEY RD. ON THE
       GRASS VALLEY SIDE OF THE DUMP

The white margin along the edge of the leaves of Swertia is unforgettable. This plant is fairly uncommon but with the unique leaves and four-petaled waxy blue-white flowers on a stalk it will be remembered. The McCourtney road area, which is attractive for homesites (except the site near the dump), Goodyears Bar-Indian Trail, and possibly near Englebright Reservoir are the only locations we found for this plant.

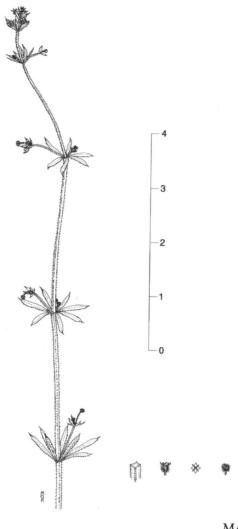

BEDSTRAW   MADDER
Galium aparine   Rubiaceae
Height: 4-40 IN.   Annual   ❀ WHITE ❀
Habitat: SLOPES, SHADE
Elevation: BELOW 7,000 FT.
Locale: MANY

This delicate weak-stemmed annual, found in shade, with small white four-petaled flowers, is a relative of Sweet Woodruff, or *Galium odorata*, used to flavor May Wine. The whorls of leaves on the stem are the most noticeable characteristic of this common shade plant. Another species of Bedstraw, *Galium nuttallii* ssp. *nuttallii*, has a similar leaf pattern on a much smaller scale. It forms a tangled mass of tiny stems and little greenish-yellow flowers that climb and rest on other plants.

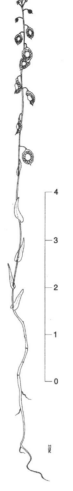

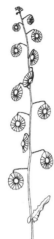

SPOKEPOD	MUSTARD	*LACEPOD, FRINGEPOD*
Thysanocarpus radians	Brassicaceae	*Thysanocarpus curvipes*
	❀ WHITE ❀	

Height: 5-22 IN.　　　　　Annual　　　　　　　　　　　　8-20 IN.
Habitat: GRASSLAND, MOIST　　　　　　　　　　　　　　　SLOPES
Elevation: BELOW 3,000 FT.　　　　　　　　　　　　BELOW 5,000 FT.
Locale: McCOURTNEY RD. NEAR　　　　　　　　WARDS FERRY RD. IN
　　　　GRASS VALLEY　　　　　　　　　　　　　　TUOLUMNE CO.

These two members of the Mustard family, with their tiny white flowers, are not noticeable until they are in seed. They have beautiful rounded silicles, like Money Plant, instead of the sleek silique of field Mustard. Spokepod has veins to the edge of the flat round seed, and Lacepod is often perforated around the edge of the flat elliptical seed. Both plants are a delight to photograph with backlighting.

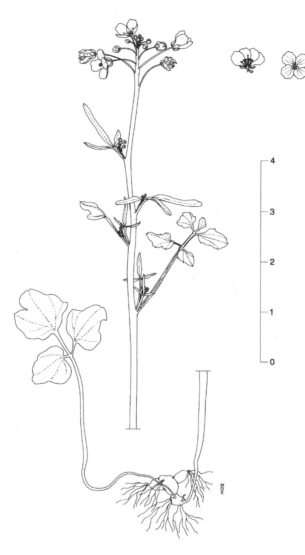

TOOTHWORT, MILKMAIDS
Dentaria californica; Cardamine californica
Height: 4-16 IN.   Perennial
Habitat: ROAD BANKS, OAK FOREST SHADE
Elevation: BELOW 2,500 FT.
Locale: YANKEE JIMS RD. OFF I-80 JUST BELOW COLFAX

MUSTARD
Brassicaceae
❀ WHITE/PINK ❀

This is an early spring bloomer, along with Isopyrum and Hound's Tongue, appearing in February or March. Milkmaids have four white petals and a cross created by the stamens, four of which are long and two short. The flower hangs its head when rain is expected, thus protecting the pollen from moisture.

WILD RADISH   WEED   MUSTARD
Raphanus sativa   Brassicaceae

Height: 2-4 FT.   Annual or biennial   ❀ WHITE, YELLOW, LAVENDER ❀
Habitat: ROADSIDE
Elevation: THROUGHOUT CALIFORNIA
Locale: MANY ROADSIDES

The most common color of Wild Radish is white, although yellow and lavender can be found growing at the same location. The yellow Wild Radish is very similar to the several species of weedy, but pretty, wild mustards. The difference, in general, is the seed pod, which in mustards is slender and in Wild Radish, while still elongated, is fatter with constrictions about the seed.

123

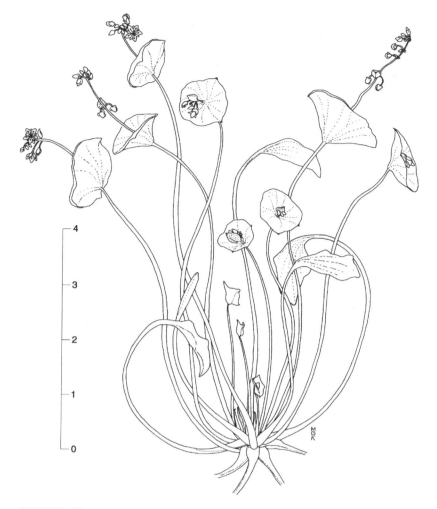

MINER'S LETTUCE
Montia perfoliata
Claytonia perfoliata ssp. *perfoliata*
Height: 4-12 IN.   Annual
Habitat: MOIST
Elevation: BELOW 5,000 FT.
Locale: PONDEROSA WAY

PURSLANE
Portulacaceae

❀ WHITE/PINK ❀

The species name *perfoliata* refers to the leaf surrounding the stem. Miner's Lettuce is easy to recognize because of this characteristic. However, not all Miner's Lettuce leaves have this shape; some are elongated or reniform. Add Miner's Lettuce to your sandwich; it is safe to eat. Another plant with perfoliate leaves is Jewel Flower, *Streptanthus tortuosus*, which generally has some elongated seed pods on the plant so one can't confuse the two plants.

CANTELOW'S LEWISIA   PURSLANE
Lewisia cantelovii   Portulacaccae
Height: ROSETTE   Perennial   ❀ **WHITE** ❀
Habitat: ROCKY
Elevation: 1,200-4,000 FT.
Locale: CARIBOU RD. OFF FEATHER RIVER HWY. / EDWARDS CROSSING
Rare Cantelow's Lewisia covering the mossy rocks at the entry to Caribou
Road is an announcement that this road is paradise for plant lovers. The
basal rosette of spoon-shaped, dentate-edged leaves has one or more deli-
cate stems with panicles of white to pale pink flowers. The blooming
period is fairly long but usually ends by Mother's Day.

ISOPYRUM	***MECONELLA***
Isopyrum occidentale	*Meconella californica*
BUTTERCUP ❀ WHITE ❀	POPPY
Ranunculaceae	Papaveraceae
Height: 4-12 IN. Perennial	Annual TO 8 IN.
Habitat SLOPES, SHADE	OPEN, ROCKY
Elevation: BELOW 5,000 FT.	BELOW 3,500 FT.
Locale: YANKEE JIMS RD. OFF I-80	RED HILL RD. NEAR
NEAR COLFAX	CHINESE CAMP

Meconella is a delicate little annual that covers the ground at Red Hill Road near the trail head. It is bright white. The Poppylike seed pod helps identify the plant family. It has a similar appearance to *Isopyrum occidentale* as far as both being delicate, small, and white. They differ in petal (sepal) number, the habitat they prefer, and leaf shape. Isopyrum closely resembles Anemone but has seed follicles like Columbine, while Anemone has achenes similar to, but smaller than, those of Clematis.

126

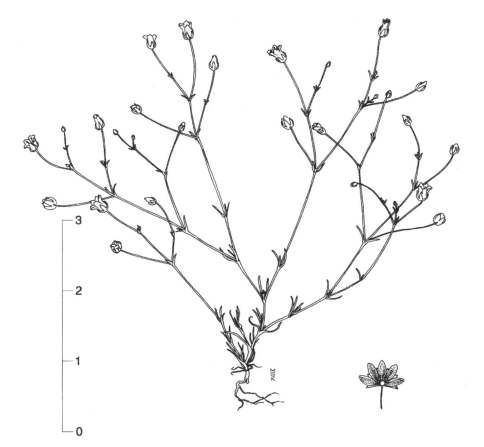

SANDWORT

Arenaria douglasii; Minuartia douglasii

Height: TO 8 IN.   Annual

Habitat: SLOPES, GRAVELLY OR SERPENTINE

Elevation: BELOW 7,000 FT.

Locale: RED HILL RD. OFF SR 120

PINK
Caryophyllaceae
❀ WHITE ❀

The genus *Arenaria* is derived from the Latin word *arena*, meaning sand, in which many of the *Arenaria* species grow. This delicate plant has opposite tiny threadlike leaves and wiry stems. The plant forms an airy mound of little white flowers that shiver to the touch.

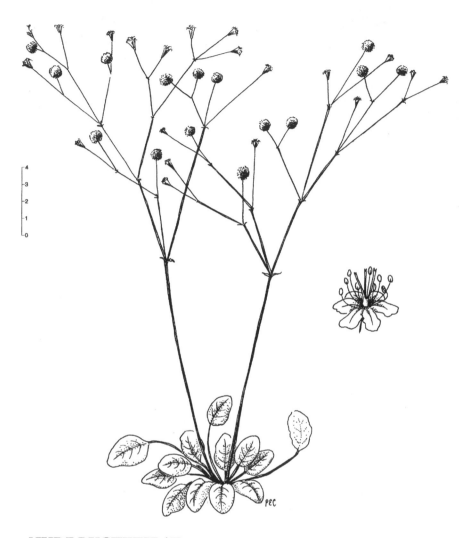

NUDE BUCKWHEAT

Eriogonum latifolium ssp. *nudum*
Eriogonum nudum var. *nudum*

Height: TO 25 IN.   Perennial

Habitat: ROCKY

Elevation: BELOW 8,000 FT.

Locale: COMMON ALONG ROADSIDES

BUCKWHEAT
Polygonaceae

❀ WHITE/PINK ❀

This Buckwheat chooses to grow along hot gravelly roadsides. The basal leaves are covered with tomentose hairs, especially on the underside, which needs insulation from the hot gravel in which the plants grow. The flower clusters are off-white to pinkish puffs on a tall stem naked of leaves, hence the derivation of the common name.

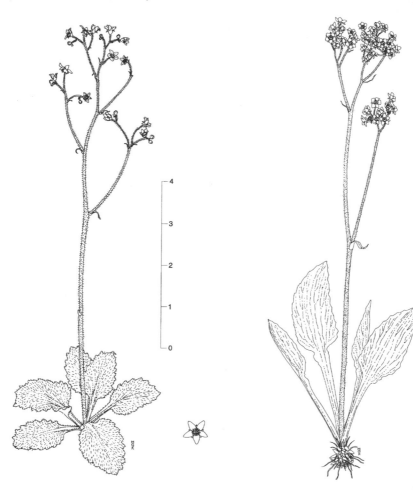

| CALIFORNIA SAXIFRAGE | SAXIFRAGE | BOG SAXIFRAGE, OREGON SAXIFRAGE |

CALIFORNIA
SAXIFRAGE
Saxifraga californica

SAXIFRAGE
Saxifragaceae
❀ WHITE ❀
Herb/Perennial

BOG SAXIFRAGE,
OREGON SAXIFRAGE
Saxifraga oregana

Height: BASAL LEAVES, 4-12 IN. FLOWER STEM — BASAL LEAVES, 12-24 IN. FLOWER STEM.

Habitat: MOIST, SHADE — WET

Elevation: BELOW 2,500 FT. — BELOW 3,500 FT.

Locale: PONDEROSA WAY AFTER CROSSING TO SOUTH SIDE OF AMERICAN RIVER — BOWMAN LAKE RD. OFF SR 20

Saxifrage is a tidy little plant with a rosette of leaves and stalks of delicate white flowers that show off beautifully against a background of dark mossy rocks. The genus name is derived from the Latin *saxum*, rock, and *frango*, to break. *Saxifraga oregana*, Bog Saxifrage, has a basal cluster of oval leaves that are narrow at the base and flare into a broad petiole. The flowering stem on both plants is more or less glandular pubescent.

129

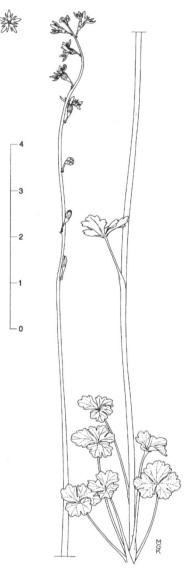

WOODLAND STAR
Lithophragma affine
Height: 8-24 IN.   Perennial
Habitat: SLOPES, SHADE
Elevation: BELOW 3,500 FT.
Locale: WARDS FERRY RD.

SAXIFRAGE
Saxifragaceae
❋ WHITE ❋

The genus name is of Greek derivation, *lithos* for rock and *phragma* for hedge. The common name is perfect for this beautiful woodland plant. It is very noticeable sticking up above the grass. It does well in a garden that mimics the native habitat.

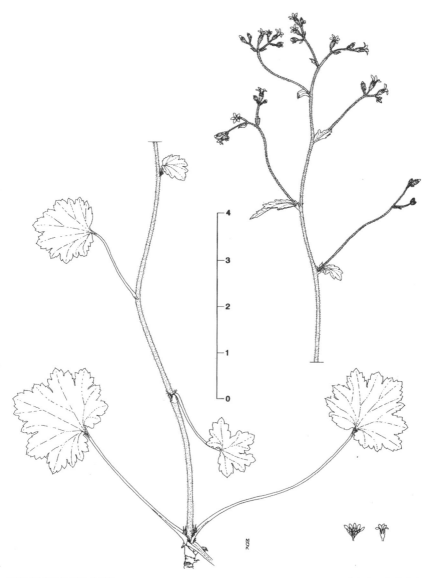

BROOK FOAM

Boykinia elata; Boykinia occidentalis

Height: 8-15 IN.   Perennial

Habitat: RIPARIAN

Elevation: BELOW 5,000 FT.

Locale: BOWMAN LAKE RD. OFF SR 20

SAXIFRAGE
Saxifragaceae
❀ WHITE ❀

A delicate wandlike cluster of small white flowers atop lush green leaves growing in shade at the edge of a stream can usually be identified as a member of the Saxifrage family. Most members have palmate or maplelike leaves and a slender stalk with delicate flowers.

131

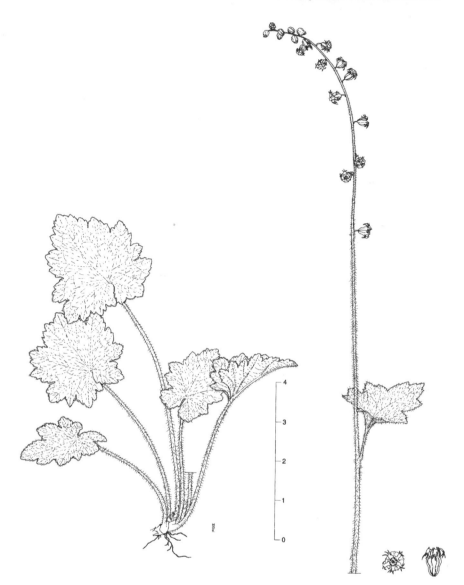

FRINGE CUPS
Tellima grandiflora

SAXIFRAGE
Saxifragaceae

Height: 16-32 IN.   Perennial   ❀ **WHITE TO ROSE** ❀

Habitat: FORESTS, MOIST

Elevation: BELOW 5,000 FT.

Locale: FEATHER RIVER HWY.

Fringe Cups is found from the coast to 5,000 feet. It is a common plant, pretty in woodland gardens when combined with native Iris, and beautiful in flower arrangements because of the long graceful stalks. Notice the fringed petals.

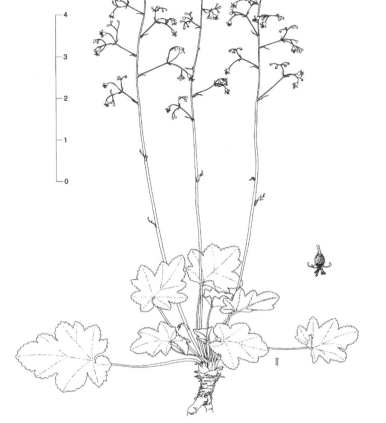

ALUM ROOT   SAXIFRAGE
Heuchera micrantha   Saxifragaceae
Height: BASAL LEAVES, 12-28 IN.   Perennial   ❀ WHITE ❀
Habitat: MOIST
Elevation: BELOW 2,000 FT.
Locale: FEATHER RIVER HWY. / YANKEE JIMS RD.

Alum Root is fairly common on north-facing shady, sometimes mossy, banks growing with *Saxifraga californica* and *Sedum spathulifolium*. Looking up at a north-facing bank, one must admire the master landscape architect. The combination of airy wands of tiny *Heuchera* flowers, the blue-green rosettes of the Sedum, and the mossy background would win a blue ribbon in any landscape show.

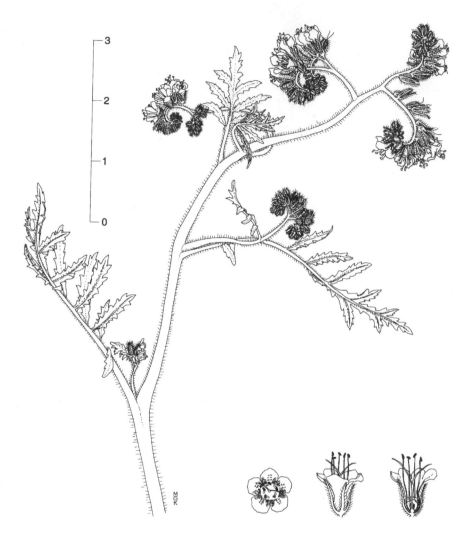

CATERPILLAR PHACELIA

Phacelia cicutaria

Height: 12-36 IN.   Perennial

Habitat: SLOPES, ROCKY

Elevation: BELOW 4,000 FT.

Locale: EL PORTAL

WATERLEAF

Hydrophyllaceae

❀ **WHITE TO OFF-WHITE** ❀

Caterpillar Phacelia has a very pretty coiled cluster of whitish flowers that have exserted stamens. It is too bad that the flowers are often dirty white. The leaves are ferny and the weak stems clamber over other plants.

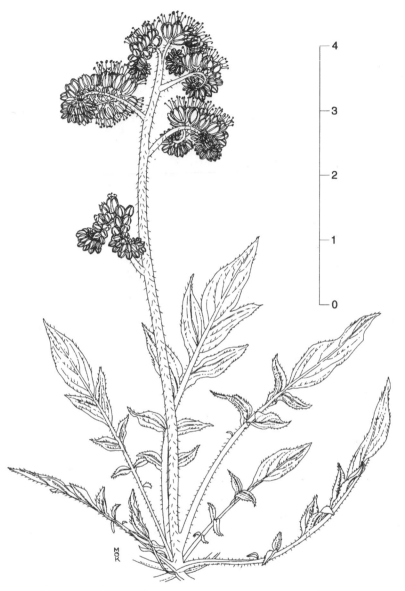

VARILEAF PHACELIA
Phacelia heterophylla
Height: 12-48 IN.　　　Perennial

WATERLEAF
Hydrophyllaceae
❀ **WHITE TO LAVENDER** ❀

Habitat: SLOPES, ROCKY
Elevation: BELOW 7,000 FT.
Locale: TIGER CREEK OFF SR 88

Phacelia heterophylla is entirely stiff-hairy including hair on the filaments. It has grayish, mostly basal leaves and a tall, robust flowering stalk above the leaves. The flower color varies from white to pale lavender.

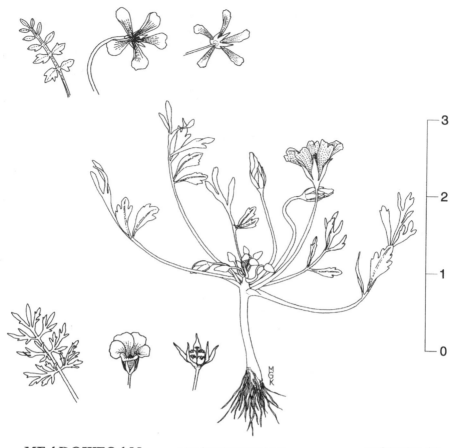

MEADOWFOAM	MEADOWFOAM	DOUGLAS
Limnanthes striata	Limnanthaceae	MEADOWFOAM
	❀ WHITE ❀	*Limnanthes douglasii*

Height: 4-12 IN.   Annual   3-12 IN.
Habitat: OPEN, MOIST   VERNAL POOL
Elevation: 600-1,700 FT.   BELOW 3,000 FT.
Locale: SR 4 ABOVE MILTON RD.   LAKE McSWAIN

Douglas Meadowfoam can be distinguished from other members of the same genus by the notch in its petals. Large colonies of this plant form white concentric circles around vernal pools found just as the terrain begins to rise above the Central and San Joaquin valleys. The genus name is derived from the Greek *limne*, marsh, and *anthos*, flower, describing the habitat where Meadowfoam is found. *Limnanthes striata* is found in moist ditches along roads at an elevation just below the Foothill Pine belt. The species name means striped, which refers to the delicate purplish-brown stripes on the petals. An important identifying characteristic is the incurled petal as it wilts.

WHITE NEMOPHILA	WATERLEAF	**FIVE SPOT NEMOPHILA**
Nemophila heterophylla	Hydrophyllaceae	*Nemophila maculata*
❀ WHITE ❀		❀ WHITE WITH PURPLE SPOTS ❀
Height: 4-12 IN.	Annual	4-12 IN.
Habitat: SLOPES, SHADE		SLOPES, MOIST
Elevation: BELOW 5,000 FT.		BELOW 5,000 FT.
Locale: EL PORTAL, HITE'S COVE TRAIL		RED HILL RD. OFF SR 120
EAST OF MARIPOSA		NEAR CREEK CROSSING

The genus name *Nemophila*, from the Greek *nemos*, grove, and *phileo*, to love, is indicative of the shaded banks where Nemophila grows. The species name *heterophylla* describes the leaves, which vary in shape. It has small pretty white flowers a half inch in diameter. *Nemophila maculata* has a larger flower, up to an inch and a half across, with a purple blotch on the tip of each petal. *Maculata* means spotted.

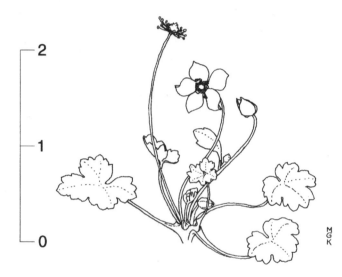

WATERFALL BUTTERCUP   BUTTERCUP
Ranunculus hystriculus   Ranunculaceae
Kumlienia hystricula
Height: 2-16 IN.   Perennial   ❀ WHITE ❀
Habitat: WET ROCKS
Elevation: 3,000-6,000 FT.
Locale: FEATHER RIVER HWY., SEEPING GRANITE CLIFFS

By the time real wildflower season has arrived, Waterfall Buttercup is on
the wane. Feather River Canyon is colder than many of the other sites,
such as Stevens Trail and the waterfalls on Cherry Lake Road, so the
bloom there usually lasts into mid-April. It has rounded, slightly lobed,
lush green leaves with bright white flowers.

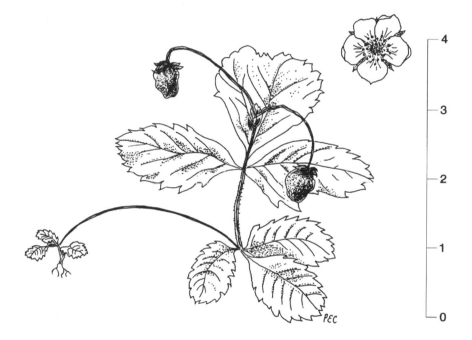

WILD STRAWBERRY

ROSE

Fragaria vesca

Rosaceae

Height: 4-5 IN.   Perennial   ❀ WHITE ❀

Habitat: FORESTS

Elevation: BELOW 7,000 FT.

Locale: CALAVERAS BIG TREES STATE PARK

Wild Strawberry is most often found at the edge of a forest or on road banks. Delicious little Strawberries appear in early summer. The genus name is from the Latin *fragrans*, fragrant, alluding to the perfume of the Strawberry.

COW PARSNIP   CARROT
Heracleum lanatum   Apiaceae
Height: 3-9 FT.   Perennial   ❀ WHITE ❀
Habitat: OPEN/SHADED
Elevation: BELOW 9,000 FT.
Locale: MANY

Cow Parsnip is attractive as a background plant in a large garden. The big six-to-eight-inch umbel of lacy white flowers is named after Hercules, who supposedly used this giant herb as a medicine. The lower young stems can be peeled and eaten raw or cooked, or the stems can be dried and burned to retrieve the salty ash. Be careful not to confuse Cow Parsnip with Poison Hemlock, *Conium maculatum*, another large plant with Carrotlike leaves, red spots on the lower stem, and an unpleasant odor.

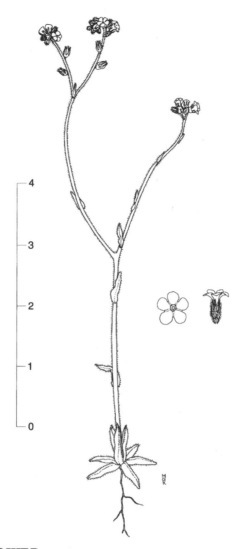

POPCORN FLOWER
Plagiobothrys nothofulvus

BORAGE
Boraginaceae

Height: 8-20 IN.   Annual   ❀ WHITE ❀

Habitat: GRASSLAND/SLOPES/ FIELDS

Elevation: BELOW 2,500 FT.

Locale: MANY

Popcorn Flower can turn hillsides white with its pretty forget-me-not flower. Often when the plant is bruised or picked a purple dye remains on one's hands. There are similar species and another genus, *Cryptantha*, which is easily confused with *Plagiobothrys*. The Borage family keying characteristic is often the arrangement of the prickles on the seed or the way the seed (nutlet) is attached to the receptacle. They are difficult to identify.

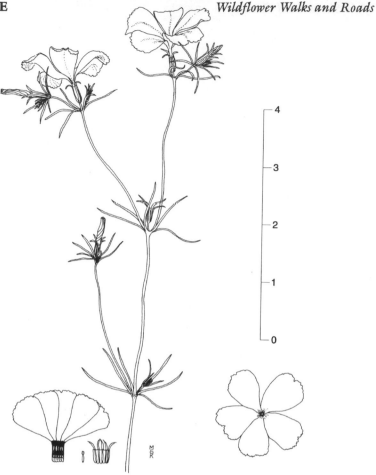

EVENING SNOW   PHLOX
Linanthus dichotomus   Polemoniaceae
Height: 2-8 IN.   Annual   ❀ WHITE ❀
Habitat: ROCKY, SERPENTINE
Elevation: BELOW 5,000 FT.
Locale: TRAVERSE CREEK BOTANICAL AREA 3 MILES SOUTH OF
          GEORGETOWN, GROWING WITH BITTERROOT / CODFISH FALLS
          OFF PONDEROSA WAY

Alice Eastwood, quoted in the Parsons book of 1916, writes: "At four
o'clock in the afternoon [it] begins to whiten the hillside. Before expan-
sion the flowers are hardly noticeable; the dull pink of the edges, which
are not covered in the convolute corolla, hides their identity and makes
the change which takes place when they unveil their radiant faces to the
setting sun the more startling. They intend to watch all night and by
sunset all are awake. In the morning they roll up their petals again when
daylight comes on, and when the sun is well up all are asleep, tired out
with the vigil of the night."

JIMSONWEED, THORNAPPLE   NIGHTSHADE
Datura meteloides; Datura wrightii   Solanaceae
Height: 2-5 FT.   Perennial   ❀ WHITE ❀
Habitat: ROADSIDES, DRY, OPEN
Elevation: BELOW 4,000 FT.
Locale: KNIGHTS FERRY STATE PARK OFF SR 120

Jimsonweed grows along the roads in the vicinity of Knights Ferry. It has a huge trumpet-shaped white to very pale lavender flower somewhat resembling the Morning-glory flower. The large silvery leaves sprawl along the ground. The plant has narcotic properties and has killed people who have tried to figure out how Indians used it in ceremonies.

HANSEN'S DELPHINIUM

Delphinium hansenii

Height: 2-3 FT. Perennial

BUTTERCUP

Ranunculaceae

❀ WHITE/PINK/BLUE ❀

Habitat: ROAD BANKS, CHAPARRAL

Elevation: BELOW 3,700 FT.

Locale: WARDS FERRY RD.

This tall, robust Delphinium has a densely packed stalk of flowers. They are later blooming than many of the Delphiniums and put on quite a show on the road banks along the Groveland side of the Wards Ferry Bridge. The flowers at this location are very light pink.

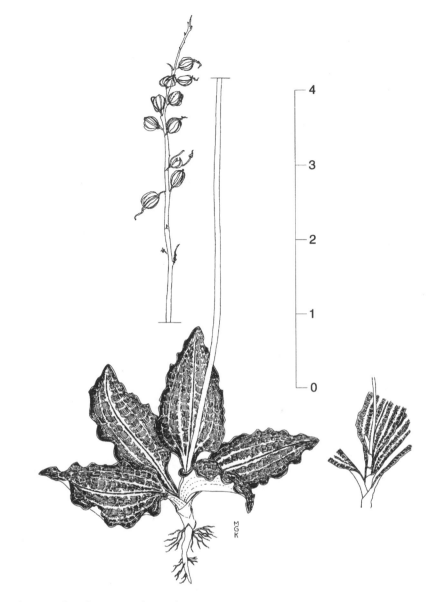

RATTLESNAKE PLANTAIN   ORCHID
Goodyera oblongifolia   Orchidaceae
Height: ROSETTE   Perennial   ❀ WHITISH ❀
Habitat: FORESTS, DRY
Elevation: BELOW 5,500 FT.
Locale: INDIAN VALLEY TRAIL, SR 49 BELOW DOWNIEVILLE

The white vein pattern of the basal leaves, rather than the stalk of tiny
Orchids, is what is most noticeable about this plant along a forest trail. The
leaves are fairly common, but one doesn't often see *Goodyera* in bloom.

145

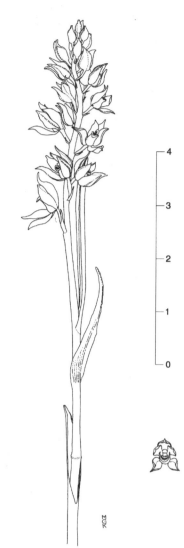

PHANTOM ORCHID   ORCHID
Cephalanthera austiniae; Eburophyton austiniae   Orchidaceae
Height: 8-20 IN.   Perennial   ❀ WHITE ❀
Habitat: FORESTS, DRY
Elevation: BELOW 6,000 FT.
Locale: SKILLMAN FLAT CAMPGROUND ON SR 20
           EAST OF GRASS VALLEY

This entire plant is pure white and has a stalk of perfect little Orchid flowers. It grows in deep shade under trees and shrubs and is very showy in the dark green forest. Phantom Orchid usually blooms in late April at Skillman Flat.

HOT ROCK	FIGWORT	***YAWNING PENSTEMON,***
PENSTEMON	Scrophulariaceae	***GAPING PENSTEMON***
Penstemon deustus	❀ WHITE-CREAM ❀	***Keckiella breviflora***

Height: 8-24 IN.　　Perennial　　　　　　　　Shrub　　2-6 FT.
Habitat: ROCKY　　　　　　　　　　　　　　　　　　ROCKY
Elevation: BELOW 8,200 FT.　　　　　　　　　BELOW 8,500 FT.
Locale: MOSQUITO RIDGE RD. NEAR FORESTHILL　　WARDS FERRY RD.

Hot Rock Penstemon is often found in gravel at the base of road banks. Look closely at the pretty white flower with dark lines that are nectar guides for the pollinators. The species name *deustus* means burned. *Keckiella breviflora* var. *breviflora*, Yawning Penstemon or Gaping Penstemon, is a shrub with small white flowers found on hot rocky slopes.

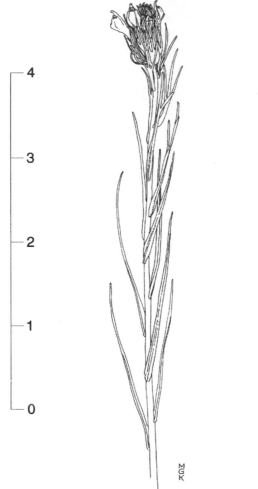

VALLEY TASSELS

Orthocarpus attenuatus; Castilleja attenuata

Height: 4-16 IN.   Annual

Habitat: GRASSLAND

Elevation: BELOW 5,000 FT.

Locale: SUTTER CREEK TO DAFFODIL HILL

FIGWORT

Scrophulariaceae

❀ WHITE ❀

Valley Tassels are sometimes cream-colored but usually white. The corolla sacs are not inflated like *Orthocarpus erianthus*, or Butter and Eggs. *Orthocarpus linearilobus*, or Pallid Owl's-clover, has white bracts with yellow corolla sacs and seems to bloom later than the other species mentioned. The species name *attenuatus* means narrowing to a point, which is descriptive of the tips of the leaves.

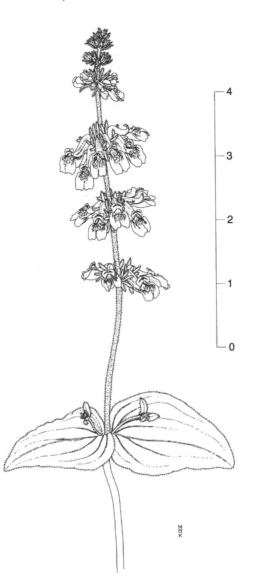

WHITE CHINESE HOUSES
Collinsia tinctoria

Height: 8-24 IN.   Annual

FIGWORT
Scrophulariaceae
❀ WHITE-CREAM ❀

Habitat: SHADE

Elevation: BELOW 2,000 FT.

Locale: DRUM POWERHOUSE RD.

White Chinese Houses are like a many-level pagoda. The flowers are cream-colored with a larger lower lip. The plant has a glandular pubescence that can leave a slight red stain on your finger from rubbing or breaking the stem, hence its species name.

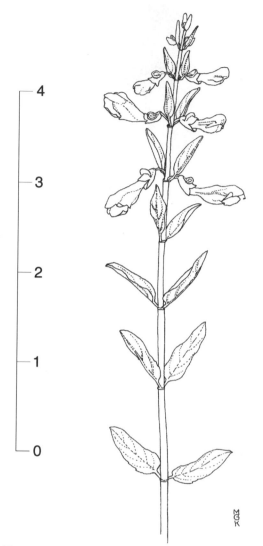

4

3

2

1

0

SKULLCAP   MINT
Scutellaria californica   Lamiaceae
Height: 4-12 IN.   Perennial   ❀ WHITE ❀
Habitat: GRAVEL, DRY
Elevation: BELOW 7,000 FT.
Locale: INDIAN TRAIL, ALONG THE AMERICAN RIVER, ON YANKEE JIMS RD.
This plant often grows in large colonies. Because of the opposite leaves
and two-lipped flowers, sometimes Skullcap is confused with Penstemon.
Most Mints are aromatic (this does not have a Mint odor) and have square
stems. The common name is descriptive of the shape of the upper fused
petals.

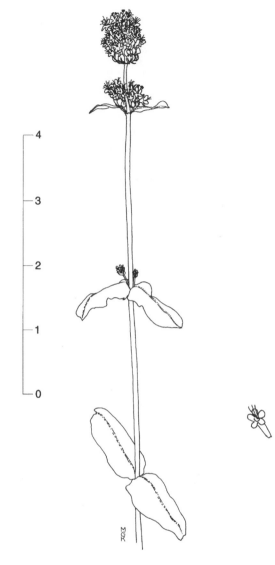

PLECTRITIS
Plectritis ciliosa

VALERIAN
Valerianaceae

Height: 4-16 IN.   Annual   ❀ **WHITE TO PALE PINK** ❀

Habitat: SLOPES/ WOODLAND, OPEN

Elevation: BELOW 4,000 FT.

Locale: BLM NATURAL BRIDGES NATURE TRAIL
        NORTH OF PARROTTS FERRY

Plectron in Greek means spur. The corolla is five-lobed with a basal spur; the calyx is missing. From a distance the flower head resembles a Clover flower head, but on close examination the tiny flowers are not at all like a Pea flower.

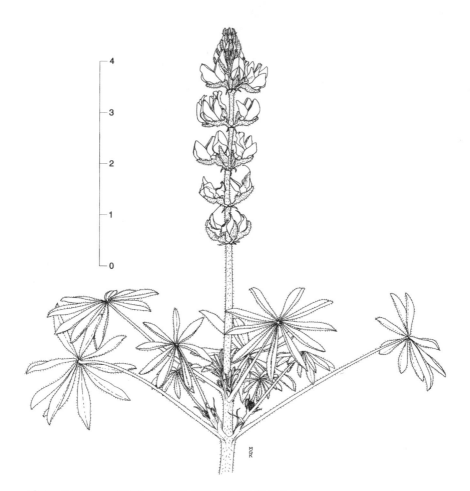

CHICK LUPINE, WHORLED LUPINE   PEA
Lupinus densiflorus   Fabaceae
Lupinus microcarpus var. *densiflorus*

Height: 8-16 IN.   Annual   ❀ WHITE/YELLOW/PINK/LAVENDER ❀
Habitat: GRASSLAND/ROADSIDES
Elevation: BELOW 2,000 FT.
Locale: SR 120 / WARDS FERRY RD.

Whorled Lupine varies greatly in color. The stacks or whorls of flowers are the characteristic that makes this common species recognizable. It is most often white or yellow on slopes or along the edge of the road. The best display of pink is along Wards Ferry Road. *Lupinus densiflorus* flowers grow in tidy whorls; as the plant forms seed, the stem bends and the seeds migrate to the top side of the stem, making a tangled mess of bent stems. Do the seeds need more heat and sunlight to mature?

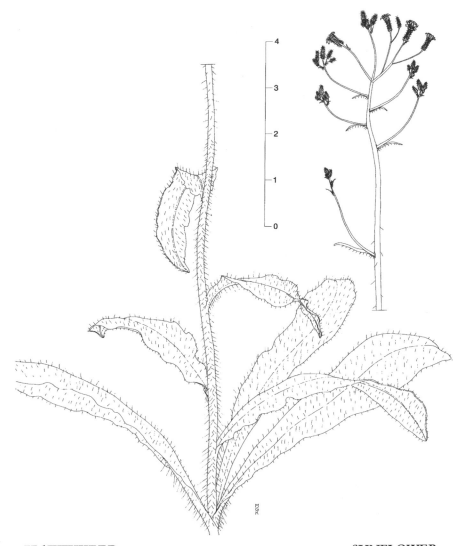

HAWKWEED SUNFLOWER
Hieracium albiflorum Asteraceae
Height: 24-36 IN. Perennial ❀ WHITE ❀
Habitat: FORESTS, DRY
Elevation: BELOW 9,000 FT.
Locale: CALAVERAS BIG TREES STATE PARK

This plant is a member of the Dandelion tribe of the Sunflower family. Typical of this tribe, it has milky juice when a stem is broken, and like its relatives Lettuce and Dandelion, it has only ray flowers. The leaves are very hairy. There are not many flowers that bloom in the forest, so Hawkweed is easy to identify.

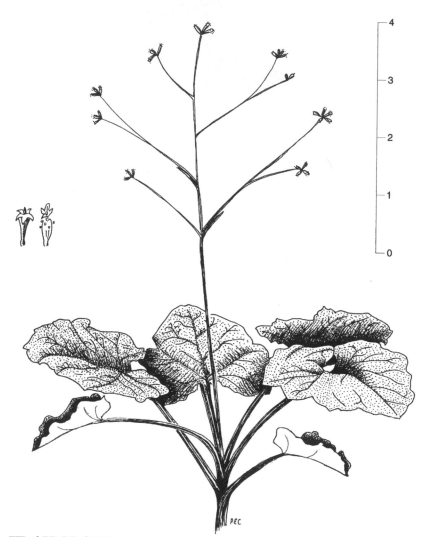

TRAIL PLANT   SUNFLOWER
Adenocaulon bicolor   Asteraceae
Height: 12-36 IN.   Perennial   ❀ SMALL WHITE ❀
Habitat: FORESTS
Elevation: BELOW 6,000 FT.
Locale: INDEPENDENCE TRAIL SR 49 NORTH OF NEVADA CITY
The genus *Adenocaulon* is from the Greek *aden,* meaning gland, and
kaulos, stem. Look with the hand lens for stem and fruit glands. On a hot
day the leaves will turn over and show a white underside, shaped like an
arrow, pointing the way along the trail. The top of the leaf is green, the
bottom whitish, hence the species name *bicolor.*

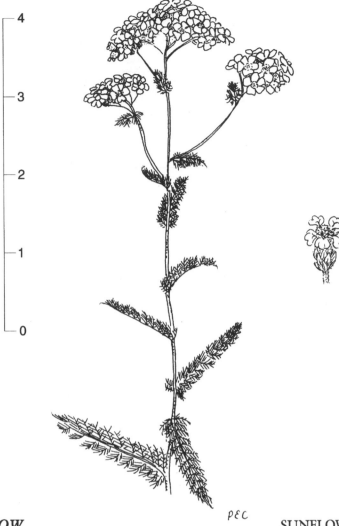

pec

YARROW   SUNFLOWER
Achillea millefolium   Asteraceae
Height: 4-40 IN.   Perennial   ❀ WHITE ❀
Habitat: ROADSIDES
Elevation: BELOW 11,000 FT.
Locale: MANY

This common aromatic plant is said to have been used by Achilles to heal wounds and stop bleeding. It has such common names as Soldier's Woundwort, Bloodwort, Staunchgrass, and Staunchweed and does stop bleeding. The flower color in nature varies from white to pale pink. There are many nursery varieties, including almost a true red and all gradations of yellow, as well as dwarf forms. A useful, hardy garden plant native or cultivated.

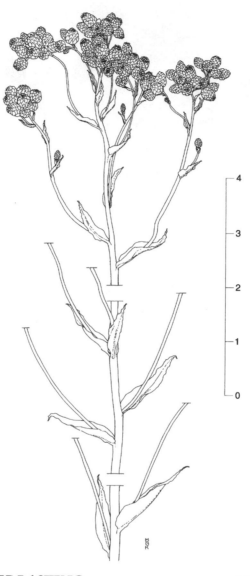

PEARLY EVERLASTING
Anaphalis margaritacea

SUNFLOWER
Asteraceae

Height: 6-30 IN. Perennial ❀ WHITE ❀

Habitat: FORESTS, OPEN

Elevation: BELOW 9,000 FT.

Locale: EL PORTAL EAST OF MARIPOSA

An Edelweiss relative, this aromatic plant has pretty dried flowers that are fun to use in botanical crafts. They are tiny papery daisies with a speck of yellow in the center. The plants are fuller and more attractive along the roads in northwestern California, where there is more moisture.

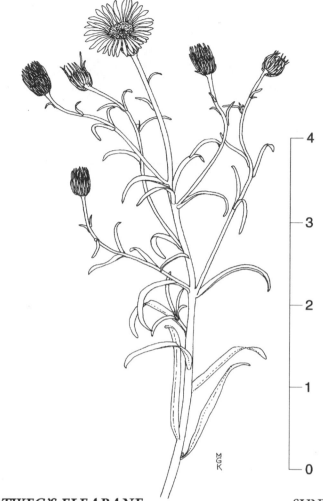

HARTWEG'S FLEABANE　　　　　　　　　　SUNFLOWER
Erigeron foliosus var. *hartwegii*　　　　　　　　Asteraceae
Height: 9-20 IN.　　　　　Perennial　　　❀ WHITE, PINKISH ❀
Habitat: ROCKY, DRY
Elevation: BELOW 3,000 FT.
Locale: MOSQUITO RIDGE RD. NEAR FORESTHILL SOUTHEAST OF AUBURN
Hartweg's Fleabane forms about a foot-wide mass of showy small white daisies that beckon you to climb the rocks to get a closer look. *Erigeron* typically has tidy even bracts on the underside of the flower. Asters, which are similar, have phyllaries that overlap like shingles and often the tips turn back, giving a messy appearance. A similar plant, *Erigeron philadelphicus,* sometimes has clasping leaves and the flowers arise mid-stem, whereas *Erigeron foliosus* leaves do not clasp the stem and the flowering heads arise near the stem tips.

BUSH POPPY   POPPY
Dendromecon rigida   Papaveraceae
Height: 3-9 FT.   Shrub/evergreen   ❀ YELLOW ❀
Habitat: SLOPES, DRY
Elevation: BELOW 6,000 FT.
Locale: MAGALIA ABOVE PARADISE

This beautiful drought-tolerant plant is wonderful for a rocky dry land-scape situation. It doesn't respond well to transplanting or to disturbance of the area around it once it is established. The seeds germinate readily after a fire. To germinate these seeds for a plant sale, the seeds can be placed on a large pie tin of sand, covered with Pine-needle duff, and then burned.

APRICOT	FIGWORT	*STICKY*
MONKEYFLOWER	Scrophulariaceae	*MONKEYFLOWER*
Mimulus bifidus	❀ APRICOT/ORANGE ❀	*Mimulus aurantiacus*
Height: 2-4 FT.	Shrub	2-4 FT.
Habitat: SLOPES, ROCKY		SLOPES, ROCKY
Elevation: BELOW 3,000 FT.		BELOW 3,000 FT.

Locale: MOSQUITO RIDGE RD. NEAR FORESTHILL AND AUBURN

Mimulus bifidus is sometimes called Apricot Monkeyflower or Azalea Monkeyflower. It is especially beautiful on Mosquito Ridge Road in mid-April or along the Feather River Highway in early May. Sticky Monkeyflower, *Mimulus aurantiacus*, is orange-yellow with sticky narrow leaves. It is very common from the coast to about 3,000 feet. Both of these Monkeyflowers have been placed in the species *bifidus* by *The Jepson Manual*. Both species are woody, are easily propagated by cuttings, and need fall pruning in a garden situation.

159

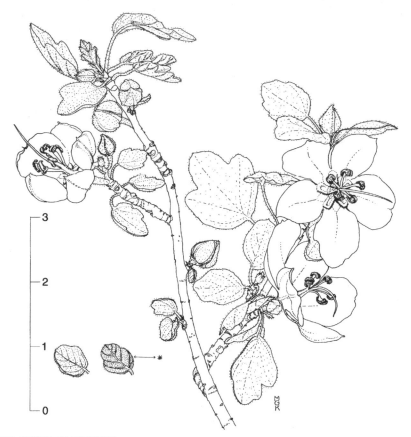

FLANNEL BUSH
Fremontia californica "Margo"; Fremontodendron
californicum cultivar form "Margo"
Height: 4-27 FT.   Tree/evergreen
Habitat: SLOPES, DRY
Elevation: BELOW 6,000 FT.
Locale: McCOURTNEY RD. ON THE LAST LITTLE ROAD
            ON THE LEFT BEFORE THE DUMP

CACAO
Sterculiaceae

❀ YELLOW ❀

There are several species and cultivar forms of the drought-tolerant Flannel Bush available to gardeners. The illustration is drawn from a plant at Tilden Botanical Garden and was collected from Dobbins, California. This very yellow cultivar form has been hard to reproduce. *Fremontia* is especially beautiful when combined with a blue *Ceanothus*, such as the cultivar form "Dark Star." Be careful when handling *Fremontia*; the stellate hairs (interesting through a hand lens) on the leaves and stems can cause a contact allergic reaction. Pine Hill, west of Placerville, has a rare species, *Fremontodendron californicum* ssp. *decumbens*, that is less than three feet tall and much wider. The flowers are copper-colored.

160

OREGON GRAPE, MAHONIA
Berberis aquifolium var. *dictyota*

BARBERRY
Berberidaceae

Height: TO 5 FT.   Shrub/evergreen   ❀ YELLOW ❀

Habitat: SLOPES, SHADED

Elevation: BELOW 7,000 FT.

Locale: PIPI CAMPGROUND OFF SR 88 IN EL DORADO CO.

Oregon Grape is easy to recognize, with its Hollylike leaves and terminal clusters of bright yellow flowers that turn into blue-purple tiny grapelike clusters of fruit. The inner bark has been used to make dye and the fruits to make jelly. This useful plant is a good landscape plant under Monterey Pines, where not much will grow.

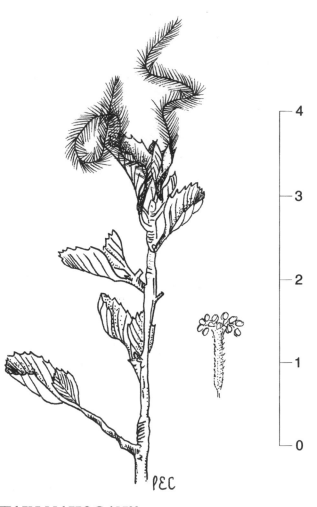

PEC

MOUNTAIN MAHOGANY   ROSE
Cercocarpus betuloides   Rosaceae
Height: 6-30 FT.   Shrub, Tree/deciduous   ❀ TINY, PALE YELLOW ❀
Habitat: SLOPES, DRY
Elevation: BELOW 6,000 FT.
Locale: CAMP NINE RD. IN CALAVERAS CO.

Mountain Mahogany has small yellow flowers and is not a very noticeable plant until you see the hairy seeds backlit by the sun. The small leaves are heavily veined, toothed, and slightly resemble those of Cream Flower (*Holodiscus discolor*) and Hazelnut. Hazelnut has very soft leaves and Cream Flower usually has last year's persistent flower heads, thus making identification among these three easy even when not in bloom.

WEED

FRENCH BROOM	PEA	*SPANISH BROOM*
Cytisus monspessulanus	Fabaceae	*Spartium junceum*
Genista monspessulana	❀ YELLOW ❀	
Height: 3-9 FT.	Shrub/deciduous	TO 7 FT.
Habitat: DISTURBED, FIELDS		SLOPES, DRY
Elevation: BELOW 2,000 FT.		BELOW 2,000 FT.
Locale: SR 49 NORTH OF NEVADA CITY		I-80 IN COLFAX AREA

Spanish Broom has simple leaves and rush-like branches with brilliant yellow, almost one inch long, fragrant flowers. The leaves on French Broom are three foliate, with terminal racemes of tiny, almost one half inch, Pea flowers. Though pretty they are terribly invasive non-native shrubs in the foothills and ruin lots of grazing land and wildflower habitats.

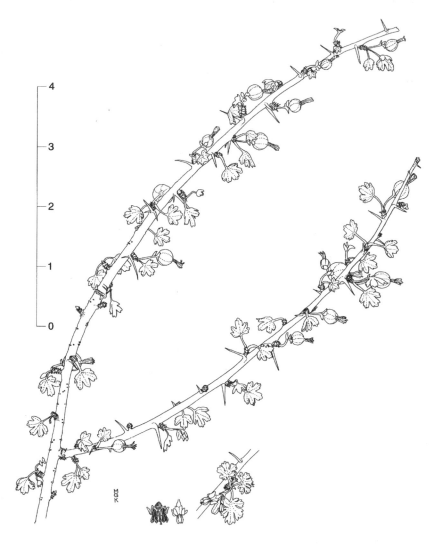

OAK GOOSEBERRY
Ribes quercetorum

GOOSEBERRY
Grossulariaceae

Height: 2-5 FT.   Shrub/deciduous   ❀ YELLOW ❀

Habitat: SLOPES/OPEN FLATS

Elevation: BELOW 4,000 FT.

Locale: ROCK RIVER RD.

The leaves on this Gooseberry are like little Oak leaves, hence its common name. The sepals are yellow and the petals cream-colored, giving the plant a pale yellow appearance when in bloom. The outstanding characteristic of this Gooseberry is the stiff arching stem. The plant has a wide range even though it is not common. The author has seen it in the flats northwest of Mount Shasta, in the foothills, and west of Bakersfield.

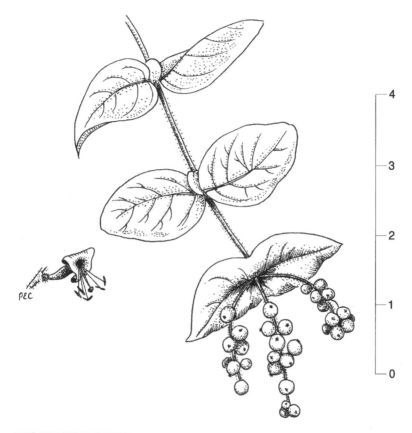

PEC

HONEYSUCKLE   HONEYSUCKLE
Lonicera hispidula **var.** *vacillans*   Caprifoliaceae
Height: 6-20 FT.   Vine   ❀ YELLOW/PINK ❀
Habitat: FORESTS, OPEN
Elevation: BELOW 2,500 FT.
Locale: FOOTES CROSSING RD. ON MIDDLE FORK OF THE YUBA RIVER
Honeysuckle climbs on other shrubs and is not very noticeable until it is
at eye level on the trail. Then one becomes aware of the spike of pink
flowers and the one or two pairs of leaves that are fused around the stem,
like Miner's Lettuce, just under the inflorescence. Later in the season a
cluster of red translucent fruit will ripen at the tip of the stem. Cream-
colored Honeysuckle, *Lonicera interrupta*, is another species found in the
same area. It climbs and sprawls, from a woody base, over other shrubs
and is beautiful when covered with cream-colored flowers.

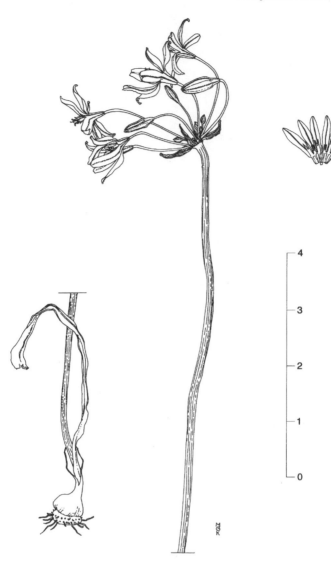

GOLDEN BRODIAEA, FOOTHILL PRETTY FACE   LILY
Triteleia ixiodes ssp. *scabra*   Liliaceae
Height: 8-16 IN.   Bulb   ❀ YELLOW ❀
Habitat: GRASSLAND
Elevation: 500-7,000 FT.
Locale: CAMP FAR WEST RD. NORTH OF LINCOLN
Golden Brodiaea has wide open straw-yellow flowers with a dark stripe on each petal. The distinguishing characteristic of this species of yellow Brodiaea is the forked appendage that surrounds each anther and the flat-open flower. Golden Brodiaea is profuse in the grasslands surrounding Camp Far West Reservoir.

GOLDEN	LILY	*YELLOW STAR-TULIP,*
MARIPOSA LILY	Liliaceae	*YELLOW PUSSY EARS*
Calochortus luteus	❀ YELLOW ❀	*Calochortus monophyllus*
Height: 15-24 IN.	Bulb	3-8 IN.
Habitat: GRASSLAND		SLOPES
Elevation: BELOW 3,000 FT.		1,200 FT. OR MORE
Locale: PENTZ-MAGALIA RD. BELOW PARADISE		CLINTON RD. OFF I-88

The Golden Mariposa Lily appears in fields just as the grass begins to turn from green to gold. This showy bowl or tulip-shaped *Calochortus* has a reddish-orange spot in the center of each petal. The nectary or gland is crescent or oblong-shaped. *Calochortus monophyllus* blooms along many of the back roads of the Gold Country. This species of *Calochortus* can be recognized by the single leaf: *mono* meaning single and *phyllus* referring to leaf.

TUOLUMNE FAWN LILY   LILY   **FAWN LILY**
Erythronium   Liliaceae   *Erythronium*
tuolumnense   ❀ YELLOW ❀   *multiscapoideum*
Height: 5-8 IN.   Perennial/corm   5-7 IN.
Habitat: FOREST   FOREST
Elevation: 1,000-2,000 FT.   1,200-3,000 FT.

Locale: ITALIAN BAR RD.   COUTENEC RD. NEAR MAGALIA ABOVE PARADISE
Visit Italian Bar Road in mid-March to see these bright lemon yellow
Tuolumne Fawn Lilies in their full glory. They are found growing on both
sides of the road as it descends fairly near the river and begins to level out.
Erythronium multiscapoideum, a more delicate and paler yellow than
Tuolumne Fawn Lily, is found on serpentine soil at Traverse Ridge near
Georgetown, under the Cypress on McCourtney Road in mid-March, and
could still be in bloom until the first week in April under the McNab
Cypress near Magalia. Try going up to the Magalia serpentine when you
visit Table Mountain.

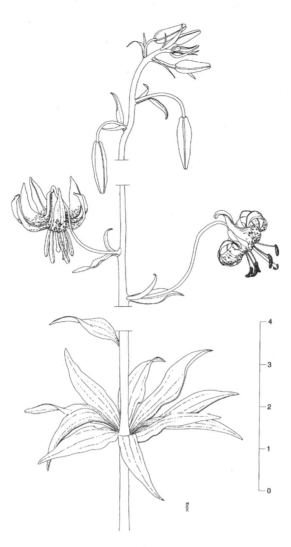

LEOPARD LILY, TIGER LILY, TURK'S CAP LILY

Lilium pardalinum

LILY
Liliaceae

Height: 40-72 IN.   Bulb/scales   ❀ **ORANGE** ❀

Habitat: MOIST

Elevation: ALL

Locale: CARIBOU RD.

Leopard Lily is very prevalent in moist areas of the foothills. The height can vary greatly, the leaves can be scattered on the stem or in one to eight whorls, and there can be from one to thirty-five pendant flowers. A similar Lily, *Lilium humboldtii*, Humboldt Lily, is found in dry shade. Jepson states that Humboldt Lily is declining. There used to be a huge colony in the Dutch Flat cemetery and now there is just one. How sad!

HARTWEG'S IRIS
Iris hartwegii

IRIS
Iridaceae

Height: 2-16 IN.   Perennial   ❁ YELLOW ❁

Habitat: SLOPES, FORESTS

Elevation: 2,000-6,000 FT.

Locale: PENTZ-MAGALIA RD. NEAR PARADISE

There is wide color variation in Hartweg's Iris. Most often it is pale yellow or cream to true yellow, but it can vary to shades of lavender. The differentiating characteristic is a short stout perianth tube. *Iris macrosiphon*, which hybridizes with Hartweg's Iris, has a long tube above the ovary.

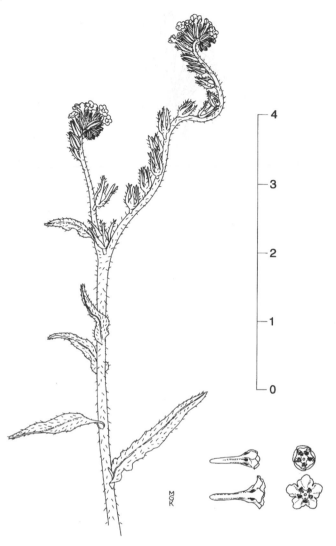

FIDDLENECK   BORAGE
Amsinckia intermedia   Boraginaceae
Height: 12-24 IN.   Annual   ❀ YELLOW/ORANGE ❀
Habitat: GRASSLAND
Elevation: BELOW 5,000 FT.
Locale: KNIGHTS FERRY OFF SR 120 WEST OF SONORA
Fiddleneck is a beautiful flower under the hand lens, with red-orange spots in the throat of the flower. This plant turns hills golden. It is disliked by farmers because the plant when dried in feed can choke a horse. It is often bristly to the touch. There are many species of *Amsinckia*. They are generally bristly, with flowers often in a slightly coiled spike.

WALLFLOWER   MUSTARD
Erysimum capitatum ssp. *capitatum*   Brassicaceae
Height: 8-32 IN.   Perennial/Biennial   ❀ YELLOW/ORANGE ❀

Habitat: SLOPES, ROCKY

Elevation: BELOW 8,000 FT.

Locale: DRUM POWERHOUSE RD. NEAR DUTCH FLAT, PLACER CO.

Wallflower is one of the most fragrant wildflowers in the foothills. The color varies from orange to yellow. Wallflowers are useful landscape plants that need sun and good drainage.

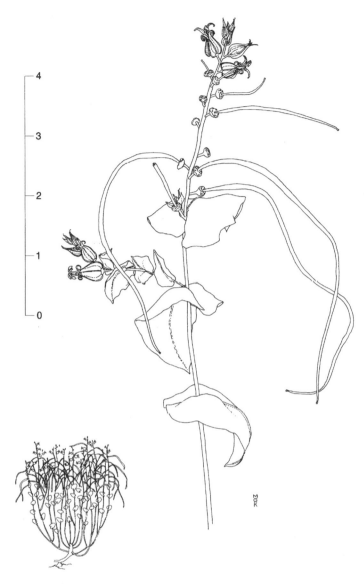

MOUNTAIN JEWEL FLOWER

MUSTARD

Streptanthus tortuosus var. *tortuosus*

Brassicaceae

Height: 8-40 IN.   Annual/Biennial   ❋ YELLOW OR PURPLE, PALE ❋

Habitat: SLOPES, ROCKY

Elevation: 1,000-6,500 FT.

Locale: EL PORTAL NEAR SCHOOL

The stem-clasping chartreuse leaves of Jewel Flower are much more noticeable than the small yellow or pale purple flowers. These leaves remind one of Miner's Lettuce leaves, which wrap around the stem. The long seed pods, "sleek siliques," are typical of the Mustard family.

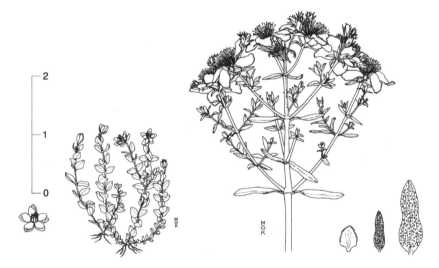

TINKER'S PENNY   ST. JOHN'S WORT   **KLAMATHWEED**
Hypericum   Hypericaceae   *Hypericum*
anagalloides   ❀ YELLOW ❀   *perforatum*
Height: PROSTRATE   Perennial   12-40 IN.
Habitat: WET   ROADSIDES
Elevation: 500-5,000 FT.   BELOW 4,500 FT.
Locale: CALAVERAS BIG TREES STATE PARK   TABLE MOUNTAIN RD.

Tinker's Penny looks as if flakes of gold had been dropped on a green mat. It can be found in sunny moist areas, such as seeps near creeks or lake banks. Look carefully at the tiny flower and you can see that the flower is a miniature of the garden Hypericum. *Hypericum perforatum,* Klamath-weed, is a wiry plant found along roadsides. It has been used medicinally to reduce depression. The toxin hypericin inhibits the human immune deficiency virus, according to Jepson. This plant is highly toxic to live-stock and is considered a noxious weed. Notice the "windows" in the leaves and the dots on the petal edge.

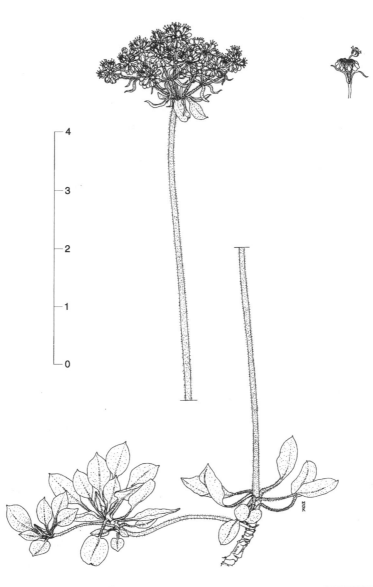

BEAR BUCKWHEAT   BUCKWHEAT
Eriogonum ursinum   Polygonaceae
Height: 8-12 IN.   Perennial   ❀ YELLOWISH ❀
Habitat: GRAVELLY
Elevation: 3,500-8,000 FT.
Locale: BOWMAN LAKE RD. JUST BEYOND YUBA RIVER CROSSING
This is a very pretty Buckwheat that is good in foothill and Tahoe gardens. Its garden requirements are sun, super drainage, and companion plants like *Monardella odoratissima* that have similar habitat requirements.

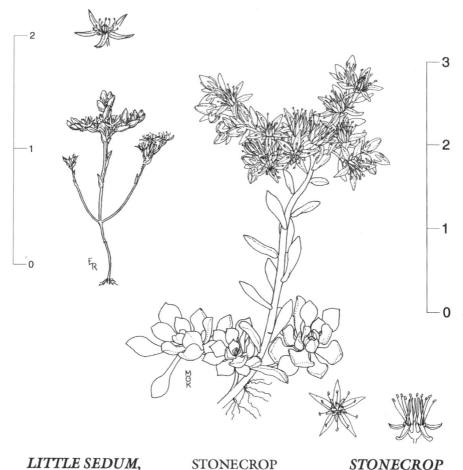

LITTLE SEDUM, GOLDEN ROCK FRINGE *Parvisedum pumilum*	STONECROP Crassulaceae ❀ YELLOW ❀	STONECROP *Sedum spathulifolium*
Height: TO 2 IN.	Annual　　Perennial	BASAL ROSETTE
Habitat: VERNAL POOLS, ROCKY SOIL		ROCKY
Elevation: BELOW 4,000 FT.		BELOW 7,500 FT.
Locale: TABLE MOUNTAIN, ESPECIALLY ON ROCKY AREAS ALONG CHEROKEE RD.		YANKEE JIMS RD.

Little Sedum, or Golden Rock Fringe, turns the parking area at Table Mountain into a carpet of yellow. As you look across the tableland, the black volcanic outcroppings have a yellow fringe of *Parvisedum* at the edge of the rocks. *Parvi* means small and *pumilum*, dwarf. *Sedum spathulifolium* or Stonecrop is very common in the foothills and is beautiful even when it is not in bloom. The pale rosettes of leaves against dark moss or rock make a wonderful contrast of textures; add the bright yellow flowers and the rocks appear to glow.

LIVE-FOREVER, DUDLEYA
Dudleya cymosa

STONECROP
Crassulaceae

Height: BASAL ROSETTE WITH   Perennial   ❀ YELLOW/CORAL ❀
      4 IN. FLOWERING STEMS

Habitat: ROCKY CLIFFS

Elevation: BELOW 9,000 FT.

Locale: NIMBUS DAM TRAIL OFF US 50 IN SACRAMENTO

Nature has combined beautiful colors in Dudleya. Because its normal habitat is cliffs or rocky road banks and it is usually seen from below, the lovely orange-red or coral of the flower cluster appears to be superimposed on the large basal rosette of blue-green leaves. (See artist's Gold Medal drawing in front of book.)

177

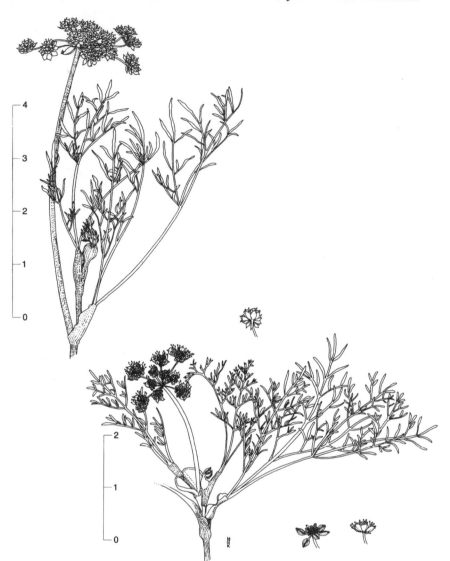

FOOTHILL LOMATIUM   CARROT
Lomatium utriculatum   Apiaceae
Height: 4-20 IN.   Perennial   ❀ YELLOW ❀
Habitat: SLOPES, GRASSY
Elevation: BELOW 5,000 FT.
Locale: PONDEROSA WAY, WEIMAR EXIT OFF I-80

Early blooming Foothill Lomatium changes its appearance greatly as it matures. The flowers start as a bright tight little cluster of yellow nestled in the leaves. Three weeks later the leaves have elongated, the flower stem is above the leaves, and the flower cluster has become an open umbel of yellow balls.

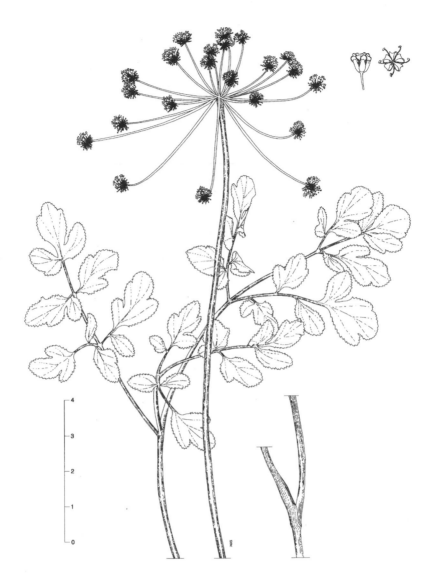

HARTWEG'S TAUSCHIA   CARROT
Tauschia hartwegii   Apiaceae
Height: 12-40 IN.   Perennial   ❀ **YELLOW** ❀
Habitat: SLOPE
Elevation: BELOW 3,500 FT.
Locale: PONDEROSA WAY, WEIMAR EXIT OFF I-80
The open umbel of Hartweg's Tauschia on a one-to-two-foot leafless stalk
is similar to Angelica or a small Cow Parsnip flower except that it is yellow
instead of white.

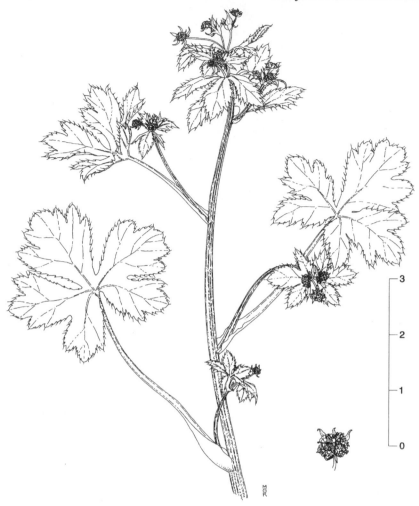

GAMBLE WEED, PACIFIC SNAKEROOT

Sanicula crassicaulis

Height: 12-24 IN.   Perennial

Habitat: SLOPES, SHADED

Elevation: BELOW 4,500 FT.

Locale: MANY

CARROT

Apiaceae

❀ YELLOW ❀

Gamble Weed is a very common plant whose leaves resemble *Heuchera*, thus fooling people into thinking it will be a beautiful plant, when really the young leaves are the prettiest part of it. A coarse stalk develops with a few hairy leaves and some tiny little yellow button flowers. *Sanicula bipinnata*, Poison Sanicle, is very similar to the yellow form of *Sanicula bipinnatifida* but does not have the toothed rachis. The genus *Sanicula* is often difficult to figure out because the key characteristic is generally the fruit with its hooks and prickle patterns, and by then the flower is gone.

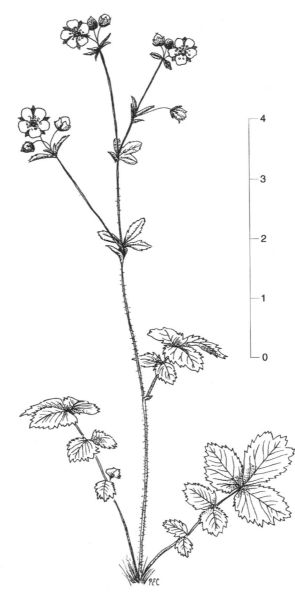

CINQUEFOIL   ROSE
Potentilla glandulosa   Rosaceae
Height: 12-24 IN.   Perennial   ❀ YELLOW ❀
Habitat: OPEN AREAS
Elevation: BELOW 8,000 FT.
Locale: EL PORTAL

The genus name is derived from *potens,* meaning powerful, referring to
medicinal properties. The flower looks like a Strawberry flower, except
that it is yellow and on a tall plant. It adapts well to garden situations.

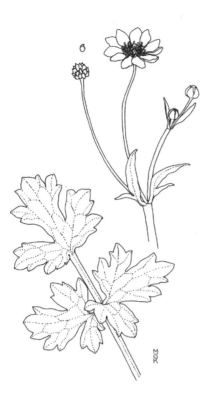

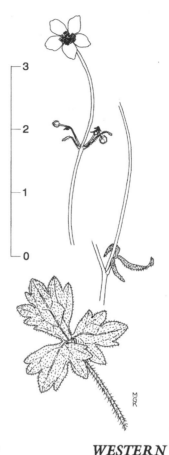

CALIFORNIA BUTTERCUP	BUTTERCUP	*WESTERN BUTTERCUP*
Ranunculus californicus	Ranunculaceae	*Ranunculus occidentalis*

❀ YELLOW, 9-16 OR MORE PETALS ❀   ❀ YELLOW, 5 PETALS ❀

Height: 12-28 IN.   Perennial   12-28 IN.

Habitat: SLOPES, MOIST   OPEN, MOIST

Elevation: BELOW 3,000 FT.   300-6,000 FT.

Locale: TELEGRAPH RD. OFF   MANY LOCATIONS; DRIFTS OF

SR 4, CALAVERAS CO.   YELLOW IN EARLY SPRING

Western Buttercup, *Ranunculus occidentalis*, is hairy like Foothill Butter-cup, *Ranunculus canus*, but has fewer petals than *Ranunculus canus* and *Ranunculus californicus*. The differences, according to Munz and Jepson, are the seed size and a straight prickle in *Ranunculus canus* versus a curved prickle in *Ranunculus californicus*. Prickleseed Buttercup, *Ranunculus muricatus*, has curvy spines all over the seed. It grows in wet areas, has shiny palmate leaves, and is a cascade of yellow. At least three species of Buttercups grow on Telegraph Road, off SR 4, near the stone corral.

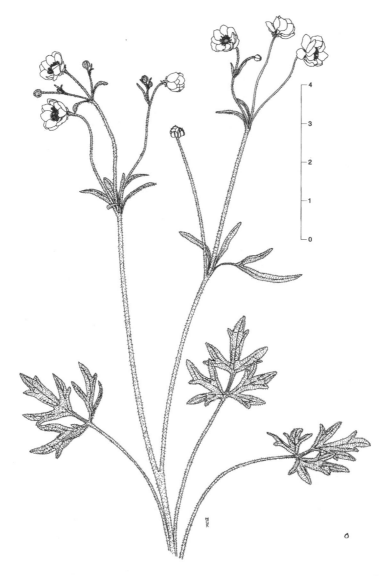

FOOTHILL BUTTERCUP,　　　　　　　BUTTERCUP
SACRAMENTO VALLEY BUTTERCUP　　Ranunculaceae
Ranunculus canus
Height: 16-36 IN.　　　　　Perennial　　　❀ YELLOW ❀
Habitat: OPEN, CLAY SOIL
Elevation: BELOW 1,000 FT.
Locale: TELEGRAPH RD. OFF SR 4, CALAVERAS CO.

Foothill Buttercup is a very hairy Buttercup, with deeply lobed basal leaves. It has from 5 to 17 petals. *Ranunculus californicus* has 9-16 or more petals, but is not as hairy as Foothill Buttercup.

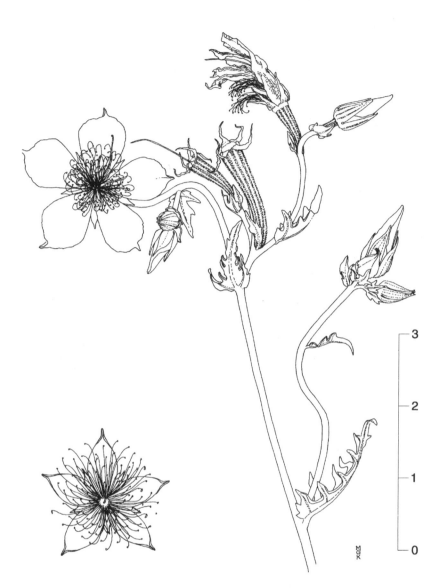

BLAZING STAR   LOASA
Mentzelia lindleyi   Loasaceae
Height: 3-24 IN.   Annual   ❀ YELLOW ❀
Habitat: SLOPES, ROCKY, HOT
Elevation: BELOW 2,500 FT.
Locale: SR 49 ABOUT 2 MILES SOUTH OF MOCCASIN POWERHOUSE
Blazing Star is well named; the flower can be two and a half inches across,
with five shiny yellow petals and an orange-red spot at the base. *Mentzelia*
has distinctive seed pods, useful for identifying this genus.

184

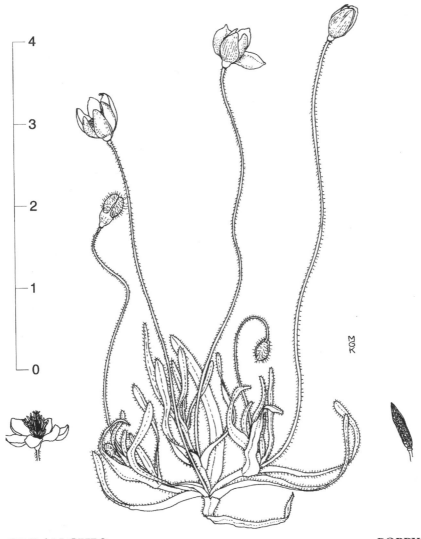

CREAM CUPS
Platystemon californicus
Height: 4-12 IN.   Annual
Habitat: GRASSLAND
Elevation: BELOW 3,000 FT.
Locale: RED HILL RD. AND ON TO CHINESE CAMP OFF SR 120

POPPY
Papaveraceae
❀ YELLOW, PALE ❀

Cream Cups color fields a pale yellow. They are often present in vernal pool areas, though not restricted to them. Like most members of the Poppy family, the sepals fall off when the flower blooms. The genus *Platystemon* is derived from the Greek meaning wide stamen. On the road between Chinese Camp and Red Hill Road there is a private driveway bordered with Cream Cups.

FRYING PANS POPPY,	POPPY	*CAESPITOSE,*
LOBB'S POPPY	Papaveraceae	*TUFTED POPPY*
Eschscholzia lobbii		*Eschscholzia caespitosa*
❀ YELLOW ❀		❀ YELLOW/ORANGE ❀
Height: 4-12 IN.	Annual	4-15 IN.
Habitat: GRASSLAND, GRAVELLY, ROCKY		SLOPES, DRY
Elevation: BELOW 2,000 FT.		BELOW 3,500 FT.
Locale: COPPEROPOLIS ON SR 4		TABLE MOUNTAIN ON CHEROKEE RD.

Lobb's or Frying Pans Poppy, typical of rock garden plants, is all flowers with delicate Fernlike leaves. It grows in gravelly hot locations and does well in a garden when given these conditions. Tufted Poppy can be almost as small as Lobb's Poppy and can be yellow as well as orange. The difference is the leaf divisions.

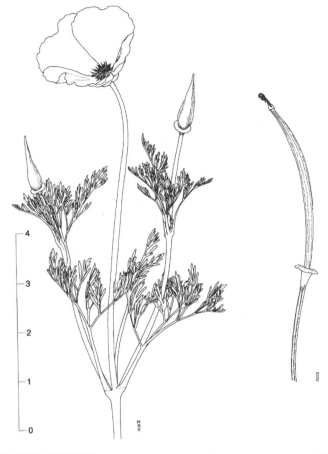

CALIFORNIA POPPY
Eschscholzia californica

POPPY
Papaveraceae

Height: 8-24 IN. Annual or Perennial ❀ ORANGE/YELLOW ❀

Habitat: GRASSLAND, SLOPES

Elevation: BELOW 6,500 FT.

Locale: MANY

Our state flower is found from the coast to Truckee, at 6,000 feet. This poppy can be distinguished from the other Poppies in the foothills by the double torus, a little red platform just below the flower. California Poppy can sometimes be invasive in a garden, and yet it can also be hard to get started. Sow the seed while the weather is still warm in early fall, sprinkle gravel over it so the doves and ants won't get all the seeds, and let nature do the watering. Children love to take the caps (sepals) off the Poppies causing them all to bloom at once. Tufted or Caespitose Poppy (*Eschscholzia caespitosa*) is usually smaller than California Poppy and lacks the obvious torus under the petals. It is generally orange but can be yellow. Tufted Poppy is a better size for landscape use.

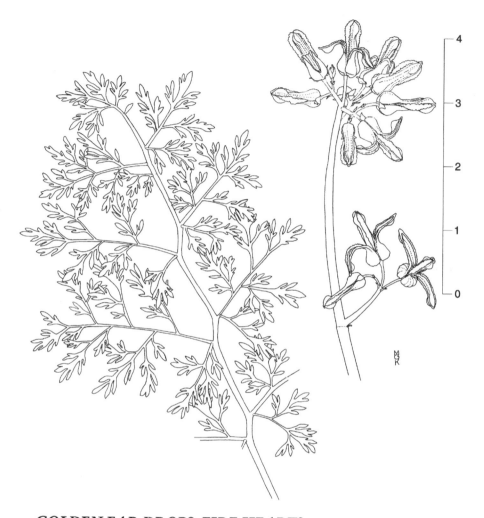

GOLDEN EAR DROPS, FIRE HEARTS   FUMATORY/POPPY
Dicentra chrysantha   Papaveraceae

Height: 20-60 IN.   Perennial   ✿ YELLOW ✿

Habitat: SLOPES, BURNED

Elevation: BELOW 5,000 FT.

Locale: NEAR HORNITOS WEST OF MARIPOSA

Golden Ear Drops are usually found for several years following a fire. This Bleeding Heart relative has similar blue-green, bipinnate leaves that are rather stiff. Since it is a perennial, it does not usually bloom until the second spring after a fire.

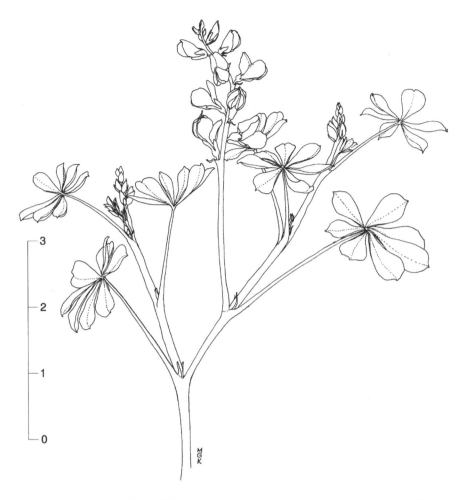

HARLEQUIN LUPINE PEA
Lupinus stiversii Fabaceae
Height: 3-14 IN. Annual ❀ YELLOW, ROSE, AND WHITE ❀
Habitat: GRAVEL
Elevation: 1,600-4,600 FT.
Locale: EL PORTAL/FEATHER RIVER HWY.

Lupinus stiversii seems to like to grow in roadside ditches and on banks just above ditches. Harlequin Lupine grows throughout the gold country from El Portal to Feather River, but never in very large colonies, so it is always a pleasure to find it. It is easy to recognize because of the color combination in the flowers and the wide green leaflets.

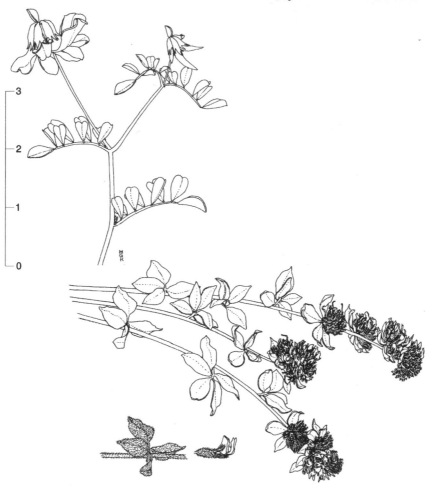

GRAND LOTUS	PEA	*SILVERLEAF LOTUS*
Lotus grandiflorus	Fabaceae	*Lotus argophyllus* var.
	❀ YELLOW ❀	*fremontii*
Height: 10-15 IN.	Perennial	8-40 IN.
Habitat: SLOPES, DRY		GRAVEL
Elevation: BELOW 5,000 FT.		BELOW 5,000 FT.
Locale: SALMON FALLS TRAIL, IOWA HILL RD.		STEVENS TRAIL

Showy Grand Lotus or *Lotus grandiflorus* has very large banner petals. The flowers age red just like the diminutive fuzzy *Lotus humistratus* that is so common in gravel at the bottom of road banks. *Lotus argophyllus* var. *fremontii* (the species name refers to the silver leaf) is covered with downy hairs that give the plant a silver appearance. It has puffs of pale yellow flowers that are beautiful cascading down the dark shale walls of the American River canyon on Stevens Trail. It would make a beautiful rock garden plant.

SULPHUR PEA   PEA
Lathyrus sulphureus   Fabaceae
Height: TO 9 FT. LONG   Perennial vine   ❀ YELLOW ❀
Habitat: SLOPES, WOODED
Elevation: ABOVE 1,200 FT.
Locale: MANY

It is very common to find Sulphur Pea hanging out of branches onto the trail. Because of the prevalence of Poison Oak in the foothills, any plant that is on the trail should be regarded carefully. Sulphur Pea has soft yellow flowers that age to tan, and six to twelve leaflets with a large terminal tendril.

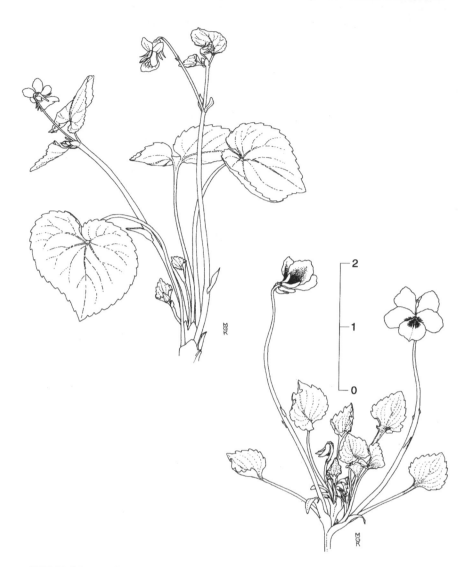

STREAM VIOLET	VIOLA	JOHNNY-JUMP-UP,
Viola glabella	Violaceae	*WILD PANSY*
	❀ YELLOW ❀	*Viola pedunculata*

Height: 4-12 IN.	Perennial	4-14 IN.
Habitat: FORESTS, WET		SLOPES, GRASSY
Elevation: BELOW 8,000 FT.		BELOW 2,500 FT.
Locale: MANY		GRASSLANDS

Stream Violet grows all the way from the coast up to 8,000 feet. It is a lush-appearing Violet. Violet leaves and flowers are edible. *Viola pedunculata,* found in the lower foothills, is a bright, cheery Pansy lookalike. This plant has very long taproots and wilts quickly if picked.

PINE VIOLET	VIOLA	*DOUGLAS'S VIOLET*
Viola	Violaceae	*Viola*
lobata	❀ YELLOW ❀	*douglasii*
Height: 4-12 IN.	Perennial	2-6 IN.
Habitat: DRY, OPEN FORESTS		GRASSLAND, OPEN
Elevation: 1,000-6,500 FT.		100-4,000 FT.
Locale: SKILLMAN FLAT		TABLE MOUNTAIN, BUTTE CO.

There are three yellow Violets with cut leaves that are covered in this book, all three having dark brown or black on the back of the two upper petals. *Viola douglasii* grows at the lowest elevation, often in rocky, grassy areas. The overall shape of the cut blue-green leaves is slightly pointed. *Viola lobata*, or Pine Violet, is larger, with lobes rather than finely cut leaves, and grows in open forests. *Viola sheltonii* is very similar to Douglas's Violet except that it has fan-shaped blue-green leaves and grows at a higher elevation in rocky open forests. Look for Steer's Head with Shelton's Violet. The leaves are similar and they are often found together.

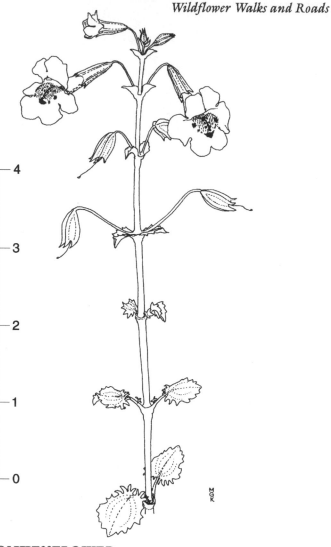

YELLOW MONKEYFLOWER   FIGWORT
Mimulus guttatus   Scrophulariaceae
Height: 2-40 IN.   Perennial   ❀ YELLOW ❀
Habitat: WET
Elevation: BELOW 10,000 FT.
Locale: COPPEROPOLIS ON SR 4

Monkeyflower, *Mimulus guttatus*, which varies greatly in both plant and leaf size, is very common. The flowers are bright yellow, with or without red freckles. The lush leaves are said to be edible raw or cooked. *Mimulus bicolor*, true to its species name, has two colors on the flowers. Generally the two upper petals are white and the three lower petals are yellow with red dots. The location listed above has a beautiful display, usually in mid-April.

WOOLLY MULLEIN $\boxed{\text{WEED}}$ FIGWORT
Verbascum thapsus   Scrophulariaceae
Height: 2-6 FT.   Perennial or Biennial   ❀ YELLOW ❀
Habitat: ROADSIDES
Elevation: BELOW 7,000 FT.
Locale: MANY

Mullein appears in late spring with a large basal rosette of soft fuzzy leaves. The plant is usually in hot disturbed areas, such as along a road or railroad track, so perhaps the hairs help insulate it from heat. The flowers are on a tall spike and are canary yellow. In autumn yellow goldfinches look like flowers that forgot to fall as they perch on the thick stalks and feed on ripe seed. *Verbascum blattaria*, Moth Mullein, is similar to Woolly Mullein but lacks hair. Both are non-native.

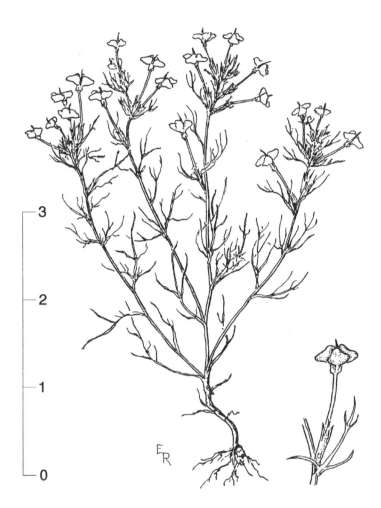

BUTTER AND EGGS, JOHNNY TUCK   FIGWORT
Orthocarpus erianthus; Tryphysaria eriantha   Scrophulariaceae
Height: 2-13 IN.   Annual   ❀ YELLOW ❀
Habitat: GRASSLAND
Elevation: BELOW 2,000 FT.
Locale: 7.5 MILES DOWN McCOURTNEY RD. NEAR GRASS VALLEY

Butter and Eggs color a field pale yellow with a touch of red. There is so little actual red on the plant—bracts and sometimes the stem—that it is amazing the plant can be identified by its red cast when driving by a field at 40 miles an hour. It is very common in the lower foothills.

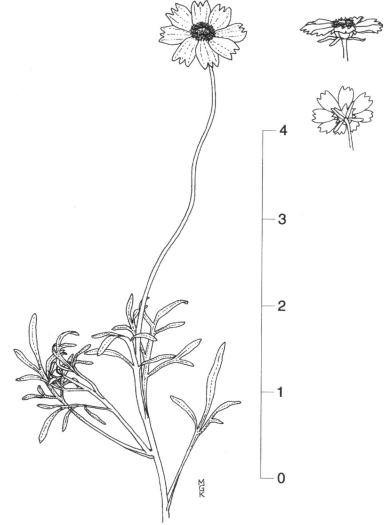

COREOPSIS
Coreopsis stillmanii

Height: 4-10 IN. Annual

Habitat: SLOPES, GRASSY

Elevation: 100-3,000 FT.

Locale: RED HILL RD. OFF SR 120

SUNFLOWER
Asteraceae
❀ YELLOW ❀

These bright yellow flowers often cover acres. Coreopsis is readily distinguished from other Daisies by the extra ring of fleshy green bracts just below the main involucral bracts on the underside of the flower heads. There are beautiful displays in early April at Hites Cove along the Merced River, Ponderosa Way near Colfax, and Red Hill Road off SR 120 near Chinese Camp.

GOLDFIELDS	SUNFLOWER	*FOOTHILL*
Lasthenia chrysantha	Asteraceae	*PSEUDOBAHIA*
Lasthenia californica	❀ YELLOW ❀	*Pseudobahia heermannii*
Height: 2-6 IN.	Annual	4-12 IN.
Habitat: GRASSLANDS		SLOPES, ROCKY
Elevation: BELOW 3,000 FT.		800-3,000 FT.
Locale: TABLE MOUNTAIN ON CHEROKEE RD.		EL PORTAL EAST OF
NORTH OF OROVILLE		MARIPOSA

The little half-inch golden-yellow flowers in these two small annuals are responsible for turning the hillsides gold in spring. *Pseudobahia* is woolly white and has pinnately lobed alternate leaves, whereas Goldfields, *Lasthenia chrysantha*, has glabrous, narrow, opposite leaves. The species name *chrysantha* is from the Greek *chrysos*, gold, and *anthos*, flower.

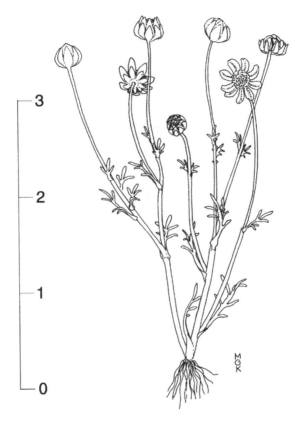

BLENNOSPERMA   SUNFLOWER
Blennosperma nanum   Asteraceae
Height: 2-8 IN.   Annual   ❊ YELLOW, PALE ❊
Habitat: VERNAL POOLS, WET
Elevation: BELOW 1,500 FT.
Locale: TABLE MOUNTAIN ON CHEROKEE RD. NORTH OF OROVILLE
This small, pale yellow Daisy is often found around vernal pools. It is about the same size as Goldfields but not as brilliant. The disk flowers look as if they have been sprinkled with salt; these are the protruding stigmas that can be seen with a lens.

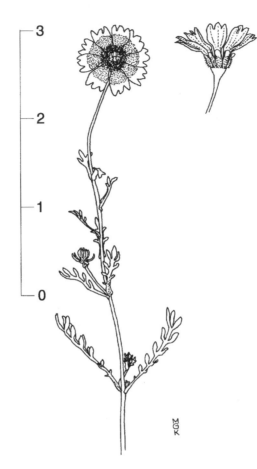

FREMONT'S TIDY-TIPS   SUNFLOWER
Layia fremontii   Asteraceae
Height: 4-16 IN.   Annual   ❀ **YELLOW** ❀
Habitat: GRASSLAND
Elevation: BELOW 2,000 FT.
Locale: SR 4 NEAR TELEGRAPH RD.

Tidy-tips are found bordering vernal pools just as the foothills begin to rise above the Central Valley. They are yellow Daisies with clean white tips on their petals. A field of Tidy-tips has a cream-colored cast while Gold-fields are old Chinese gold in color. *Layia fremontii* has pappus on its seeds and lacks glands, while *Layia platyglossa* does not have any pappus but is glandular. *Layia pentachaeta* is generally all yellow and has purple anthers, glands, and an odor.

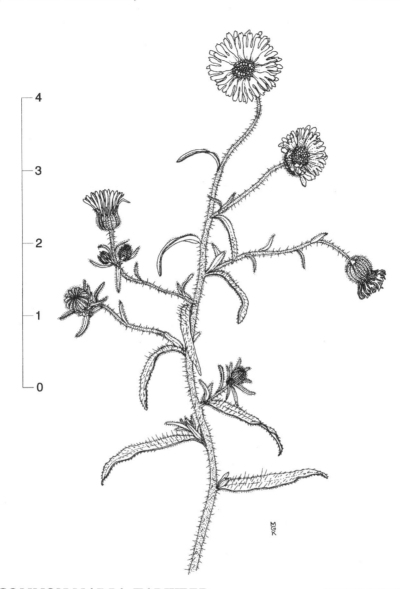

COMMON MADIA, TARWEED
Madia elegans

Height: 8-32 IN.   Annual

Habitat: SLOPES, DRY

Elevation: 3,000-8,000 FT.

Locale: EL PORTAL

SUNFLOWER
Asteraceae
❀ YELLOW ❀

Use a hand lens to see the stem glands on Tarweed, especially those near the flower. These glands are sticky and can stain clothing. Tarweed covers acres of slopes in the foothills, usually in late spring. Goldfields, Coreopsis, and Pseudobahia start the annual spring show in late March.

BALSAMROOT SUNFLOWER *CALIFORNIA SUNFLOWER*
Balsamorhiza   Asteraceae   *Helianthella californica*
deltoidea   ❀ YELLOW ❀   var. *nevadensis*
Height: 8-32 IN.   Perennial   8-24 IN.
Habitat: SLOPES, OPEN   SLOPES, DRY
Elevation: 600-7,000 FT.   800-7,000 FT.
Locale: PINE HILL PRESERVE   WOLF MOUNTAIN RD.
     OFF US 50   OFF McCOURTNEY RD.

The genus name is derived from the Greek *helios*, sun, and *anthos*, flower. *Helianthella* is the diminutive of *Helianthus*. This is a more delicate plant than Mule Ears. The key characteristic of this Sunflower is the leaflike bracts at the base of the involucre. Balsamroot, *Balsamorhiza deltoidea*, has large green triangular leaves that are long-petioled and the one to few flower heads have long peduncles, giving the plant a more graceful appearance than Mule Ears.

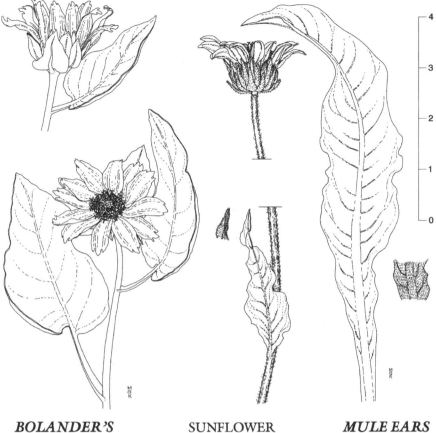

BOLANDER'S	SUNFLOWER	*MULE EARS*
MULE EARS	Asteraceae	*Wyethia*
Wyethia bolanderi	❀ YELLOW ❀	*angustifolia*
Height: 5-15 IN.	Perennial	8-25 IN.
Habitat: GRASSLAND		SLOPES, GRASSY
Elevation: 1,000-3,000 FT.		BELOW 5,500 FT.
Locale: WOLF MOUNTAIN RD.		McCOURTNEY RD.
OFF McCOURTNEY RD.		NEAR GRASS VALLEY

Wyethia bolanderi is a very showy Mule Ears; it is abundant on Wolf Mountain Road near the Grass Valley dump. The leaves are shiny green and more oval than the leaves of most members of this genus. This plant would be nice in a drought-tolerant garden. The owner of Far Star Nursery, who lives just off McCourtney Road, grows *Wyethia angustifolia*, also native to the McCourtney Road area. It has oblanceolate leaves and is a larger plant than Bolander's Mule Ears. *Wyethia reticulata* grows only in El Dorado County and has very prominent venation on its triangular leaves.

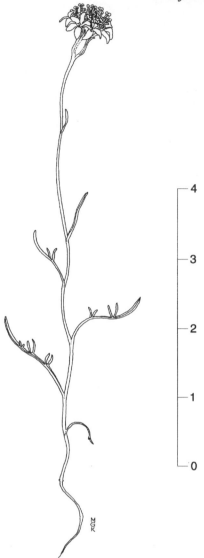

YELLOW-FLOWERED CHAENACTIS,   SUNFLOWER
YELLOW PINCUSHION FLOWER   Asteraceae
Chaenactis glabriuscula var. *megacephala*

Height: 5-16 IN.   Annual   ❀ YELLOW ❀
Habitat: SLOPES, GRAVEL
Elevation: 100-4,000 FT.
Locale: EL PORTAL EAST OF MARIPOSA

A bright yellow-gold flower combined with whitish-gray soft fuzzy foliage makes this plant stand out on a hillside of wildflowers. The rounded flower head has larger flowers around the outer edge; these are bilaterally symmetrical, giving the appearance of a fringe of petals.

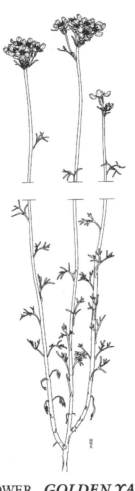

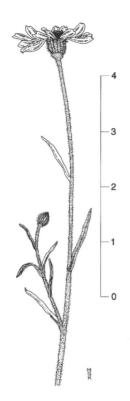

WOOLLY SUNFLOWER,	SUNFLOWER	*GOLDEN YARROW*
OREGON SUNSHINE	Asteraceae	*Eriophyllum*
Eriophyllum lanatum	❋ YELLOW ❋	*confertiflorum*
Height: 5-11 IN.	Perennial	12-30 IN.
Habitat: DRY OPEN AREAS		SLOPES, ROCKY
Elevation: BELOW 10,000 FT.		BELOW 8,000 FT.
Locale: ROAD BELOW DAM AT	SR 49 A FEW MILES SOUTH OF	
NEW HOGAN RESERVOIR	MOCCASIN POWERHOUSE	

The woolly covering on the leaves and stems of *Eriophyllum* helps protect it from the heat on west-facing rocks where it grows. The hairs insulate the plant and reflect the sun. The genus name is derived from Greek *erion,* wool, and *phyllon,* leaf. The species name, *confertiflorum,* refers to flowers crowded together. The flower head does resemble Yarrow, but the leaves are not Fernlike as they are in Yarrow. *Eriophyllum lanatum,* Woolly Sunflower, is very common and cheery on road banks in the foothills. It has a Daisylike flower and is an excellent drought-tolerant landscape plant.

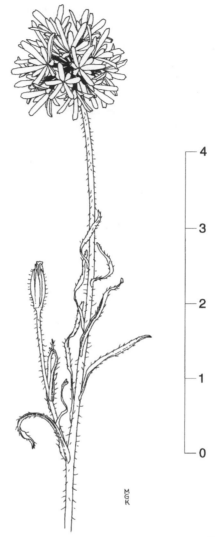

BLOW WIVES   SUNFLOWER
Achyrachaena mollis   Asteraceae
Height: 4-16 IN.   Annual   ❀ **YELLOW, INCONSPICUOUS** ❀
Habitat: GRASSLAND
Elevation: BELOW 1,000 FT.
Locale: PHOENIX PARK OFF US 50 NEAR SACRAMENTO

Blow Wives in bloom is not noticeable. However, when in fruit, as in the illustration, it is similar to a Dandelion head that persists with shiny papery flowerlike pappus. It is then, if you look carefully, that you may find some plants in bloom, with small orange-yellow flowers that barely stick up above the green involucre.

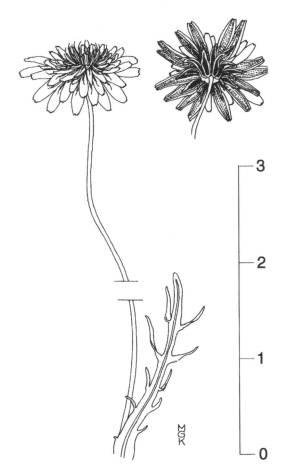

DANDELION

Agoseris heterophylla

Height: 14 IN. Perennial

Habitat: GRASSLAND, SLOPES

Elevation: BELOW 7,000 FT.

Locale: MANY

SUNFLOWER

Asteraceae

❀ YELLOW ❀

All Dandelions have milky juice and ray flowers. They are members of the Chicory tribe and lack the typical center of the Daisy, that is composed of disk flowers. The large showy yellow flower heads of Mountain Dandelion (*Agoseris retrorsa*, not illustrated) stick up above the groundcover of Mountain Misery along Mather Road, near Groveland. During World War II, German children who lived in mountain villages picked Dandelion greens for army troops stationed nearby.

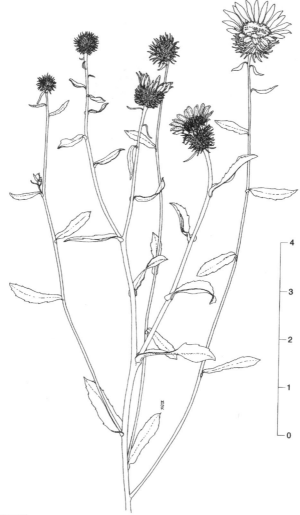

GUM WEED   SUNFLOWER
Grindelia camporum   Asteraceae
Height: 20-50 IN.   Perennial   ❀ YELLOW ❀
Habitat: FIELDS, DRY, ROCKY
Elevation: BELOW 4,000 FT.
Locale: WOLF MOUNTAIN RD. OFF McCOURTNEY RD.
This tall perennial has green leaves that look as if they were covered with shiny varnish. The rounded involucre is covered with reflexed or coiled phyllaries that give a heavy look to a pretty yellow Daisy. The buds have a white gummy resin that Indians have used as a treatment for Poison Oak and for pulmonary problems.

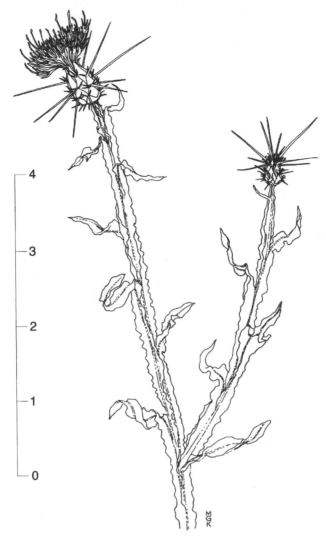

STAR THISTLE   WEED   SUNFLOWER
Centaurea solstitialis   Asteraceae
Height: 12-50 IN.   Annual   ❀ YELLOW ❀
Habitat: DISTURBED AREAS
Elevation: BELOW 4,000 FT.
Locale: IN FIELDS ALONG MANY ROADS, SUCH AS SR 120
       EAST OF OAKDALE

This plant, native to southern Europe, has taken over many acres of pasture land. Walking through it is painful. The bristles feel as if they contain a poison and leave an ache after the initial prick. The plant is cumulatively toxic to livestock. Fortunately for the flower folk most of the field flowers are finished by the time Star Thistle is tall in late May.

WHITELEAF MANZANITA
Arctostaphylos viscida

Height: 4-14 FT.   Shrub/evergreen

Habitat: SLOPES, DRY, CHAPARRAL

Elevation: 2,000-6,000 FT.

Locale: SR 174 JUST NORTHEAST OF COLFAX

HEATH
Ericaceae
❀ WHITE/PINK ❀

Whiteleaf Manzanita, *Arctostaphylos viscida*, is very noticeable because of the beautiful color combination of red bark, bluish leaves, and usually pink flower clusters. Look with a hand lens at the glands on the flower clusters or just cup your hand about the flowers and understand the species name *viscida* (sticky). This plant is especially beautiful on road banks in the Colfax area. Greenleaf Manzanita, *Arctostaphylos patula,* has very shiny flat leaves, and grows at a higher elevation.

WESTERN AZALEA
Rhododendron occidentale

HEATH
Ericaceae

Height: 3-10 FT.   Shrub/deciduous   ❀ **WHITE/PINK/YELLOW** ❀
Habitat: MOIST
Elevation: BELOW 7,500 FT.
Locale: CARIBOU RD. OFF FEATHER RIVER HWY.

Western Azalea is one of the most beautiful and fragrant plants in our native flora, and it does well in a garden when it receives normal garden water. Western Azalea is usually white to yellow with pink tints. Our native Azalea can be found along creeks in the Coast Range, in the Napa area, on exposed slopes along the coast in northern California, in Yosemite Valley, and in the foothills. If it is in a swampy area, lift up the "skirts" (branches on the ground) and you may see a little branchlet with roots. Many nurseries carry *Rhododendron occidentale*.

SPICEBUSH   SWEET-SHRUB
Calycanthus occidentalis   Calycanthaceae
Height: 4-10 FT.   Shrub/deciduous   ❀ RED-BROWN ❀
Habitat: MOIST, RIPARIAN
Elevation: BELOW 4,000 FT.
Locale: HONEYRUN RD. NEAR PARADISE

Large green leaves and a two- to three-inch many-petaled magenta flower head, usually in a damp location, make Spicebush easy to identify. Yosemite ladybugs like to spend the winter packed into the urn-shaped seed pods. At lower elevations, during the winter the ladybugs mass on top of one another in large clumps in the forest. Insert a hand into this mass and feel the warmth.

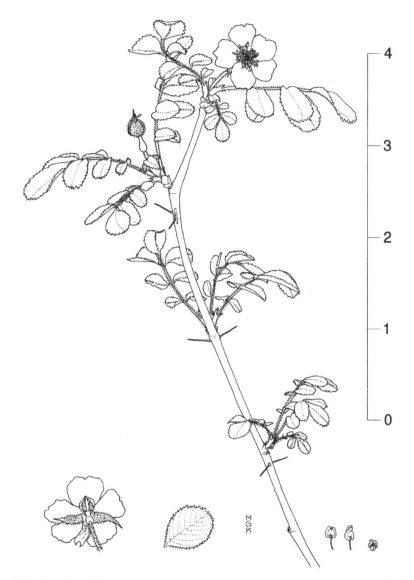

WOOD ROSE
Rosa gymnocarpa

Height: TO 8 FT. Shrub/deciduous

Habitat: CANYONS, FORESTS

Elevation: BELOW 6,500 FT.

Locale: PONDEROSA WAY NEAR AUBURN

ROSE
Rosaceae
❀ PINK ❀

This delicate Rose has slender prickles and is generally found in partial shade whether from a forest or north-facing canyon exposure. The flowers are very fragrant and pretty. The Rose hips are edible when bright orange-red. The skin has a citrus taste; spit the seeds out so new plants can grow.

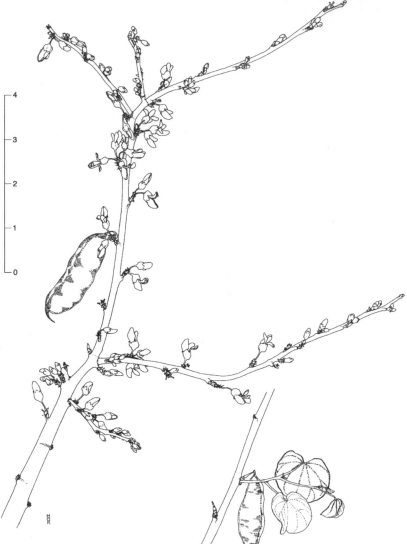

REDBUD
Cercis occidentalis
Height: 7-18 FT.   Tree, Shrub/deciduous
Habitat: SLOPES, DRY
Elevation: BELOW 4,000 FT.
Locale: EL PORTAL EAST OF MARIPOSA

PEA
Fabiaceae
❀ **MAGENTA** ❀

Redbud is a wonderful drought-tolerant landscape plant. The magenta flowers are beautiful in a planting with *Ceanothus*. The heart-shaped to kidney-shaped leaves range from pale green to a beautiful yellow or sometimes red in the fall, and the persistent brown-magenta seed pods add interest after the flowers and the leaves have gone. Even in the winter the shiny gray bark and delicate form of this tree are attractive.

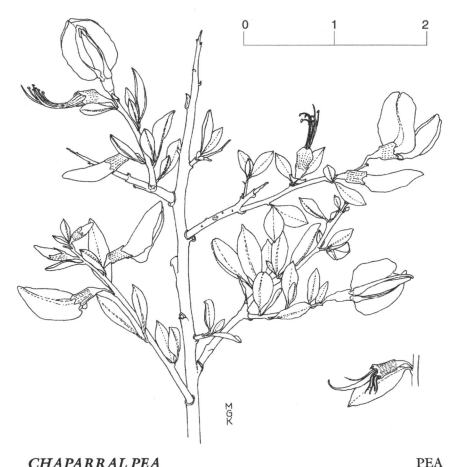

CHAPARRAL PEA

PEA

Pickeringia montana

Fabaceae

Height: 2-7 FT.   Shrub/evergreen   ❀ **MAGENTA** ❀

Habitat: SLOPES, DRY

Elevation: BELOW 5,000 FT.

Locale: WOLF RD. OFF McCOURTNEY RD.

Chaparral Pea in bloom, with its magenta Pea flowers and stiff spiny branches, is easy to recognize. When the plant is not blooming, however, it is possible to drive right past and never see it. This plant can also be found on Mount Tamalpais, in Marin County, hanging over the main road to the summit.

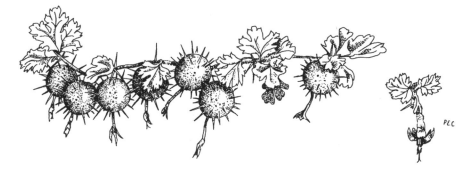

SIERRA GOOSEBERRY	**SIERRA CURRANT, MOUNTAIN PINK CURRANT**
Ribes roezlii	GOOSEBERRY · Grossulariaceae	*Ribes nevadense*

❀ WHITE AND MAROON ❀		❀ PINK ❀
Height: 3-6 FT.	Shrub/deciduous	5-10 FT.
Habitat: SLOPES, DRY, OPEN		FOREST OPENINGS
Elevation: 3,500-8,500 FT.		2,000-6,500 FT.
Locale: CHERRY CREEK INTAKE HIKE NEAR		CANYON CREEK HIKE
GROVELAND / BOWMAN LAKE RD.		OUT OF GRASS VALLEY

The very spiny attractive Sierra Gooseberry makes delicious jelly. The fruit is ripe when it is rose-colored and soft to pressure. To harvest the fruit, usually in September, lay a piece of plastic under the shrub and hit it with a stick, or wear ski gloves, hold the tip of the branch, and rake it with a fork. The flowers have purplish-red turned-back sepals and white petals. The leaves are shiny and palmate and turn bright red in the fall. *Ribes nevadense* or Mountain Pink Currant is a wonderful landscape shrub for the foothills and mountains. It tolerates some garden water or drought if it is in part shade. Plant the Currant in early fall if it will not be watered. It is early blooming and deer resistant.

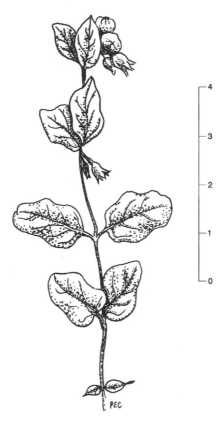

SNOWBERRY

Symphoricarpos albus var. *laevigatus*

Height: 2-5 FT. Shrub/deciduous

Habitat: SLOPES, FOREST SHADE

Elevation: BELOW 4,000 FT.

Locale: MANY

HONEYSUCKLE

Caprifoliaceae

❀ **PINK, PALE** ❀

It is rare to see the flowers and only in fall will you spot the little white berry. The flower is hairy inside, which is the keying characteristic of this species of Snowberry. One of the most notable Snowberries in the foothills has a common name of Trip Vine or Creeping Snowberry, *Symphoricarpos mollis*, with soft downy leaves. The leaves can be slightly lobed or entire on the same plant and it resembles Honeysuckle, to which it is related.

SCARLET FRITILLARY   LILY
Fritillaria recurva   Liliaceae
Height: 12-36 IN.   Bulb/scales   ❀ RED ❀
Habitat: SLOPE, DRY
Elevation: 2,000-6,000 FT.
Locale: CANYON CREEK TRAIL ON SR 49 NORTH FORK YUBA RIVER
Scarlet Fritillary is beautiful and can easily be spotted from the car in areas
where it is prolific, such as SR 89 north of Graeagle and near Quincy in
Feather River country. Occasionally it is seen in the area of the Pioneer
Grave east of Nevada City on SR 20. The stalk is tall and the flowers are
bright. It often survives deer predation by growing through shrubs. See
the description of *Fritillaria* seed leaves on page 307 *Fritillaria micrantha.*

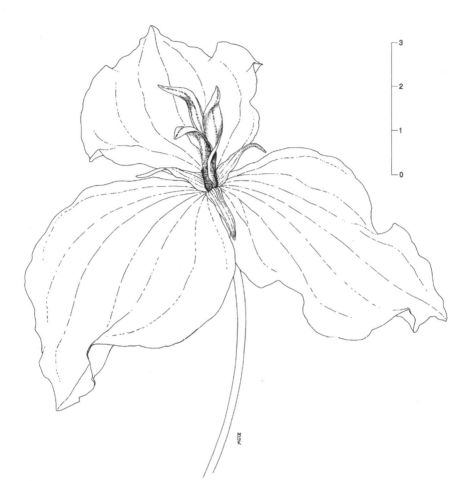

WAKE ROBIN, GIANT TRILLIUM
Trillium chloropetalum

LILY
Liliaceae

Height: 10-14 IN.　　　Perennial/rhizome　　　❀ PURPLE ❀

Habitat: FOREST

Elevation: BELOW 6,000 FT.

Locale: PONDEROSA WAY

Trillium has a single stalk topped by three large, sometimes blotched leaves and three erect purple, yellow-green, or occasionally white-to-pinkish petals. Do not pick Trillium; the plant needs the energy from the leaves to produce seeds and next year's bloom. Pipi Campground has exceptionally large Trillium.

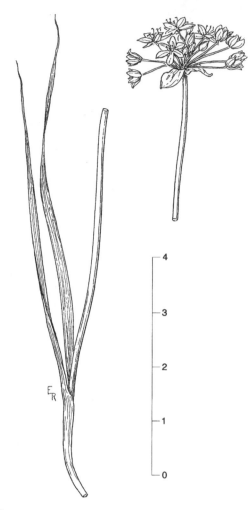

WILD ONION   LILY
Allium peninsulare   Lilaceae
Height: 8-16 IN.   Bulb   ❀ ROSE-PURPLE ❀
Habitat: SLOPES, DRY
Elevation: BELOW 3,000 FT.
Locale: CLARK TUNNEL RD. NEAR PENRYN

Wild Onions are often difficult to distinguish from one another because the key characteristic is frequently the pattern of the bulb coat, which can be seen only by digging up the plant—a no-no! This Onion has three central crests on the ovary, with flowers that are almost a half-inch long, in an open umbel. *Allium campanulatum* is very similar but has six crests on the ovary. *Allium sanbornii* var. *sanbornii* has a single leaf, and many crowded deep pink flowers with exserted stamens, and is found in serpentine soil.

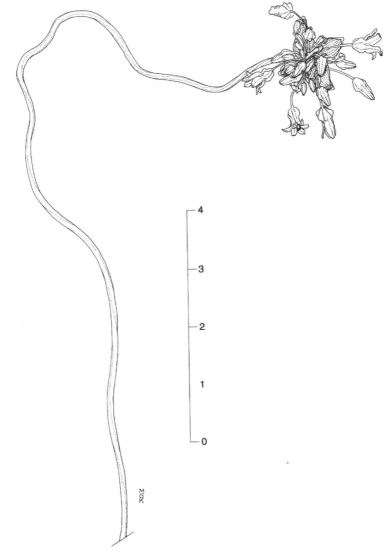

TWINING BRODIAEA   LILY
Brodiaea volubilis; Dichelostemma volubile   Liliaceae
Height: 20-40 IN.   Bulb   ❀ PINK ❀
Habitat: SLOPES, BRUSHY
Elevation: BELOW 2,500 FT.
Locale: HONEYRUN RD. NEAR PARADISE

This plant's showy pink flower heads, often twining in Poison Oak or on grass stems, are seen on shaded road banks throughout the foothills. Be sure to look at the stem as well as the flower; it is really an amazing adaptation to get more light.

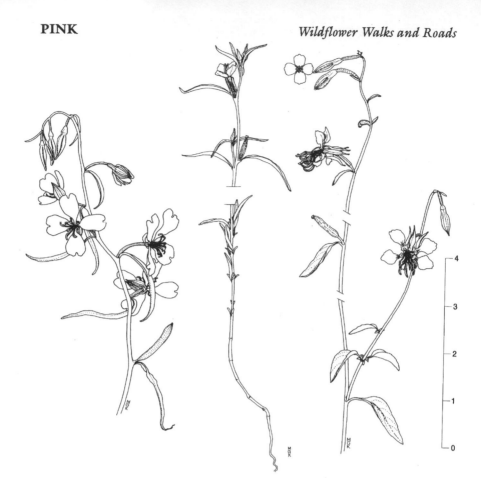

CLARKIA,	*WINECUP CLARKIA*	*TONGUE*
FAREWELL TO	*Clarkia purpurea*	*CLARKIA*
SPRING	ssp. *quadrivulnera*	*Clarkia*
Clarkia biloba	❀ PALE TO	*rhomboidea*
❀ PINK/LAVENDER/ROSE ❀	DARK PURPLE ❀	❀ PINK ❀

EVENING PRIMROSE • Onagraceae • Annual

Height: 12-40 IN.	4-20 IN.	8-44 IN.
Habitat: SLOPES	SLOPES	SLOPES, DRY
Elevation: BELOW 4,000 FT.	BELOW 6,000 FT.	BELOW 8,000 FT.
Locale: SOUTH YUBA	HELL'S HALF ACRE	HELL'S HALF ACRE
RIVER BRIDGE	GRASS VALLEY	GRASS VALLEY

Clarkia biloba, because of the two lobes on each petal, is often seen in masses on road banks in the foothills. The flower is usually pale lavender but it can vary to shades of pink and even rose. Ponderosa Way has beautiful displays. *Clarkia purpurea* ssp. *quadrivulnera*, Winecup Clarkia, has small, usually dark pink-magenta flowers with erect buds, and is also found growing on Ponderosa Way. Tongue Clarkia, or *Clarkia rhomboidea*, is tall and has delicate flowers with the petals clawed at the base.

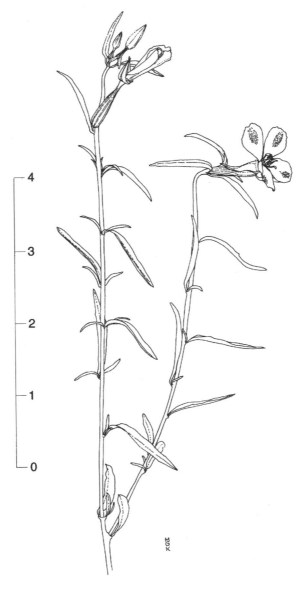

WILLIAMSON'S CLARKIA   EVENING PRIMROSE
Clarkia williamsonii   Onagraceae
Height: 12-36 IN.   Annual   ❀ DARK PINK ❀
Habitat: SLOPES
Elevation: BELOW 5,000 FT.
Locale: RAINBOW FALLS NEAR GROVELAND
This is a beautiful Clarkia with wedge-shaped, fringed petals. The erect
buds are a key characteristic. It grows on hot, dry, south-facing slopes.

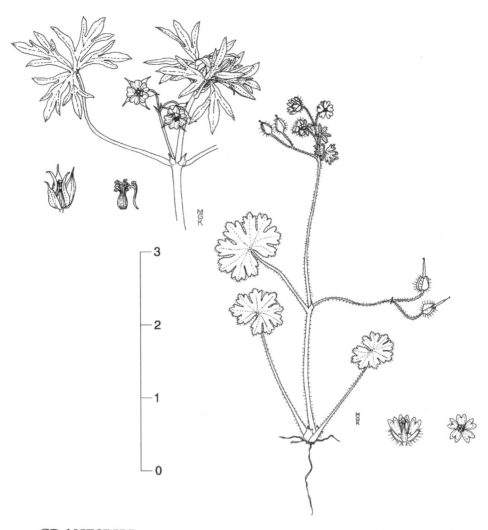

CRANESBILL	GERANIUM	SOFT CRANESBILL
Geranium	Geraniaceae	*Geranium*
dissectum	❀ ROSE ❀	*molle*
Height: 12-24 IN.	Annual	4-16 IN.
Habitat: DISTURBED AREAS		SHADE
Elevation: BELOW 3,000 FT.		BELOW 2,800 FT.
Locale: WEED, COMMON ALONG		WEED IN SHADED
ANY ROADSIDES		WOODLANDS

Geranium dissectum, Cranesbill, with a seed shaped like a short crane's bill, has deeply dissected leaves and grows in sunny spots. *Geranium molle*, Soft Cranesbill, found in shade, has very soft leaves that are lobed instead of deeply dissected. Both plants are weeds and have rosy lavender flowers. It is closely related to the genus *Erodium*.

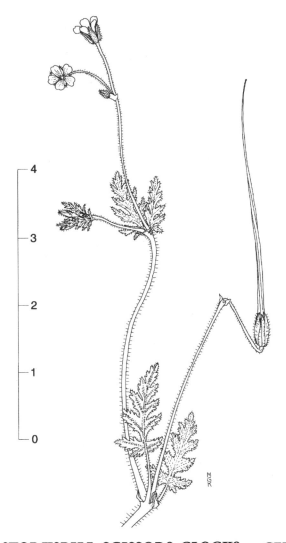

FILAREE, STORKSBILL, SCISSORS, CLOCKS

GERANIUM

Erodium botrys

Geraniaceae

Height: 4-36 IN.   Annual   ❀ ROSE ❀

Habitat: GRASSLAND

Elevation: BELOW 2,500 FT.

Locale: WEED, COMMON IN GRASSLANDS, ROADSIDES

This nuisance weed can turn a gravelly, wasted area into a photographer's delight on an overcast day. The small thumbnail-size lavender flowers can be very showy. Children like to collect the seed head and make scissors by inserting the beak of one seed head into another. Put a drop of water on a dried single seed off the cluster of seeds and watch it wind itself into the soil.

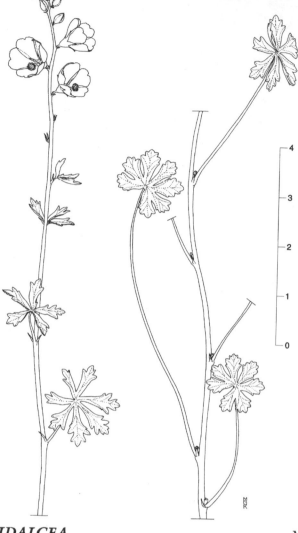

WAXY SIDALCEA
Sidalcea glaucescens
Height: 12-28 IN.   Perennial
Habitat: FIELDS, DRY
Elevation: 3,000-11,000 FT.
Locale: MOORE RD. OFF SR 120

MALLOW
Malvaceae
❀ ROSE ❀

Sometimes called Wild Hollyhock, this graceful *Sidalcea* has stems of bright pink flowers that wave and bend just above the grasses of the meadows and banks where it is found. The stamens and filaments are bound into a central column, like its cousin the garden Hollyhock. Waxy Sidalcea has waxy bluish-green glaucous leaves that are deeply divided into five lobes. *Sidalcea hartweggii*, found on slopes and serpentine, has a short undivided flower bract and divided leaves.

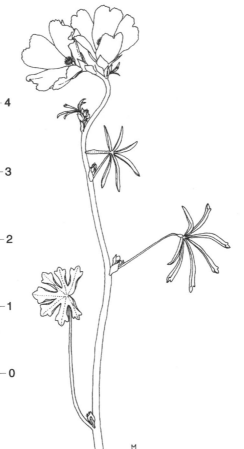

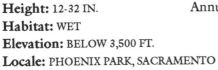

CHECKER MALLOW   MALLOW
Sidalcea calycosa ssp. *calycosa*   Malvaceae
Height: 12-32 IN.   Annual   ❀ ROSE ❀
Habitat: WET
Elevation: BELOW 3,500 FT.
Locale: PHOENIX PARK, SACRAMENTO

Sidalcea calycosa forms a sinuous pink border around the vernal pools at
Phoenix Park in Sacramento. This showy annual usually is at its peak in
early to mid-April. It can be found in moist areas throughout the eastern
edge of the Sacramento Valley. It is easily identified because of its habitat
and by the linear upper leaves.

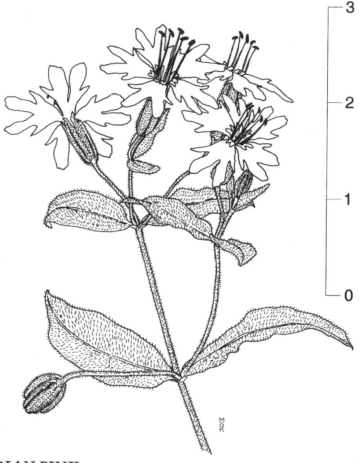

3

2

1

0

INDIAN PINK
Silene californica   PINK
                                                    Caryophyllaceae
Height: 5-20 IN.   Perennial   ❀ RED ❀
Habitat: SLOPES, BRUSHY
Elevation: BELOW 5,000 FT.
Locale: MARSHES FLAT RD. NEAR GROVELAND / HONEY RUN RD.
          NEAR PARADISE

The Pink or Carnation family can be recognized by opposite leaves at swollen nodes. A Carnation stem will always break at a node. Leave this beautiful red Carnation relative right where it is growing. It wilts very quickly after picking, even if immediately put in water. The El Niño spring of 1998 brought Indian Pinks in fantastic bloom throughout the foothills.

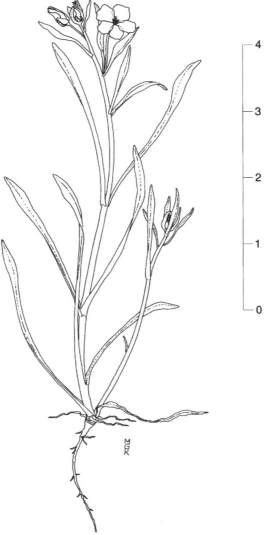

RED MAIDS
Calandrinia ciliata var. *menziesii*

Height: 2-24 IN.   Annual

Habitat: FIELDS

Elevation: BELOW 6,000 FT.

Locale: MANY

PURSLANE
Portulacaceae
❀ **MAGENTA** ❀

Red Maids have brilliant shiny magenta petals that remain closed until they get enough sunlight to open and be pollinated. That is probably why you missed the beautiful display of Red Maids beside your car when it was parked in the morning. Red Maids are not "morning flowers." They need warmth and sunlight.

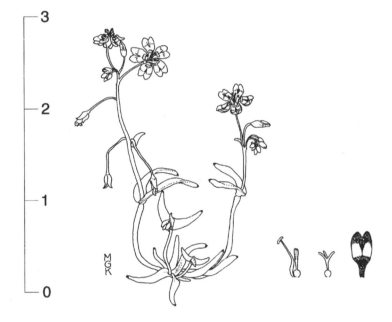

DWARF MINER'S LETTUCE   PURSLANE
Montia gypsophiloides; Claytonia gypsophiloides   Portulacaceae
Height: 2-8 IN.   Annual   ✿ WHITE/PINK ✿
Habitat: MOIST, SERPENTINE
Elevation: BELOW 4,000 FT.
Locale: CAMP NINE RD.

Dwarf Miner's Lettuce looks like pink puddles in the east-facing ditches at the top of Camp Nine Road. It also seeps down the road banks between large rocks in this same area. *Montia gypsophiloides* is often found on serpentine. The foliage is succulent and blue-green. Notice the hornlike leaves.

BITTER ROOT   PURSLANE
Lewisia rediviva   Portulacaceae
Height: ROSETTE   Perennial   ❀ WHITE/PINK ❀
Habitat: ROCKY
Elevation: 500-6,000 FT.
Locale: TABLE MOUNTAIN, EAST END OF CHEROKEE RD.
    BEFORE DESCENDING TABLELAND

The blue-green thick linear leaves form a rosette in which are nestled several 1½-inch pink or white many-petaled flowers. Often in drought years the leaves will barely extend beyond the flower petals. *Lewisia rediviva,* the state flower of Montana, has an edible root. It got the species name *rediviva* because the pressed, dried plant was sent back from the Lewis and Clark Expedition and, to the surprise of the explorers when they returned several years later, it was growing again. The thickened roots store lots of energy.

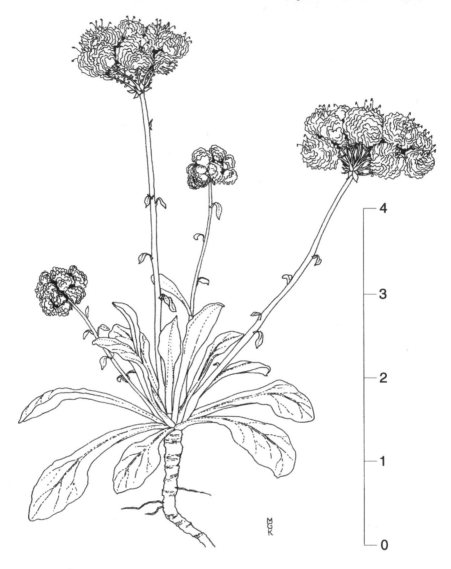

PUSSY PAWS   PURSLANE
Calyptridium umbellatum   Portulacaceae
Height: ROSETTE   Perennial   ❀ WHITE/ROSE ❀
Habitat: GRAVEL, DRY
Elevation: 2,500-11,000 FT.
Locale: SR 49 ABOVE SIERRA CITY

The flower clusters resemble soft pussy paws. The flower color varies from bright rose near the Kentucky Mine in Sierra City to a washed-out white or pale pink in other locations, such as Bowman Lake Road. The flowers are generally near the ground in the morning; as the temperature rises so do the flowers in response to the radiating heat from the ground.

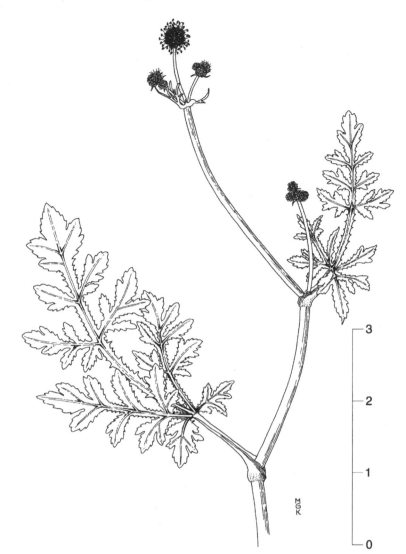

PURPLE SANICLE, SHOE BUTTONS

Sanicula bipinnatifida

Height: 6-28 IN.   Perennial

Habitat: SLOPES, OPEN

Elevation: BELOW 3,500 FT.

Locale: MANY

CARROT

Apiaceae

❀ PURPLE/YELLOW ❀

There are several common names for this plant. Children like to call it Satellites because of the round flower head with exserted stamens. People who sew call the plant Pincushions. The species name describes the leaf shape, which sometimes has a purplish rachis or midrib. Notice the toothed wing along the rachis or backbone of the leaf.

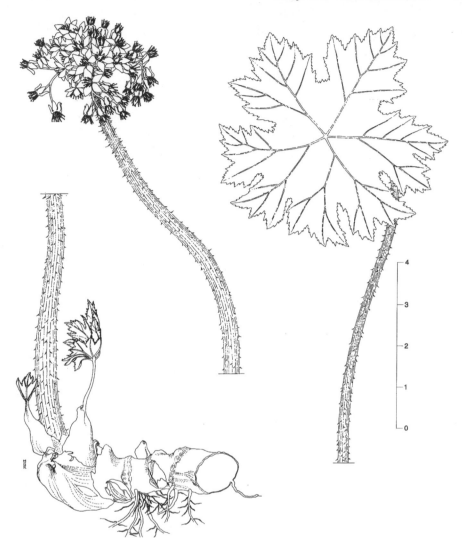

INDIAN RHUBARB
Peltiphyllum peltatum; Darmera peltata
Height: 12-40 IN.   Perennial
Habitat: STREAM
Elevation: BELOW 6,000 FT.
Locale: YANKEE JIMS RD. OFF I-80 BELOW COLFAX

SAXIFRAGE
Saxifragaceae
❀ PINK ❀

This unique plant is easily identified because it is found in running water or at the edge of streams and has a leafless stalk with a large rounded flower head about the size of a tennis ball. It is a shock to see these pink flower heads bobbing back and forth in spring streams. The leaves follow later, when the water is not as high and fast. They are large, umbrellalike, and a beautiful red and yellow in the fall.

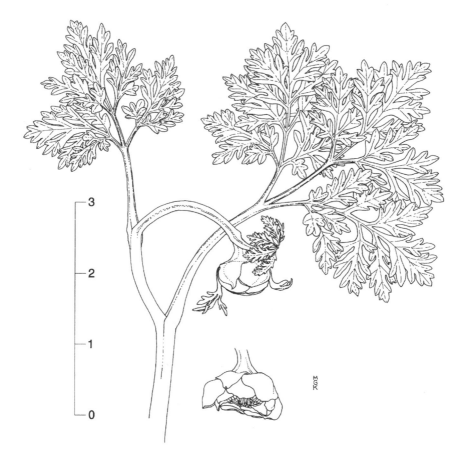

BROWN'S PEONY   PAEONY
Paeonia brownii   Paeoniaceae
Height: 8-16 IN.   Perennial   ❀ **MAROON** ❀
Habitat: SLOPES, DRY
Elevation: 3,000-7,000 FT.
Locale: BOWMAN LAKE RD. OFF SR 20 ACROSS FROM
            PARKING LOT NEAR BEAR RIVER

The genus name *Paeonia* is derived from Paeon, a physician to the gods. Brown's Peony has a heavy nodding flower that is brownish-red, with bluish-green foliage. The two to five large follicles contain several seeds each and have persistent sepals. The fruiting stage is as noticeable as when the plant is in flower.

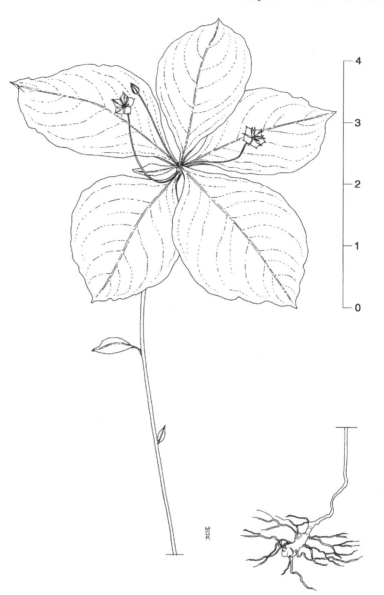

STAR FLOWER   PRIMROSE
Trientalis latifolia   Primulaceae
Height: 2-8 IN.   Perennial   ❀ **WHITE/PINK, PALE** ❀
Habitat: FORESTS, SHADE
Elevation: BELOW 4,500 FT.
Locale: MANY

Star Flower is a delicate plant that frequently almost forms a groundcover in open forests. It has a small tuberous root. It is not invasive, and is attractive in woodland gardens.

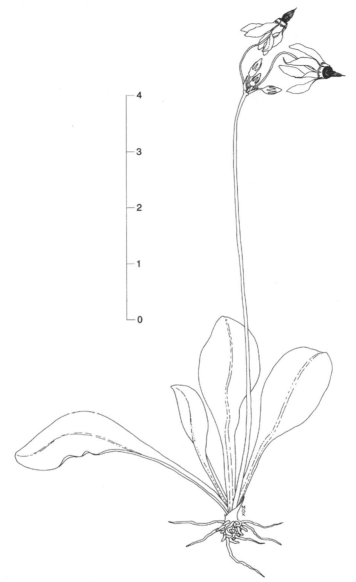

SHOOTING STAR   PRIMROSE
Dodecatheon hansenii   Primulaceae
Dodecatheon hendersonii
Height: TO 10 IN.   Perennial   ❀ MAGENTA/WHITE ❀
Habitat: GRASSLAND
Elevation: 1,000-6,000 FT.
Locale: ROAD TO ENGLEBRIGHT RESERVOIR NEAR BRIDGEPORT
A favorite of many people, Shooting Star blooms in late March or early
April. Another common name for this plant is Mosquito Bills. The genus
name is from the Greek *dodeka,* twelve, and *theos,* a god.

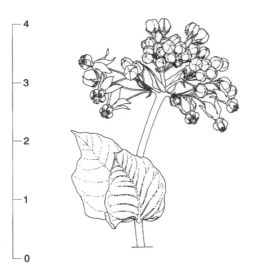

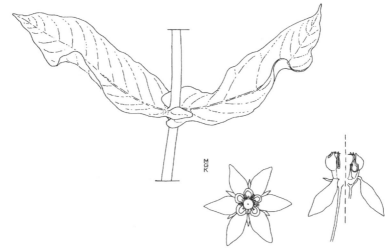

PURPLE MILKWEED
Asclepias cordifolia

Height: 12-32 IN.   Perennial

Habitat: SLOPES

Elevation: 500-6,300 FT.

Locale: HELL'S HALF ACRE, GRASS VALLEY

MILKWEED
Asclepiadaceae
❀ PURPLE ❀

Milkweed is often seen on road banks. The large leaves and showy purple flowers are eye-catchers. Monarch butterfly larva emerge from the beautiful green chrysalis, that has a touch of metallic appearing gold, to feed on Milkweed. The Milkweed seedpod is very noticeable especially when the fluffy seeds are being released. The sap of Milkweed is milky, sticky, and an eye irritant.

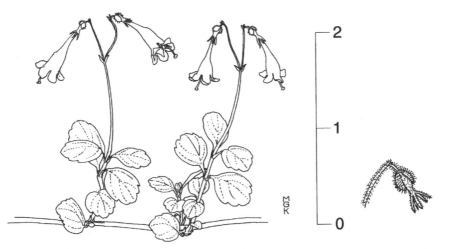

TWIN FLOWER
Linnaea borealis ssp. *longiflora*
Height: TRAILING STEMS TO 3 FT.   Perennial
Habitat: FORESTS, DAMP
Elevation: 400-8,000 FT.
Locale: SKILLMAN FLAT CAMPGROUND, SR 20, NEVADA CO.

HONEYSUCKLE
Caprifoliaceae
❀ **PALE PINK** ❀

It is a real treat to find Twin Flower. It forms a flat mat of trailing stems and shiny little green leaves. The twin flowers are held on a slender peduncle just above the leaves. They are pale pink and bell or funnel-shaped. The genus was named for Linnaeus, who established the modern scientific method of naming plants.

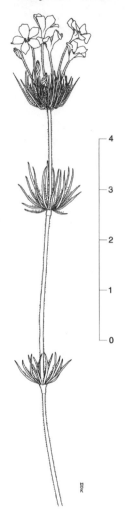

WHISKER BRUSH	PHLOX	**MUSTANG-CLOVER**
Linanthus	Polemoniaceae	*Linanthus*
ciliatus	❀ PINK ❀	*montanus*
Height: 4-12 IN.	Annual	4-24 IN.
Habitat: OPEN, DRY		GRAVELLY, DRY
Elevation: BELOW 8,000 FT.		1,000-5,000 FT.
Locale: WASHINGTON JUNCTION WITH		HITES COVE
SR 20 EAST OF NEVADA CITY		

The Greek word *linon* means flax and *anthos,* flower. The species, *ciliatus,* refers to the hairy edges of the leaves. Observe this colorful little annual with a hand lens to see the leaf hairs, the rosy dot on each petal, and the yellow center of the flower. A similar species, *Linanthus montanus,* is taller, up to 24 inches, and showier, sometimes white or lavender, and has a longer floral tube, up to 2 inches.

SHOWY PHLOX

Phlox speciosa

Height: 6-24 IN.   Perennial

Habitat: FORESTS, SHADE

Elevation: 1,500-7,000 FT.

Locale: McCOURTNEY RD. GRASS VALLEY / TABEAUD RD. OFF SR 88

PHLOX
Polemoniaceae
❀ PINK ❀

Phlox is such a bright rosy pink and it is often seen on road banks at eye level. It brings the car to a quick stop. The plant has lancelike leaves and the flower petals are bilobed. Mountain Misery is often a companion plant.

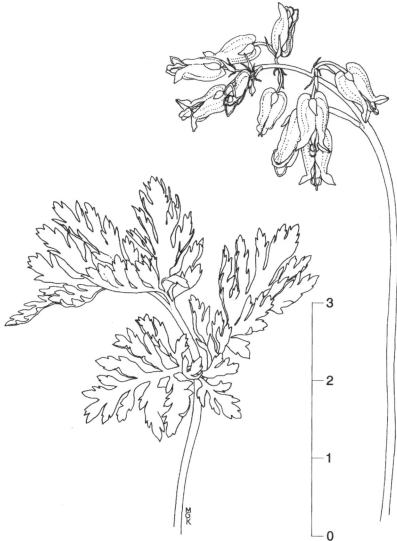

BLEEDING HEART   FUMATORY/POPPY
Dicentra formosa   Papaveraceae
Height: 8-18 IN.   Perennial   ❀ ROSE ❀
Habitat: FORESTS, SHADE
Elevation: BELOW 7,000 FT.
Locale: DRUM POWERHOUSE RD. NEAR ALTA AND DUTCH FLAT
Bleeding Heart forms a border along a stretch of Drum Powerhouse
Road. They are a beautiful garden plant, with their pendant rosy- colored
flowers and delicate blue-green Poppylike leaves. The plants should not
receive garden water once they are summer dormant.

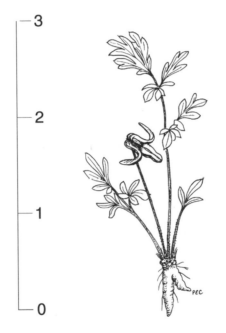

STEER'S HEAD   FUMATORY/POPPY
Dicentra uniflora   Papaveraceae
Height: 1-3 IN.   Perennial   ❀ PINK, PALE ❀
Habitat: GRAVEL
Elevation: 5,400-12,000 FT.
Locale: OMEGA REST STOP ON SR 20 EAST OF NEVADA CITY
Pale pink Steer's Head follows the snowmelt in gravelly, rocky areas. It
grows with Shelton's Violet and has a similar leaf, except that Steer's
Head is smaller, blue-green, and hard to see because it is so close to the
ground. It is at the upper elevation of the area covered in this book.

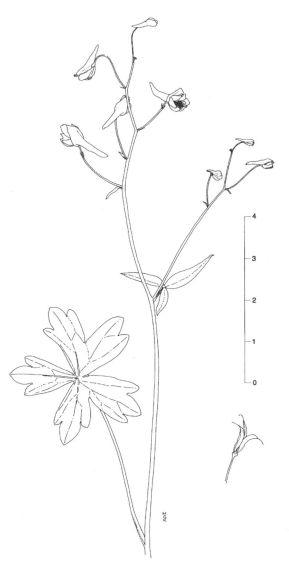

RED LARKSPUR
Delphinium nudicaule

Height: 4-24 IN.   Perennial

Habitat: SLOPES, BRUSHY

Elevation: BELOW 6,500 FT.

Locale: HONEYRUN RD. NEAR PARADISE

BUTTERCUP
Ranunculaceae
❀ REDDISH ORANGE ❀

The species name of Red Larkspur refers to the nude stem. The flower color varies from scarlet to orange-red. This is a good garden plant, given part shade and very little summer water. See the Appendix for native nurseries that may have it for sale.

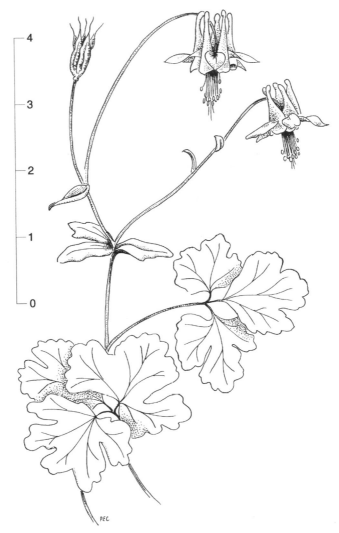

COLUMBINE   BUTTERCUP
Aquilegia formosa   Ranunculaceae
Height: 20-40 IN.   Perennial   ❀ RED ❀
Habitat: MOIST, FORESTS
Elevation: BELOW 9,000 FT.
Locale: INDEPENDENCE TRAIL ON SR 49 NEAR NEVADA CITY

Plants that are both popular and common tend to have several folk names. Columbine is also known as Granny Bonnets, Eagles, and Doves. The name Eagles is derived from the Latin *aquila,* referring to the spurred petals that resemble an eagle's claw. Columbine is easy to grow from seed; the native form is often found in nurseries. Hummingbirds love Columbine and the combination can create an exquisite photo.

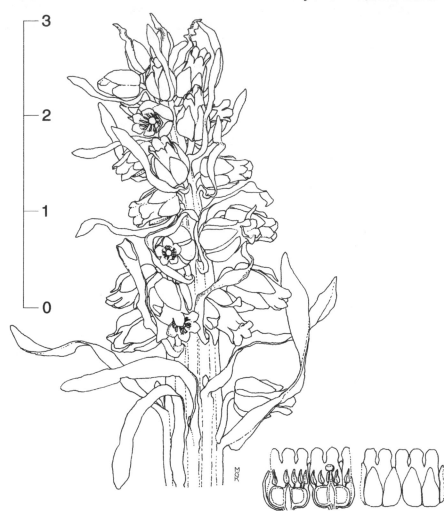

SNOW PLANT
Sarcodes sanguinea
Height: 5-12 IN.   Perennial
Habitat: FORESTS
Elevation: 4,000-8,000 FT.
Locale: SKILLMAN FLAT CAMPGROUND, SR 20

HEATH
Ericaceae
❀ RED ❀

Snow Plant is the showiest and most unusual plant of the forest. It is totally red, lacking any chlorophyll, and has urn-shaped flowers, similar to Manzanita. The genus name is derived from the Greek *sarx*, flesh, and *oeides*, like. The species name is derived from the Latin *sanguis*, blood. The plant follows the snowmelt, sometimes popping through the snow; occasionally a shaft of sunlight will highlight a Snow Plant in a dark forest, bringing photographers to their knees.

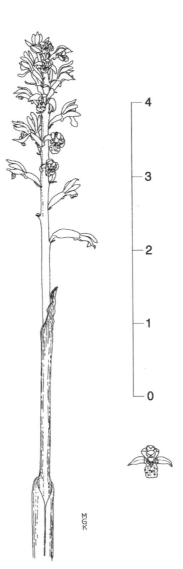

CORAL ROOT ORCHID
Corallorhiza maculata Orchidaceae

Height: 8-28 IN. Perennial ❀ WHITE, MAGENTA ❀

Habitat: FORESTS

Elevation: BELOW 9,000 FT.

Locale: SKILLMAN FLAT CAMPGROUND

Coral Root is noticeable in the forest due to the fact that often it is the only plant growing out of dense Pine-needle duff on the forest floor, usually on an uphill slope. It is easy to check the white lower lip to see if it has spots, as in *Corallorhiza maculata,* or stripes, as in *Corallorhiza striata.*

3

2

1

0

MILKWORT   POLYGALA
Polygala californica   Polygalceae
Height: 4-20 IN.   Annual   ❀ ROSE ❀
Habitat: SLOPES, BRUSHY
Elevation: BELOW 3,000 FT.
Locale: SR 88 NEAR PIONEER RD.

Milkwort is a confusing plant to identify. It slightly resembles a Pea. There are five sepals, and three united petals form one keel shaped with two laterals. The flower color varies from rose and light pink to whitish. Because it is generally found under brush, *Polygala* is not often seen.

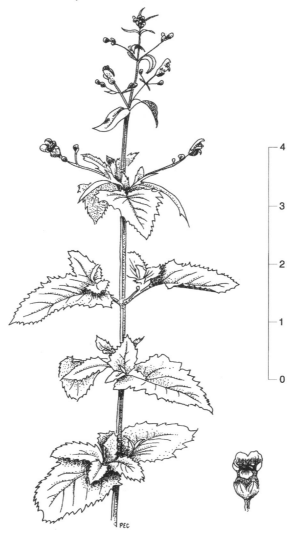

BEE PLANT, CALIFORNIA FIGWORT   FIGWORT
Scrophularia californica   Scrophulariaceae
Height: 40-60 IN.   Perennial   ❀ MAROON ❀
Habitat: MOIST
Elevation: BELOW 5,000 FT.
Locale: BELOW LAKE McSWAIN / FOOTES CROSSING,
          MIDDLE FORK YUBA RIVER

Bee Plant is a tall, rank weedlike plant that resembles Nettles. Look closely at the small two-lipped maroon flowers that are pretty but not very exciting to flower chasers. Keep in mind that this is an important agricultural plant. It is cultivated by bee keepers because it is such a good source of nectar for honey.

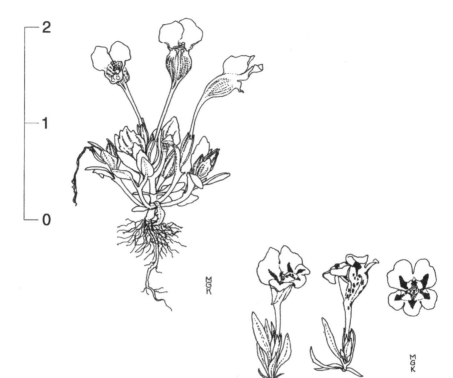

CHINLESS MIMULUS,	FIGWORT	TRICOLOR
PURPLE MOUSE-EARS	Scrophulariaceae	*MONKEYFLOWER*
Mimulus douglasii	❀ MAGENTA ❀	*Mimulus tricolor*
Height: TO 2 IN.	Annual	TO 4 IN.
Habitat: DAMP		VERNAL POOL
Elevation: BELOW 3,000 FT.		BELOW 2,000 FT.
Locale: EL PORTAL, EAST OF		NIMBUS DAM OVERLOOK OFF
MARIPOSA		US 50 IN SACRAMENTO

Mimulus douglasii, Chinless Mimulus or Purple Mouse-ears, has an upper lip that is erect and arched (like mouse ears) and the lower lip is rudimentary or lacking. *Mimulus tricolor* is small, rose-magenta, has a dark spot on each petal, and has a long throat. *Mimulus kelloggii,* another magenta Mimulus, has a reduced lower lip, a red dot in a yellow throat, and a long narrow tube. *Mimulus torreyi* is larger, up to ten inches tall, pinkish-rose, and found in dry places.

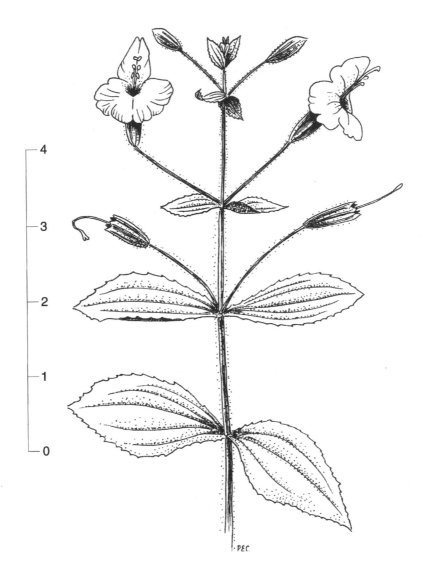

SCARLET MONKEYFLOWER
Mimulus cardinalis

FIGWORT
Scrophulariaceae

Height: 9-32 IN. Perennial ❀ RED ❀

Habitat: WET

Elevation: BELOW 8,000 FT.

Locale: ALONG STREAMS AND RIVERS

Scarlet Monkeyflower is always found in wet, generally sunny locations. It is probably best seen when rafting rivers in May. It is pretty beside a pond in a garden and easy to grow from seed. This is an herbaceous plant rather than a woody shrub like Sticky Monkeyflower.

251

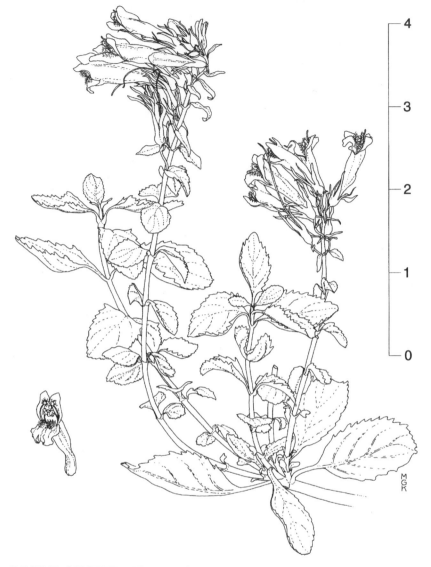

PRIDE OF THE MOUNTAIN
Penstemon newberryi

Height: 6-12 IN.   Perennial/woody

Habitat: ROCKY

Elevation: ABOVE 5,000 FT.

Locale: FEATHER RIVER CANYON

FIGWORT
Scrophulariaceae
❀ **ROSE-RED** ❀

Pride of the Mountain Penstemon with its blue-green leaves and magenta flowers is easy to grow from seed in mountain gardens. It is a beautiful contrast against the granite. This plant is at the upper elevation covered in this book.

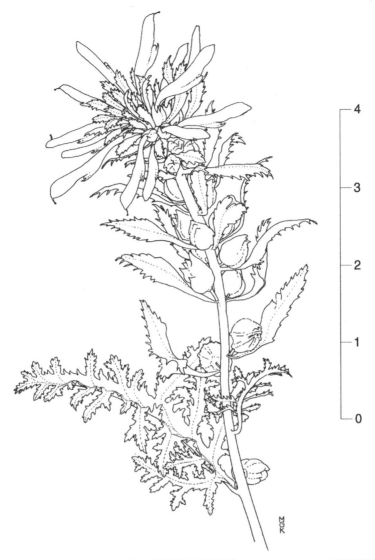

LOUSEWORT, INDIAN WARRIORS
Pedicularis densiflora

FIGWORT
Scrophulariaceae

Height: 4-20 IN.   Perennial   ❀ RED-PURPLE ❀

Habitat: SLOPES, SHADED

Elevation: BELOW 6,000 FT.

Locale: INDEPENDENCE TRAIL ON SR 49 NEAR NEVADA CITY

The color of Lousewort varies from the more common magenta, on the Independence Trail, to a rusty red in the De Sabla Reservoir area in Butte County. It usually blooms in late March, when the Fawn Lilies are blooming in Magalia. Lousewort has a thick stem and Fernlike leaves. It wilts very quickly if picked.

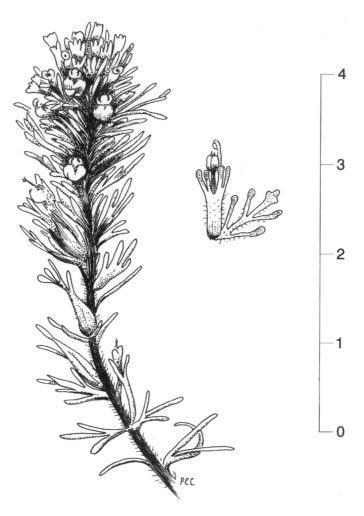

PURPLE OWL'S-CLOVER, ESCOBITA

Orthocarpus purpurascens; Castilleja exserta

Height: 4-16 IN.   Annual

Habitat: GRASSLAND

Elevation: BELOW 3,000 FT.

Locale: TABLE MOUNTAIN ON CHEROKEE RD. NORTH OF OROVILLE

FIGWORT
Scrophulariaceae
❀ ROSE-PURPLE ❀

The Spanish Californians gave this plant the common name of Escobita, meaning little whisk brooms. This Owl's-clover has a hooked beak on the upper lip and three lower yellowish sacs. *Orthocarpus densiflorus,* a similar species, has a straight upper lip or beak. They both turn grassy fields magenta.

FUZZY PAINTBRUSH,	FIGWORT	ASH
WOOLLY INDIAN	Scophulariaceae	*PAINTBRUSH*
PAINTBRUSH		*Castilleja*
Castilleja foliolosa	❀ RED ❀	*pruinosa*
Height: 12-24 IN.	Perennial	12-27 IN.
Habitat: ROCKY, DRY, ROAD BANKS		ROCKY
Elevation: BELOW 5,000 FT.		ABOVE 1,400 FT.
Locale: CAMP NINE RD. ABOVE	WOLF MOUNTAIN RD. OFF McCOURTNEY	
ANGELS CAMP	RD. AT GRASS VALLEY DUMP	

Brilliant orange-red flowers with very fuzzy stems and leaves, on hot, often west-facing rocky slopes, make Fuzzy Paintbrush one of the easier Paintbrushes to identify. Ash Paintbrush, *Castilleja pruinosa,* has grayish stems. Large orange-red flowers are set off by the dark gray stems and leaves. Using a hand lens notice the branched hairs on the gray stem of Ash Paintbrush. Wavy-leaf Paintbrush, *Castilleja applegatei,* with its rippled leaves, is usually seen above 2,000 feet.

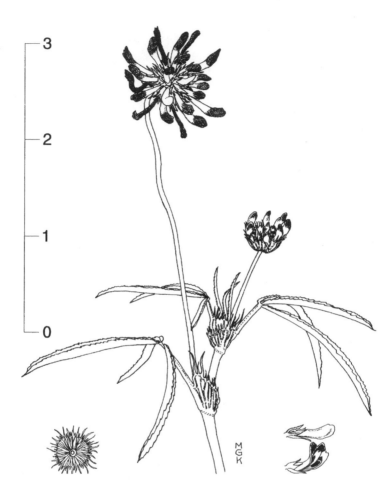

TOMCAT CLOVER   PEA
Trifolium tridentatum; Trifolium willdenovii   Fabaceae
Height: 4-16 IN.   Annual   ❀ MAGENTA AND WHITE ❀
Habitat: SLOPES, GRASSY, ROAD BANKS
Elevation: BELOW 5,000 FT.
Locale: WARDS FERRY

Beautiful native Tomcat Clover has narrow serrated lancelike leaves. The
flower heads are quite showy and often in large colonies on road banks
giving a rosy-purple appearance. The shape of the involucral bracts, just
below the flower head, is often important in determining different species
of Clover.

COW'S UDDER CLOVER,	PEA	WHITE-TIPPED
BALLOON CLOVER	Fabaceae	**CLOVER**
Trifolium depauperatum		*Trifolium*
var. *depauperatum*	❀ PURPLE AND WHITE ❀	*variegatum*

Height: 2-3 IN.   Annual   4-16 IN. ERECT OR PROSTRATE

Habitat: MOIST   WET, MEADOWS

Elevation: BELOW 2,500 FT.   BELOW 7,000 FT.

Locale: TABLE MOUNTAIN ON CHEROKEE RD.   TABLE MOUNTAIN

NORTH OF OROVILLE

Balloon Clover is a small, pretty little matlike Clover that needs to have the flower head hung upside down to understand its common name of Cow's Udder Clover. The tiny flowers are inflated and have a milky white tip on each flower. The involucre is vestigial and ringlike. *Trifolium wormskioldii*, found in the same habitat, has large showy flower heads with bristles on the lobes of the involucre. *Trifolium variegatum*, or White-tipped Clover, also from the same habitat, has somewhat narrow oblong leaves with a sawtooth margin.

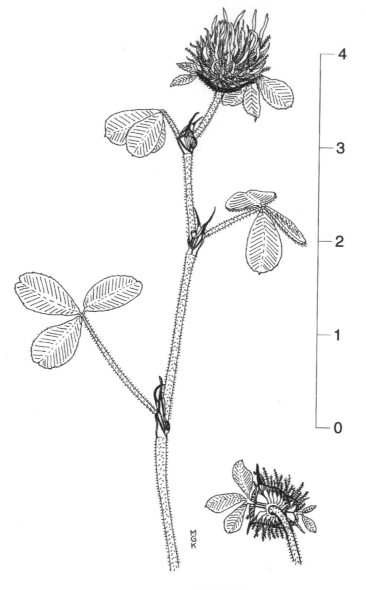

ROSY CLOVER   WEED   PEA
Trifolium hirtum   Fabaceae
Height: 4-16 IN.   Annual   ❁ PINK ❁
Habitat: ROADSIDES, BANKS
Elevation: BELOW 6,500 FT.
Locale: McCOURTNEY RD. NEAR GRASS VALLEY
The dense long hairs that cover Rosy Clover give the leaves a gray cast.
The plant blankets roadsides in the foothills and has been declared a weed
in Butte County.

PERENNIAL SWEET PEA

| WEED |

PEA

Lathyrus latifolia

Fabaceae

Height: 24-80 IN.   Perennial   ❀ MAGENTA ❀

Habitat: SLOPES, FIELDS, GARDENS

Elevation: BELOW 6,200 FT.

Locale: GARDEN ESCAPE, I-80 NEAR COLFAX

This colorful magenta Sweet Pea is native to Europe and very aggressive but people like it and continue to plant it. It can be easily recognized by wings less than an eighth of an inch wide that run the length of the stem and by the leaflets in pairs. It has jumped fences throughout the Gold Country and mountains and, though pretty, it is a weed and toxic to humans and livestock. Another magenta weed, Rose Campion or Mullein Pink, *Lychnis coronaria*, is in the Carnation family. The opposite leaves are densely hairy giving a gray appearance to the plant. It is common in the state park in Coloma.

THISTLE   SUNFLOWER
Cirsium andersonii   Asteraceae
Height: 24-48 IN.   Perennial   ❀ RED ❀
Habitat: OPEN, DRY
Elevation: 1,600-10,000 FT.
Locale: WOLF MOUNTAIN RD. OFF McCOURTNEY RD.
        NEAR GRASS VALLEY DUMP

This tall, beautiful red Thistle is green on the upper leaf surface and
woolly white on the underside. It is extremely spiny and feels as if there
are toxins in the spines because of the residual pain after being stuck. A
weedy common Thistle is *Silybum marianum,* or Milk Thistle, with purplish flowers and shiny white-splashed large basal leaves that look as if a
pitcher of milk had been spilled on them. It is a very invasive non-native.

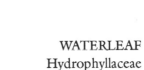

YERBA SANTA
Eriodictyon californicum
Height: 20-90 IN. Shrub/evergreen

WATERLEAF
Hydrophyllaceae
❋ **LAVENDER, PALE** ❋

Habitat: SLOPES, DRY, ROCKY
Elevation: BELOW 5,500 FT.
Locale: RAILROAD GRADE, TUOLUMNE CITY

New young shrubs of Yerba Santa are much more attractive than the older plants, whose dark green sticky leaves seem to attract a fungus and turn black. The leaves are prominently net-veined and serrated; the flowers are off-white to pale lavender.

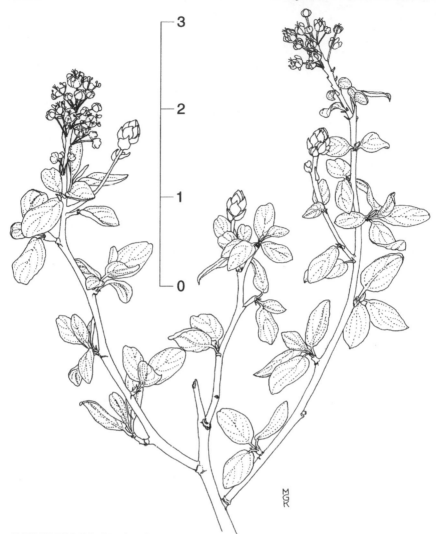

LEMMON'S CEANOTHUS   BUCKTHORN
Ceanothus lemmonii   Rhamnaceae
Height: 12-24 IN.   Shrub/evergreen   ❀ BLUE ❀
Habitat: SLOPES, OPEN
Elevation: 1,200-3,500 FT.
Locale: WOLF MOUNTAIN RD. OFF McCOURTNEY RD.
          NEAR GRASS VALLEY DUMP

This Ceanothus can be identified by bright blue flower clusters with shiny
green leaves and stiff branches that have a whitish bloom on the tops of
the stems. In general *Ceanothus* provides about seventy percent of a deer's
diet. They seem to prefer the softer three-veined leaves, such as Deer
Brush has, to the spiny Hollylike leaves of Mahala Mat or the tough leaves
of Lemmon's Ceanothus.

MAHALA MAT, SQUAW CARPET   BUCKTHORN
Ceanothus prostratus   Rhamnaceae
Height: 3-7 FT. WIDE   Shrub, prostrate/evergreen   ❀ **BLUE, PALE** ❀
Habitat: FORESTS, OPEN PINE
Elevation: 3,000-6,500 FT.
Locale: SR 20 NEAR BEAR VALLEY EAST OF GRASS VALLEY

In May and early June lavender, off-white and sometimes pinkish flower clusters adorn this groundcover shrub. The mat, formed by pale green Hollylike leaves, invites one to sit down and lean against the trunk of a Ponderosa Pine while having lunch, but often the leaves are too stiff and prickly without heavy fabric between leaf and skin. Another prostrate evergreen Ceanothus is the rare *Ceanothus roderickii*, or Pine Hill Ceanothus, with off-white to bluish flower clusters. This plant is rare and found only in the Pine Hill region.

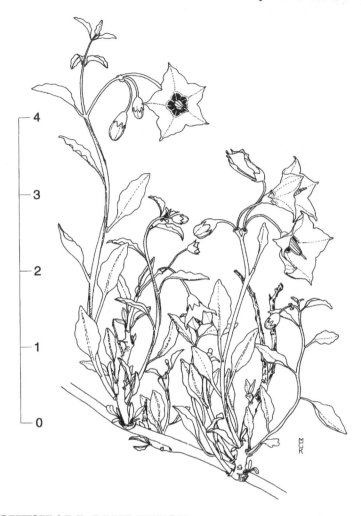

NIGHTSHADE, BLUE WITCH
Solanum xanti

NIGHTSHADE
Solanaceae

Height: 16-36 IN.   Shrub   ❀ VIOLET ❀

Habitat: CHAPARRAL

Elevation: BELOW 4,000 FT.

Locale: McCOURTNEY RD. NEAR GRASS VALLEY

Some species of *Solanum* make nice drought-resistant landscape plants, and some are too leggy. The genus is derived from the Latin *solamen,* quieting, because of the narcotic properties of some species. Europeans were concerned about tomatoes when they were first brought from the New World because they knew of the dangers of some members of this plant family. Potatoes, eggplant, and peppers are also in the same family. The flowers of all these species may differ in color but the relationship is visible in the flower.

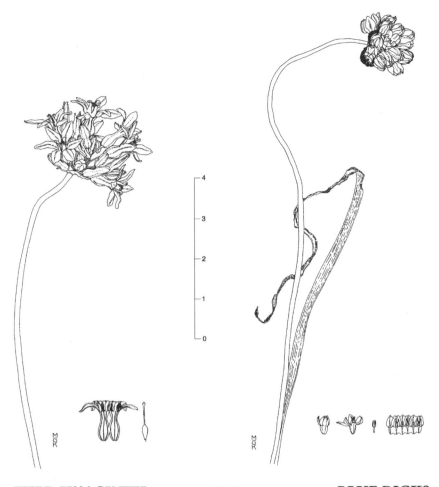

WILD HYACINTH	LILY	BLUE DICKS
Brodiaea multiflora	Liliaceae	*Brodiaea pulchella*
Dichelostemma		*Dichelostemma*
multiflorum	❀ VIOLET ❀	*capitatum*
Height: 12-24 IN.	Bulb	12-14 IN.
Habitat: SLOPES, ROAD BANKS		FIELDS, ROAD BANKS
Elevation: BELOW 5,000 FT.		BELOW 6,000 FT.

Locale: CHEROKEE RD. NORTH OF OROVILLE

Wild Hyacinth has a dense, rounded umbel, more than two inches across, of lavender-blue flowers. Each flower tube has a tightly constricted neck just above the ovary. There are three fertile anthers and three staminodia (toothlike projections easily mistaken for anthers), in this case rounded at the tips. *Dichelostemma capitatum,* or Blue Dicks, has a crowded flower head subtended by dark purple bracts. Each bulbous flower tube has six anthers within.

265

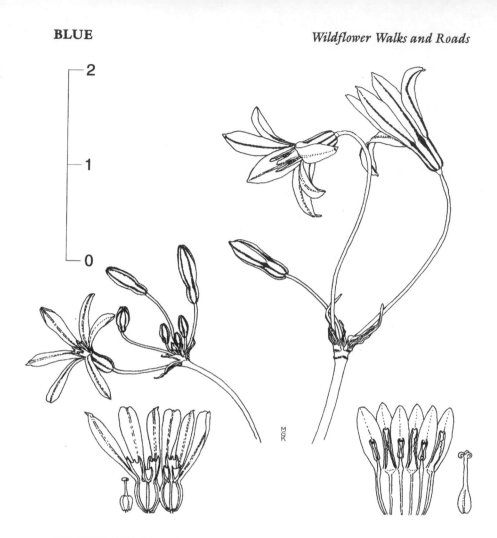

CROWN BRODIAEA	LILY	APPENDAGED BRODIAEA
Brodiaea coronaria	Liliaceae	*Brodiaea appendiculata*
❀ VIOLET-ROSE ❀		❀ BLUE/VIOLET ❀
Height: TO 10 IN.	Bulb	TO 2 FT.
Habitat: OPEN FIELDS		GRASSLAND
Elevation: BELOW 5,000 FT.		BELOW 1,800 FT.
Locale: MEISS RD. NORTH OF IONE		EASTERN EDGE OF VALLEY

Brodiaea coronaria varies in color from blue-violet to rose. The petal lobes are recurved at the tips. The flower has three hornlike whitish staminodia that enclose the stamens. This small flower is common along the gravelly grasslands of the eastern edge of the valley just as the hills begin to rise. *Brodiaea appendiculata* has funnel-shaped flowers with brilliant blue-violet waxy-appearing petals that are a showy contrast against the drying grasses. It has three anthers, with two threadlike appendages on the tip of each filament, and three inrolled, wavy-margined staminodia.

ITHURIEL'S SPEAR	LILY	*BRIDGE'S BRODIAEA*
Brodiaea laxa; Triteleia laxa	Liliaceae	*Triteleia bridgesii*
❀ VIOLET ❀		❀ BLUE ❀
Height: 8-16 IN.	Bulb	10-18 IN.
Habitat: SLOPES, FIELDS		SLOPES, ROCKY
Elevation: BELOW 4,600 FT.		2,000 FT.
Locale: CHEROKEE RD. NORTH		INDEPENDENCE TRAIL ON SR 49
OF OROVILLE		NORTH OF NEVADA CITY

Ithuriel's Spear, or *Triteleia laxa,* has a large (three inches across) loose umbel of lavender-blue flowers. The filaments of the six anthers are attached within the flower at two levels. Cherokee Road just north of Oroville, on the way to Table Mountain, always has one of the most spectacular displays of this Brodiaea. Bridge's Brodiaea, or *Triteleia bridgesii,* is an exceptionally beautiful blue Brodiaea. Its petals are upturned instead of bell-like and the perianth throat is white or translucent inside. The ovary and style project above the three stamens.

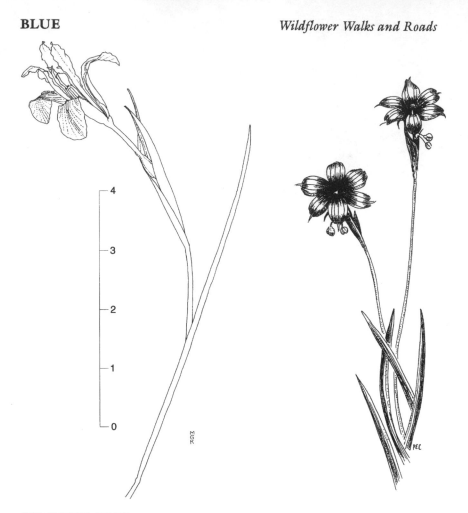

GROUND IRIS	IRIS	BLUE-EYED GRASS
Iris macrosiphon	Iridaceae	*Sisyrinchium bellum*
❀ PURPLE/YELLOW ❀		❀ BLUE-PURPLE ❀
Height: TO 9 IN.	Perennial	4-16 IN.
Habitat: SLOPES, FORESTS		GRASSLANDS
Elevation: BELOW 3,000 FT.		BELOW 3,000 FT.
Locale: SALMON FALLS RD. BETWEEN		MANY
FOLSOM LAKE AND PILOT HILL		

The *Iris macrosiphon* along Salmon Falls Road toward Pilot Hill is a brilliant purple, but it can vary to shades of yellow. The key difference between Hartweg's Iris and Ground Iris is that Ground Iris has a long tube above the ovary and Hartweg's Iris has a short perianth tube. *Sisyrinchium bellum*, Blue-eyed Grass, a very common plant, is found at lower elevations and in dry habitats. It is purple and has a deep yellow center. Idaho Blue-eyed Grass, *Sisyrinchium idahoense*, is true blue, blooming in the damp meadows in May, along Cherry Lake Road, off SR 120, near Groveland.

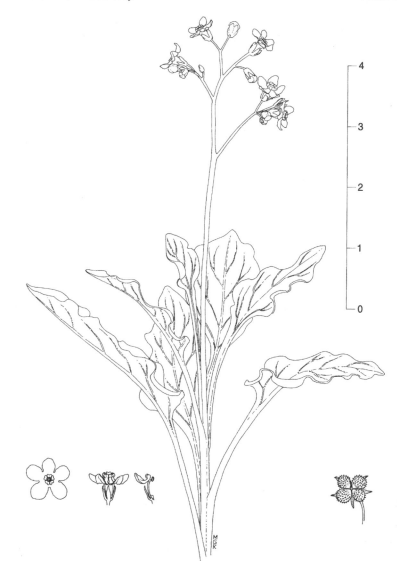

HOUND'S TONGUE
Cynoglossum grande

Height: 12-25 IN.   Perennial

Habitat: SLOPES, SHADE

Elevation: BELOW 4,000 FT.

Locale: PURDON CROSSING BRIDGE NEAR NEVADA CITY

BORAGE

Boraginaceae

❀ BLUE ❀

The genus name is derived from the Greek *kyon,* a dog, and *glossum,* tongue, referring to the leaves. The species, *grande,* is descriptive of this large Forget-Me-Not relative. The seeds of the Borage family have hooked bristles and are dispersed by pant cuffs, shoelaces, animal fur, or whatever they cling to.

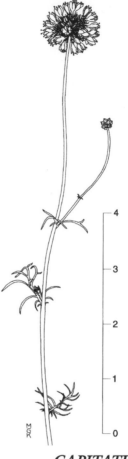

BIRD'S EYE	PHLOX	*CAPITATE GILIA,*
GILIA	Polemoniaceae	*BALL-HEADED GILIA*
Gilia tricolor		*Gilia capitata*

❀ VIOLET, PALE ❀   ❀ BLUE ❀

Height: 4-16 IN.   Annual   8-32 IN.

Habitat: SLOPES, GRASSLAND   SLOPES, OPEN

Elevation: BELOW 4,000 FT.   BELOW 6,000 FT.

Locale: KNIGHTS FERRY   MOSQUITO RIDGE RD.

      STATE PARK OFF SR 120   OUT OF FORESTHILL

Bird's Eye Gilia is a small annual with a half-inch flower that has created beautiful lavender hillsides in the Sierra foothills and elsewhere in California. Look carefully at the blossom. *Gilia tricolor* has lavender outer petals that become white toward the center, with a dark purple spot and gold in the throat. *Gilia capitata*, Ball-headed Gilia, has a ball-like cluster of blue flowers that stand out against the red dirt of the hot road banks where it is most often found. *Gilia achilleaefolia* has small deep blue single flowers.

WATERLEAF   WATERLEAF
Hydrophyllum occidentale   Hydrophyllaceae
Height: 4-24 IN.   Perennial   ❀ BLUE ❀
Habitat: SLOPES, SHADE
Elevation: 2,500-8,000 FT.
Locale: FEATHER RIVER HWY. / CANYON CREEK TRAIL, SR 49

The entire plant is showy. The pinnate white blotched leaves are eye-catchers, as is the ball-like blue flower cluster elevated on a stem above the leaves. Each flower has exserted stamens that add to the beauty of the plant.

271

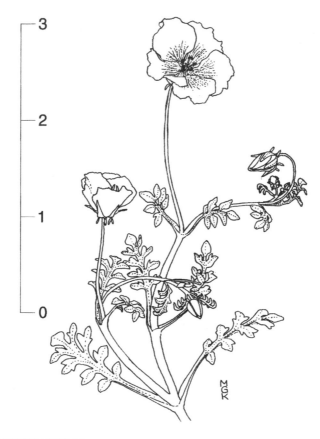

BABY BLUE EYES   WATERLEAF
Nemophila menziesii   Hydrophyllaceae
Height: 4-12 IN.   Annual   ❀ BLUE ❀
Habitat: MOIST SLOPES/FIELDS
Elevation: BELOW 2,500 FT.
Locale: INDIAN GRINDING STONE STATE PARK, VOLCANO / GOOD
          SHOW AT ENTRANCE TO STEVENOT WINERY, SHEEP RANCH RD.
Baby Blue Eyes often grow in large colonies and look like a fallen piece of
sky, they are such a beautiful blue. Seed is available in nurseries, though
young plants need protection from birds and snails. After trying to start
them in a garden, it is hard to imagine how these plants grow to fruition
in the wild.

FIESTA FLOWER   WATERLEAF
Pholistoma auritum   Hydrophyllaceae
Height: 12-40 IN.   Annual   ❀ BLUE ❀
Habitat: SLOPES, SHADE
Elevation: BELOW 4,500 FT.
Locale: KNIGHTS FERRY STATE PARK OFF SR 120

The specific name refers to the ears (auricles) between the calyx lobes. This plant forms a tangle of weak stems resting on other plants for support. The stem has retrorse prickles that help the plant climb. The violet-blue flowers are large; the shape should remind you of Baby Blue Eyes and Five Spot Nemophila, which are in the same family.

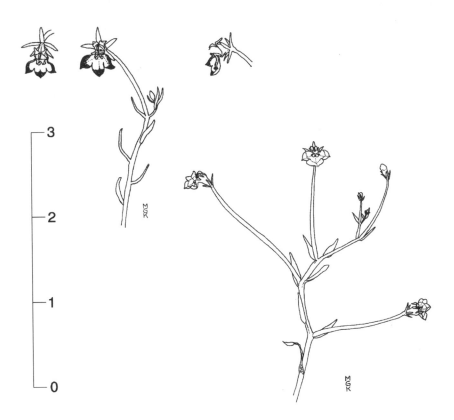

DOUBLE-HORN	CAMPANULA	*DOWNINGIA*
DOWNINGIA	Campanulaceae	*Downingia*
Downingia bicornuta	❀ BLUE ❀	*ornatissima*
Height: TO 3 IN.	Annual	TO 12 IN.
Habitat: VERNAL POOLS		VERNAL POOLS
Elevation: BELOW 6,000 FT.		CENTRAL VALLEY
Locale: PHOENIX PARK, SACRAMENTO, OFF US 50		MEISS RD.

Downingia looks like a piece of fallen sky when all the water has evaporated from a vernal pool. It is always a pleasure to time it right and get to see Downingia. Depending on the seasonal rainfall, the pools start to evaporate and produce a bull's-eye effect, due to the different plants in the pool, in early April and generally are through by the third week in April. Vernal pools go through their cycle quickly if there is a drying north wind. The lower lip of *Downingia bicornuta* has a large white center with small yellow spots. A similar species, *Downingia cuspidata*, also found at Phoenix Park, has a large white central area with a large yellow spot. *Downingia ornatissima* has twisted, folded-back upper petal lobes. The central lip area is white with yellow on the two middle ridges.

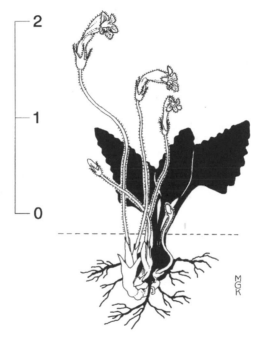

NAKED BROOM-RAPE
Orobanche uniflora

BROOM-RAPE
Orobanchaceae

Height: TO 2 IN.　　　　　Parasite　　　❀ **PURPLE TO YELLOW** ❀
Habitat: SLOPES
Elevation: BELOW 10,000 FT.
Locale: CHERRY CREEK INTAKE HIKE NEAR GROVELAND

Naked Broom-rape is a non-green root parasite on herbs, most often *Sedum, Saxifragaceae*, and *Asteraceae*. In the illustration the Saxifraga root ball has been parasitized and the host plant has died. The upper 2 lips of the flower are erect to reflexed, the lower 3 spreading. The flower can also be yellow.

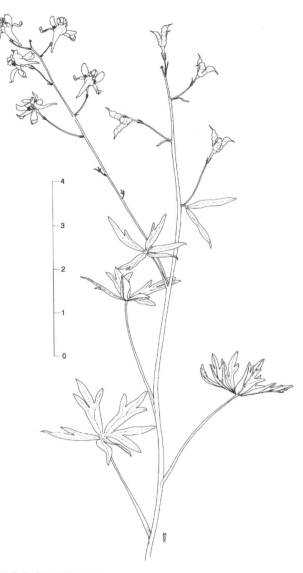

SPREADING LARKSPUR   BUTTERCUP
Delphinium patens   Ranunculaceae
Height: 6-20 IN.   Perennial   ✿ BLUE, WHITE ✿
Habitat: FOREST, EDGES
Elevation: BELOW 3,500 FT.
Locale: 7.5 MILES DOWN McCOURTNEY RD. NEAR GRASS VALLEY

Ted Niehaus, in his book *Pacific States Wildflowers*, calls this plant Zigzag
Delphinium, which describes the wiry stem. The dark blue spur typically
points upward. The buds of *Delphinium* resemble a dolphin, hence the
derivation from the Latin *delphinius*.

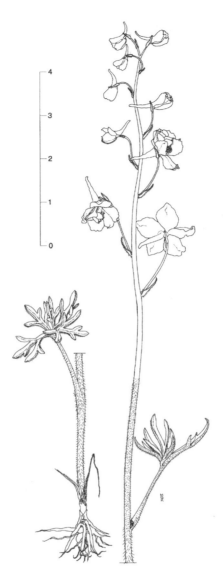

ROYAL DELPHINIUM   BUTTERCUP

Delphinium variegatum   Ranunculaceae

Height: 1-2 FT.   Perennial   ❀ **BLUE, DARK** ❀

Habitat: GRASSLAND

Elevation: BELOW 3,000 FT.

Locale: NIMBUS DAM OVERLOOK JUST OFF US 50 IN SACRAMENTO

This huge, beautiful royal-blue Delphinium generally stands six to ten inches taller than the adjacent grasses. The size of the plant, the hairs on the lower petal blades, the sepal spur that is straight or down-curved, and the hair on the petioles and leaves help identify the Royal Delphinium.

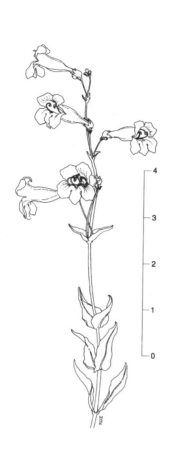

AZURE	FIGWORT	*VARIED LEAF PENSTEMON,*
PENSTEMON	Scrophulariaceae	*FOOTHILL PENSTEMON*
Penstemon azureus	❀ BLUE ❀	*Penstemon heterophyllus*

Height: 8-20 IN. Perennial/woody 8-20 IN.

Habitat: SLOPES, DRY SLOPES, DRY

Elevation: ABOVE 1,200 FT. BELOW 5,500 FT.

Locale: McCOURTNEY RD. NEAR 3 MILES DOWN McCOURTNEY RD.

GRASS VALLEY AT FRENCH RAVINE

The Penstemons on this page are among the most beautiful and are difficult to tell apart. Azure Penstemon has glaucous wider leaves at the base
that seem to clasp the stem. Foothill Penstemon has leaves in clusters that are
somewhat tapered at the base. *Penstemon heterophyllus* var. *purdi*, also common in the northern foothills, lacks the axillary leaf clusters.

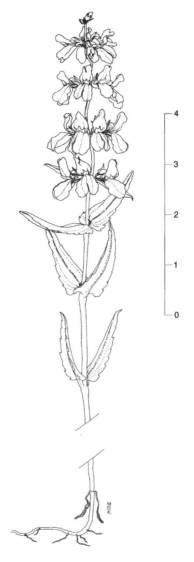

CHINESE HOUSES
Collinsia heterophylla

FIGWORT
Scrophulariaceae

Height: 8-20 IN.   Annual   ❀ PURPLE-MAGENTA/LAVENDER/WHITE ❀
Habitat: SHADE
Elevation: BELOW 2,500 FT.
Locale: DRUM POWERHOUSE RD.

Shady road banks are the preferred habitat of Chinese Houses, a pagoda-like stack of lavender and white flowers, which can vary to reddish-magenta and white. Typical of the Figwort family, the flowers are two-lipped, similar to the Snapdragon. The magenta form is beautifully displayed on the Priest-Coulterville Road, usually in early April.

PENNYROYAL	MINT	*MUSTANG MINT*
Monardella odoratissima	Lamiaceae	*Monardella lanceolata*

❋ LAVENDER-PURPLE ❋   ❋ PURPLE ❋

Height: 5-14 IN.   Perennial   Annual   8-20 IN.

Habitat: ROCKY   ROCKY/CHAPARRAL

Elevation: 2,000-11,000 FT.   BELOW 8,000 FT.

Locale: CARIBOU RD. OFF FEATHER RIVER HWY.   HETCH HETCHY

Pennyroyal has many uses. It is a wonderful aromatic drought-tolerant landscape plant. The color varies from pale lavender to rich purple. It is delicious as a tea, especially in the high country with a little rum before crawling into a cold sleeping bag. However, the medical journal *Lancet* several years ago had an article warning that *Monardella odoratissima* can cause abortion when taken in great quantities. *Monardella lanceolata* is also aromatic, with a very showy purplish flower. It is an annual and a smaller plant.

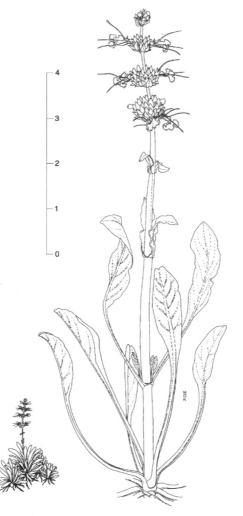

SONOMA SAGE   MINT
Salvia sonomensis   Lamiaceae
Height: 4-16 IN.   Perennial   ❀ BLUE ❀
Habitat: SLOPES, CHAPARRAL
Elevation: BELOW 6,500 FT.
Locale: PINE HILL

Salvia sonomensis, Sonoma Sage, forms an attractive silver-gray mat. It is a good drought-tolerant plant for landscape use, though it does need cutting back after blooming. Tilden Botanical Garden in Berkeley has a hillside of Sonoma Sage right behind the office. Another, prettier annual blue Sage is Chia, *Salvia columbariae*, with whorls of flowers that are brilliant blue on a stout square stem. The seeds are edible and supposedly full of energy. They can be purchased in health food stores. The plant is found growing on hot, rocky, gravelly slopes.

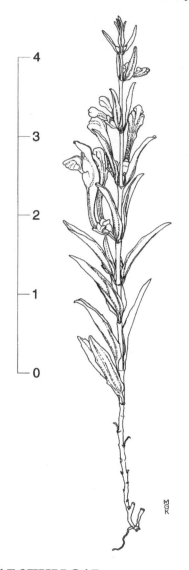

NARROWLEAF SKULLCAP   MINT
Scutellaria angustifolia; Scutellaria siphocampyloides   Lamiaceae
Height: 4-12 IN.   Perennial   ❀ PURPLE ❀
Habitat: CHAPARRAL
Elevation: BELOW 5,000 FT.
Locale: ALONG THE NORTH FORK OF THE MERCED RIVER,
      OFF MOORE RD. NEAR BOWER CAVE

Narrowleaf Skullcap has a tubular flower with an upright bend just above
the calyx, which has a little horn on the upper part. This is illustrated on
the lower left flower where the calyx and corolla meet. The narrow leaves
are gray-green, like *Scutellaria californica.*

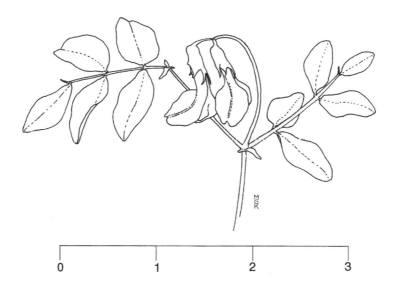

0   1   2   3

SIERRA NEVADA PEA   PEA
Lathyrus nevadensis var. *nevadensis*   Fabaceae
Height: 6-24 IN.   Perennial   ❀ BLUE ❀
Habitat: SLOPES
Elevation: ABOVE 1,500 FT.
Locale: YANKEE JIMS RD. NEAR FORESTHILL

Sierra Nevada Pea is a beautiful blue low-growing delicate plant. On Yankee Jims Road it grows with Mountain Misery and in the same habitat on Ponderosa Way. It has four to eight oval leaves and a short terminal tendril.

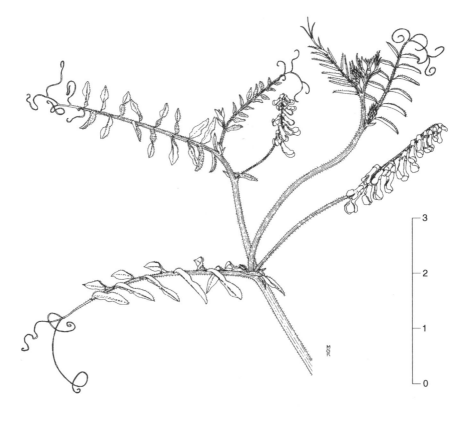

WINTER VETCH
Vicia villosa

    WEED

                PEA
                Fabaceae

Height: 24-48 IN.   Annual   ❀ **PURPLE** ❀
Habitat: SLOPES, FIELDS
Elevation: BELOW 5,000 FT.
Locale: WEED

Vicia villosa, Winter Vetch, has ten or more flowers on a raceme and up to twelve pairs of leaflets to a leaf. This Vetch is very colorful on road banks, having a bright blue cast. However, it is a terrible weed in gardens because it seeds so prolifically.

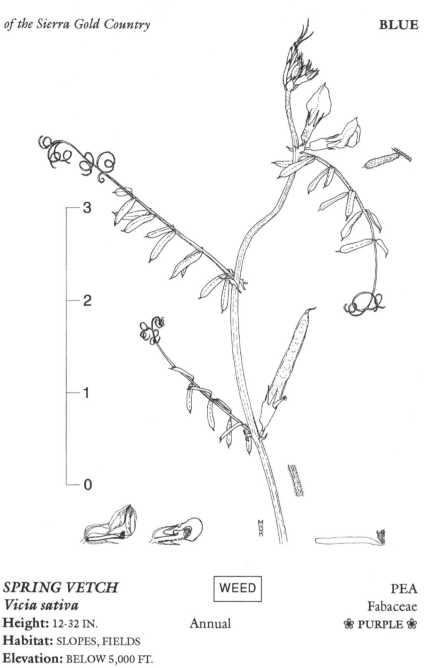

SPRING VETCH
Vicia sativa

WEED

PEA
Fabaceae

Height: 12-32 IN.   Annual   ❀ PURPLE ❀

Habitat: SLOPES, FIELDS

Elevation: BELOW 5,000 FT.

Locale: WEED

Spring Vetch is common along roadsides. It has one or two pea-like flowers at the base of each leaf. The leaves have 8 to 14 leaflets, with a tiny bristle at each leaflet tip. Using a hand lens, take the flower apart and look at the stigma. It should have tiny hairs in a bottle-brush arrangement. If the hairs are one-sided, like a toothbrush, then the plant is probably a Pea, or *Lathyrus,* not a Vetch.

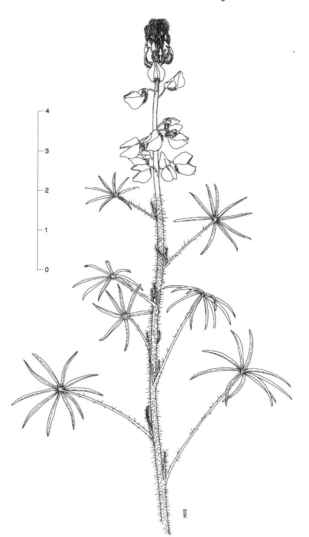

SPIDER LUPINE, BENTHAM'S LUPINE
Lupinus benthamii

PEA
Fabaceae

Height: 12-24 IN.　　　　Annual　　　　❀ **BLUE** ❀

Habitat: ROAD BANKS/SLOPES

Elevation: BELOW 3,500 FT.

Locale: TULLOCK RESERVOIR CURVE OFF SR 120

Lupinus benthamii is a graceful, slender Lupine found throughout the foothills on slopes or road banks. It is a beautiful blue with a whitish tip to the inflorescence. The white tip is created by bud scales that fall off as the flowers open. The leaflets are very narrow and remind one of spider legs. *Lupinus albifrons* is the only shrubby Lupine in the foothills. It has beautiful wands of blue-violet flowers and silver foliage.

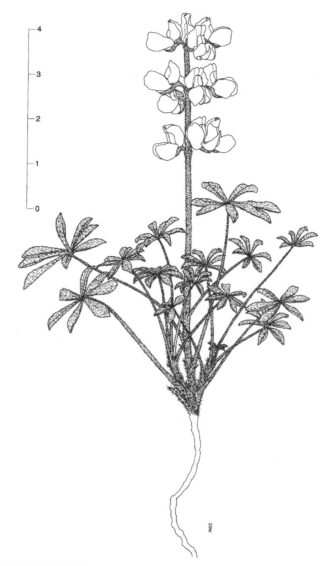

GRAY'S LUPINE PEA

Lupinus grayi Fabaceae

Height: 8-14 IN.   Perennial ❀ **BLUE WITH YELLOW SPOT ON BANNER** ❀

Habitat: SLOPES

Elevation: BELOW 2,000 FT.

Locale: CALAVERAS BIG TREES

Lupinus grayi grows in dense colonies. Each plant is entirely covered with woolly hairs that give the appearance of a silvery mat with blue flower spikes scattered throughout. The flower is bright blue, with a yellow spot on the banner that turns red with age.

SKY	PEA	MINIATURE
LUPINE	Fabaceae	*LUPINE*
Lupinus nanus	❀ BLUE WITH WHITE SPOT ❀	*Lupinus bicolor*
Height: 4-20 IN.	Annual	4-20 IN.
Habitat: SLOPES, GRASSY		SLOPES, GRAVEL
Elevation: BELOW 3,000 FT.		BELOW 3,000 FT.
Locale: TABLE MOUNTAIN ON CHEROKEE		CHEROKEE RD. NORTH
RD. NORTH OF OROVILLE		OF OROVILLE

Sky Lupine, sometimes called Blue and White Lupine or Douglas's Lupine, absolutely covers Table Mountain, generally during the first week in April. The tableland is blue and the air is perfumed. The half-inch flower has a low, rounded banner petal with a white patch in the center. *Lupinus bicolor*, or Miniature Lupine, is a smaller, rather scrawny plant with an oblong banner petal, much narrower and longer relative to the flower size than Sky Lupine. They grow together, though Miniature Lupine is more often seen on road banks.

CHICORY, BLUE SAILORS
Cichorium intybus

| WEED |

SUNFLOWER
Asteraceae

Height: 1-4 FT. Perennial ❀ BLUE ❀

Habitat: ROADSIDE, DISTURBED AREAS

Elevation: BELOW 5,000 FT.

Locale: MANY ROADSIDES JUST ABOVE THE VALLEY

The outstanding feature of this weed is the beautiful sky blue color of this member of the Sunflower family. It is a very coarse unattractive plant except for the beautiful flowers that seem to wilt within minutes of picking. The roasted roots were used as a coffee substitute during World War II.

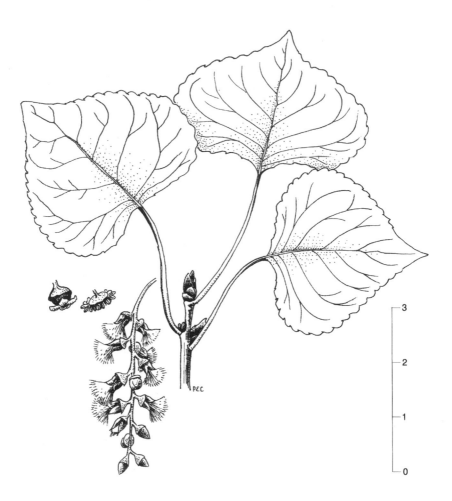

FREMONT'S POPLAR, FREMONT'S   WILLOW
COTTONWOOD   Salicaceae
Populus fremontii
Height: 36-90 FT.   Tree/deciduous
Habitat: MOIST
Elevation: BELOW 6,500 FT.
Locale: BRIDGEPORT

Fremont's Cottonwood is a large stately tree. When Cottonwood goes to seed it looks like an early summer snowstorm. The cottony fluff blows in the air, piles up against houses, and in general is quite a nuisance. Fortunately that lasts only a short time, and the tree's value for erosion control and as a beautiful tree with lemon-yellow fall color makes the nuisance worth putting up with.

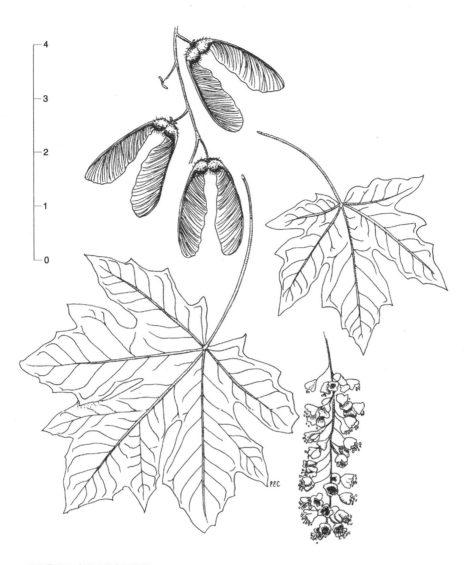

BIGLEAF MAPLE

Acer macrophyllum

MAPLE

Aceraceae

Height: 15-90 FT.   Tree/deciduous

Habitat: CANYONS, RIPARIAN

Elevation: BELOW 5,000 FT.

Locale: GRASS VALLEY TO DOWNIEVILLE ON SR 49

The species name *macrophyllum* refers to the very large leaf of this Maple. The tree has chartreuse blossom clusters that hang beneath the leaves in early spring. The bright yellow fall leaves are beautiful against the dark green of its companion plant Douglas Fir. Like eastern Maples, a large Bigleaf Maple can be tapped for sap which is boiled down into syrup.

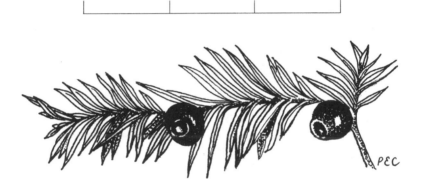

PACIFIC YEW   YEW
Taxus brevifolia   Taxaceae
Height: 15-90 FT.   Tree/evergreen
Habitat: CANYONS, MOIST
Elevation: BELOW 7,000 FT.
Locale: PONDEROSA WAY, SEVERAL MILES SOUTH OF THE
          AMERICAN RIVER CROSSING

Pacific Yew is not common in the foothills. It grows in canyon bottoms with Trillium, Ferns, and Elk Clover, all moisture-seeking plants. The seed takes two years to mature and has a fleshy red aril that wraps around the seed and is open at the top. The tree seems to shed its needles throughout the year. Pacific Yew has made the news recently as a possible breast cancer cure.

YELLOW PINE,   SUGAR   GRAY, GHOST, DIGGER,
PONDEROSA PINE   PINE   FOOTHILL PINE

Pinus ponderosa   *Pinus lambertiana*   *Pinus sabiniana*

PINE • Pinaceae • Tree/evergreen

Height: 45-210 FT.   60-235 FT.   36-54 FT.

Habitat: FORESTS   FORESTS   SLOPES, DRY

Elevation: 2,000-8,500 FT.   2,500-9,000 FT.   BELOW 4,500 FT.

Locale: I-80, BELOW AND ABOVE GOLD RUN

These pines are all located along Interstate 80; the Foothill Pine, *Pinus sabiniana*, appears as the hills begin to rise above the valley near Loomis, the Ponderosa Pine at Auburn, and the beautiful Sugar Pine can be seen between Colfax and Alta. The Foothill Pine is easily recognized by its sparse, grayish foliage and multibranch crown. The large heavy cones remain closed until there is a fire and then the sweet edible seeds are released. Ponderosa Pine is lush green with long shiny clusters of needles. The bracts on the cone stick out and prick your fingers if you pick up a cone. Mature Ponderosa Pines have flat scaly plates or "puzzle bark" on their trunks. Sugar Pine has lovely long cones, up to 18 inches, that hang in pendant groups from the tips of the branches. It has needles in bundles of five and is susceptible to White Pine Blister Rust. Perhaps the disease along with the high commercial value of the Sugar Pine is why it is not more prevalent.

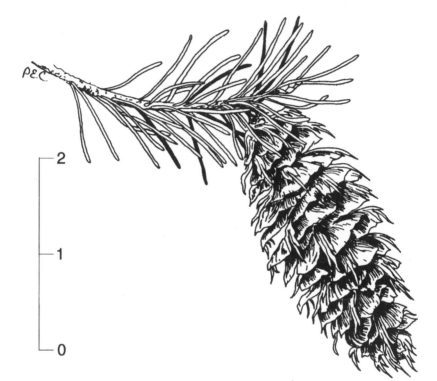

2

1

0

DOUGLAS FIR   PINE
Pseudotsuga menziesii   Pinaceae
Height: TO 210 FT.   Tree/evergreen
Habitat: SLOPES
Elevation: BELOW 5,000 FT.
Locale: MOSQUITO RIDGE RD. NEAR FORESTHILL

The genus is from Greek, *pseudos,* false, and *tsuga,* hemlock. This graceful tree is common in the foothills. It smells like Christmas and has unique 3-4 inch cones that have a prominent 3-toothed bract between the scales. The bract looks like a mouse with two back legs and a tail scooting in between the scales of the cone. This tree does well in gardens.

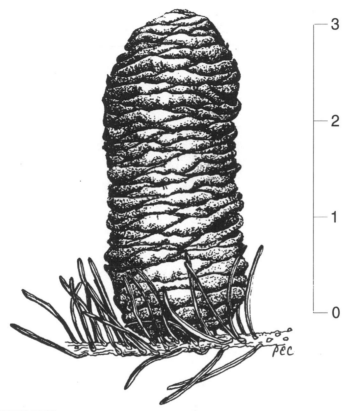

WHITE FIR   PINE
Abies concolor   Pinaceae
Height: 60-200 FT.   Tree/evergreen
Habitat: FORESTS
Elevation: 3,000-10,000 FT.
Locale: BOWMAN LAKE RD. OFF SR 20
White Fir is very widespread because it is the climax species of the upper
elevation forest. It can grow in its own shade and the seed can germinate
in forest duff or mineral soil. It grows quickly for the first 100 years and
reaches old age at 350 years. Young trees have white to silvery bark and a
traditional Christmas tree shape that is lost with age. When bruised or cut,
the tree has a foul odor.

3

2

1

0

plc

BIG TREE, GIANT SEQUOIA   BALD CYPRESS
Sequoiadendron giganteum   Taxodiaceae
Height: 150-240 FT.   Tree/evergreen
Habitat: SLOPES, MOIST
Elevation: 4,600-8,400 FT.
Locale: ISOLATED GROVES ABOVE FORESTHILL ON MOSQUITO RIDGE RD.
          OFF SR 4 / CALAVERAS BIG TREES / SR 120, THE TUOLUMNE GROVE
Spend New Year's at the Wawona Grove off SR 140 and see these trees in
all their glory. The magnificent red trunks against the white snow, the
bright green of the foliage, and the blue sky combine to make a great
Christmas card photo. In May, when the Dogwoods are in bloom in the
Tuolumne Grove, it becomes a fairyland. The trees need fire to reproduce. The fire-resistant bark is very thick and protects the inner layers
from heat damage. The purpose of controlled burns is to expose mineral
soil and eliminate the pathogens that inhibit germination; also, these burns
prevent the buildup of fuel so that fire cannot reach the crown of the tree.

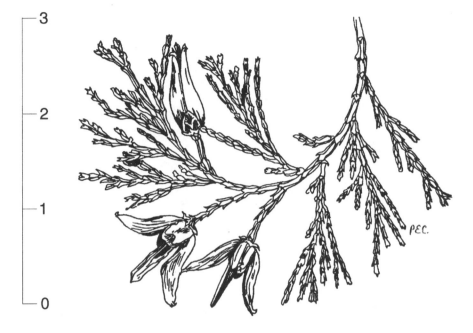

INCENSE CEDAR

CYPRESS

Libocedrus decurrens; Calocedrus decurrens   Cupressaceae

Height: 75-105 FT.   Tree/evergreen

Habitat: SLOPES

Elevation: 2,400-8,200 FT.

Locale: MANY

Incense Cedar, with its gorgeous red bark, is the climax tree species of the mid-elevation forest. This means that Cedar seeds can germinate and the plants survive with low light intensity. Bay Tree, *Umbellularia californica*, is the tree that will inherit the forest at low elevations, while White Fir, *Abies concolor*, is the upper-elevation climax species. These plants will continue to dominate a forest until a fire or land clearing opens it to sunlight. Notice the little duckbill-shaped scale containing two seeds.

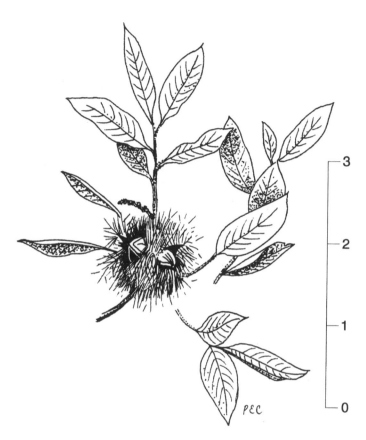

PEC

3

2

1

0

CHINQUAPIN   BEECH
Castanopsis sempervirens; Chrysolepis chrysophylla   Fagaceae
Height: 2-9 FT.   Shrub/evergreen
Habitat: SLOPES, ROCKY, CHAPARRAL
Elevation: 2,500-11,000 FT.
Locale: OMEGA REST STOP ON SR 20 ABOVE GRASS VALLEY
The genus *Chrysolepis,* from Greek, refers to the golden scale on the
underside of the leaf. This is a fairly small evergreen shrub with gold-
backed leaves and with a spiny husk burr covering one to three nuts that
take up to two years to mature. This plant forms thickets along ridges and
stump sprouts as a result of fire.

VALLEY OAK   BLACK OAK   BLUE OAK
Quercus lobata   *Quercus kelloggii*   *Quercus douglasii*

BEECH • Fagaceae • Tree/deciduous

Height: 36-110 FT.   30-75 FT.   18-69 FT.
Habitat: VALLEY, SLOPES   SLOPES   SLOPES, DRY, ROCKY
Elevation: BELOW 2,000 FT.   1,000-8,000 FT.   BELOW 3,500 FT.

Quercus lobata, or Valley Oak, is the most majestic of the Oaks and is found in the valley and lower foothills in rich soil. Blue Oak, *Quercus douglasii*, is common where the foothills begin to rise out of the valley. The leaf is smaller and the lobes are not as deeply cut as those of the other two Oaks. Blue Oak has a bluish cast once the leaves have been out for a few weeks. Black Oak, *Quercus kelloggii*, is very common at the mid-elevation. The forest looks as if it is in flower when the first leaves of Black Oak emerge in spring because of the velvety rose new growth. The trees are beautiful in fall with their yellow leaves against the black trunk. There is a prickle at the tip of each leaf lobe.

299

GOLD CUP OAK, CANYON OAK, MAUL OAK

Quercus chrysolepis

BEECH
Fagaceae

Tree/evergreen

INTERIOR LIVE OAK

Quercus wislizeni

Height: 18-60 FT.		30-70 FT.
Habitat: SLOPES, SHADED		SLOPES, CANYONS
Elevation: BELOW 6,500 FT.		BELOW 5,000 FT.
Locale: MOSQUITO RIDGE RD. NEAR FORESTHILL		MANY

Gold Cup describes the fuzzy dusty-gold cap on the acorn. As the illustration shows, the leaves can be either Hollylike or have a smooth edge on the same branchlet. Often the Hollylike leaves are young foliage, and perhaps this is an adaptation against deer browsing. The leaves are shiny green on top and silvery-blue on the underside. This leaf color is the easiest way to tell Gold Cup Oak from *Quercus wislizeni* or Interior Live Oak. Interior Live Oak also has shiny leaves but they are shiny chartreuse on the underside.

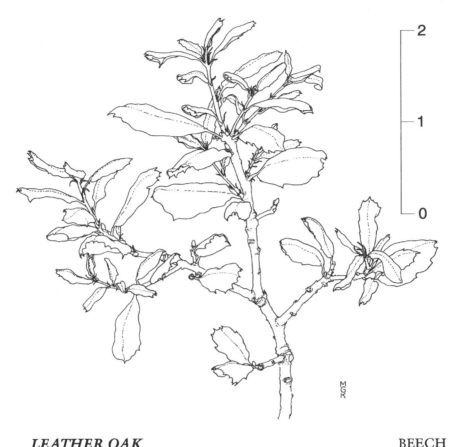

LEATHER OAK   BEECH
Quercus durata var. *durata*   Fagaceae
Height: 10-15 FT.   Shrub/evergreen
Habitat: SERPENTINE
Elevation: BELOW 5,000 FT.
Locale: TRAVERSE CREEK NEAR GEORGETOWN

It is surprising to find Oaks in shrub proportions. Leather Oak is generally found on serpentine soils. The leaf is usually a convex shape, but this is the most variable of the smaller Oaks. Perhaps this is because of its large range, from Southern California mountains to Tehama County in the Coast Range, and to the mid-elevation of the Sierra Nevada. Another small shrubby Oak, *Quercus vaccinifolia*, or Huckleberry Oak, can be seen at the upper elevations covered by this book. Acorns are scarce on Huckleberry Oak, but the showy pink-dotted galls are often evident.

REDBERRY, HOLLY-   BUCKTHORN   **COFFEEBERRY**
LEAF REDBERRY   Rhamnaceae   *Rhamnus*
Rhamnus crocea ssp. *ilicifolia*   *tomentella*
Rhamnus ilicifolia   var. *tomentella*
Height: TO 12 FT.   Shrub/evergreen   TO 15 FT.
Habitat: SLOPES, DRY   SLOPES, DRY
Elevation: BELOW 5,000 FT.   BELOW 3,000 FT.
Locale: WOLF MOUNTAIN RD. OFF McCOURTNEY RD.
          NEAR GRASS VALLEY

Large shrubs of Redberry resemble small evergreen Oaks except that there are no catkins or acorns, only tiny greenish flowers and tiny red berries. This plant has a much different appearance from Coffeeberry. *Rhamnus tomentella* var. *tomentella,* Coffeeberry, has gray-green leaves that resemble Bay leaves with a tomentose undersurface. The flowers are inconspicuous. The fruit is black and round, like a small plum or coffee bean. *Rhamnus purshiana,* Cascara, has been used as a laxative and is toxic in large amounts.

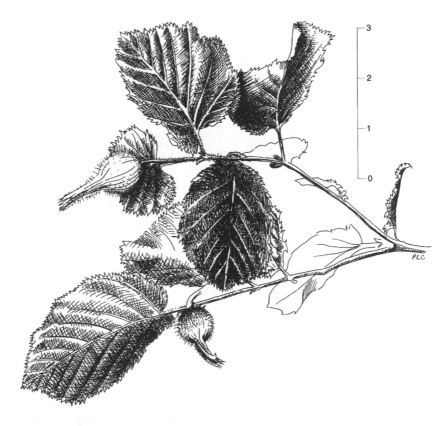

HAZELNUT, FILBERT

BIRCH

Corylus cornuta var. *californica*   Betulaceae

Height: 7-20 FT.   Shrub/deciduous   ❀ **RED, TINY** ❀

Habitat: FORESTS

Elevation: BELOW 7,000 FT.

Locale: INDIAN VALLEY TRAIL BELOW DOWNIEVILLE

This understory shrub has gray bark and a graceful shape. The serrated leaves are about 1½-3 inches long and up to 2 inches wide, with noticeable veins. Gently rub the leaf and feel the soft down on the upper surface. Cattle and sheep graze on Hazelnut foliage. The downy leaf of Hazelnut is the way to tell the difference between Cream Bush and Hazelnut when there are only leaves on the shrub.

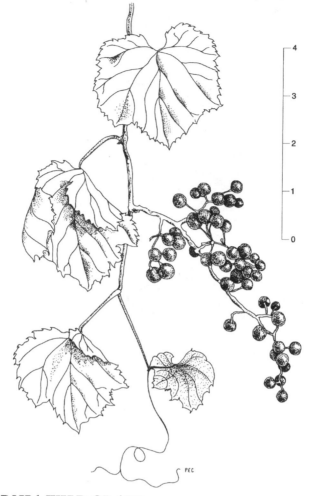

CALIFORNIA WILD GRAPE   GRAPE
Vitis californica   Vitaceae

Height: 6-45 FT.   Vine, woody   ❀ **GREENISH YELLOW** ❀
Habitat: STREAM BANKS, CANYONS
Elevation: BELOW 4,000 FT.
Locale: SR 26 AT THE MOKELUMNE RIVER BRIDGE

Wild Grapes form a curtain of gold in the autumn at the Mokelumne
River bridge on SR 26. They are beautiful in many places, but this is the
best. *Vitis californica,* "Roger's Red," is a particularly beautiful cultivar
form of this plant; it is good for landscape use on a fence, as a screen, or
on an arbor. The tiny flowers perfume the air and the grapes that follow
make good jelly. A survival tip in the California Native Plant Society newsletter suggests cutting the stem and catching the sap that drips as an
emergency water source. (When Concord Grapes are pruned too late in
the winter the sap can be heard dripping from any cut as large as a pencil.)

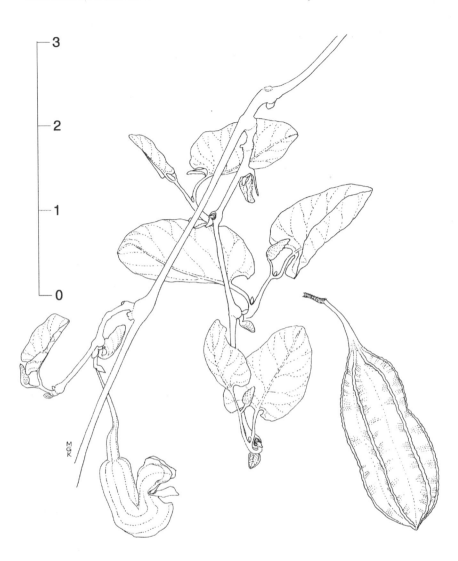

DUTCHMAN'S PIPE   PIPEVINE
Aristolochia californica   Aristolochiaceae
Height: 9-12 FT.   Vine   ❀ BROWN ❀
Habitat: RIPARIAN, OAK FORESTS, NORTH FACING
Elevation: BELOW 1,500 FT.
Locale: HONEYRUN RD. NEAR PARADISE

This is a wonderful vine to grow over a lath house. The little meerschaum pipes emerge on the stem in March, before the leaves. Later in the spring fruits develop that look like the star fruit from the grocery store. Often the plant goes unnoticed until you spot the black swallowtail butterfly, whose larva feeds on the Dutchman's Pipe.

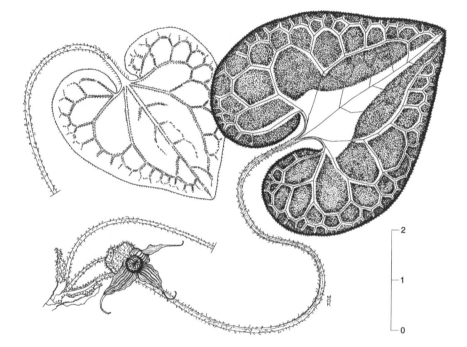

HARTWEG'S WILD GINGER
Asarum hartwegii

PIPEVINE
Aristolochiaceae

Height: 6-10 IN.   Perennial   ❀ **BROWN-PURPLE** ❀
Habitat: FORESTS
Elevation: 2,000-7,000 FT.
Locale: CARIBOU RD. OFF FEATHER RIVER HWY.

The drawing does not exaggerate the pattern on these attractive leaves. The leaf stems are aromatic; the purple-brown flowers are hidden under the leaves and are pollinated by insects attracted by their carrion odor.

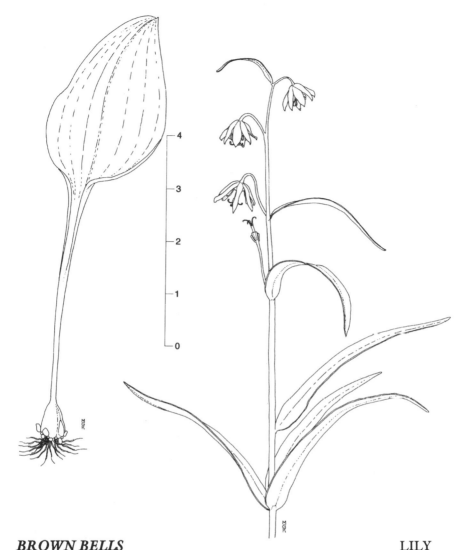

BROWN BELLS   LILY
Fritillaria micrantha   Liliaceae

Height: 15-36 IN.   Bulb/scales   ❀ BROWNISH/GREEN ❀
Habitat: SLOPES, SHADE, DRY
Elevation: 1,000-6,000 FT.
Locale: HELL'S HALF ACRE, GRASS VALLEY

This elusive Lily is hard to see. Often, when walking on a trail, you will see a relatively large single fleshy leaf, two inches by four inches, on a bank above the trail. This is the "seed leaf" of *Fritillaria*. This leaf appears for several years, storing up enough energy in the scaly bulb to send up the stalk and flowers. The seed leaf is the clue that there are some mature plants nearby.

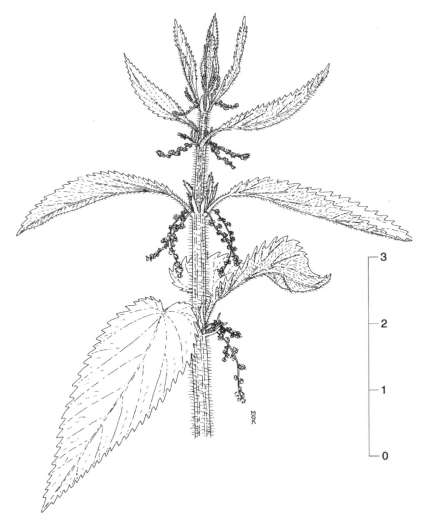

NETTLE   NETTLE

Urtica holosericea; Urtica dioica ssp. *holosericea*   Urticaceae

Height: 3-6 FT.   Perennial   ❀ **GREEN, INCONSPICUOUS** ❀

Habitat: MOIST

Elevation: BELOW 9,000 FT.

Locale: MANY

At first glance Nettle resembles a Mint or Figwort, especially Bee Plant, because of the height and serrated opposite leaves. The most obvious difference is the flowers in the axils of the leaves. The genus is derived from the Latin *urere,* to burn, referring to the stinging sensation to skin from contact with Nettles. Europeans make Nettle soup. The Germans cure Nettle sting by rubbing the area with Horsetail Fern, *Equisetum* sp., which is often found growing in the same location. It works.

CALIFORNIA MUGWORT
Artemisia douglasiana

SUNFLOWER

Asteraceae

Height: 20-60 IN.   Perennial   ❀ YELLOWISH, INCONSPICUOUS ❀

Habitat: OAK FORESTS, CHAPARRAL SHADE

Elevation: BELOW 7,000 FT.

Locale: MANY

The plant is very common, with nothing particularly outstanding about it other than the pleasant aroma, attractive leaves that are white on the underside, and the fact that it is a great Poison Oak cure. Boil a bundle of leaves in water, cool in the fridge, then sop the cold liquid on the Poison Oak rash. The author's rash disappeared as if it had been treated with cortisone.

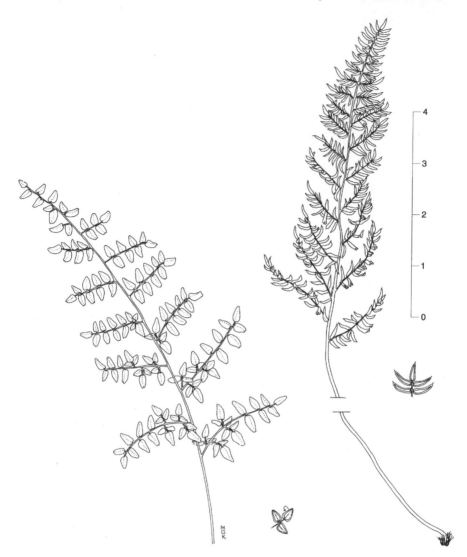

COFFEE FERN	BRAKE	*BIRD'S FOOT FERN*
Pellaea andromedaefolia	Pteridaceae	*Pellaea mucronata*
Height: 5-28 IN.	Fern	5-20 IN.
Habitat: ROCKY		ROCKY, DRY
Elevation: BELOW 4,000 FT.		BELOW 6,000 FT.

Locale: EL PORTAL, HITES COVE TRAIL

Notice the species name *andromedaefolia* from mythology: Andromeda was tied to a rock, as is Coffee Fern. *Folia* refers to foliage, which is three times pinnate. *Pellaea mucronata*, Bird's Foot Fern, has wiry-looking growth. The species name means pointed, as is the tip of each leaf segment. Both plants have bluish-gray leaves and are often in hot locations.

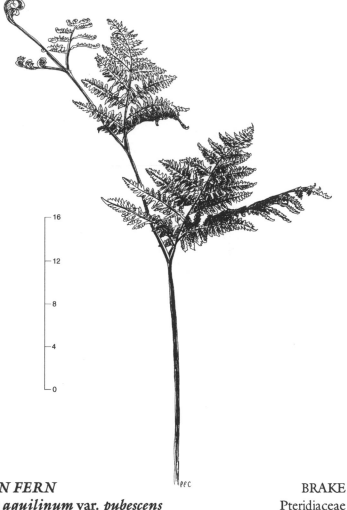

BRACKEN FERN

Pteridium aquilinum var. *pubescens*

Height: 12-45 IN.   Fern

Habitat: FORESTS

Elevation: BELOW 10,000 FT.

Locale: MANY

BRAKE
Pteridiaceae

Bracken Fern grows throughout the world. It is weedy once it gets into a garden. The very young fiddleheads are delicious steamed and are served in some elegant hotels. They have an almondy aftertaste when nibbled off the plant. (There was a warning in one of the medical journals that eaten in quantity it can cause cancer and is a known livestock poison.) The straw-colored fall fronds are pretty in dried arrangements. Bracken found in the mountains seems to dry a better color; the dry air does not permit the growth of mold, so the fronds stay yellow instead of turning gray as they do where air is moist.

MAIDENHAIR	BRAKE	*GOLDBACK FERN*
FERN	Pteridaceae	*Pityrogramma triangularis*
Adiantum jordanii		*Pentogramma triangularis*

Height: 8-20 IN.   Fern   4-16 IN.

Habitat: RIPARIAN, BANKS   ROCKY, SHADE

Elevation: GENERALLY BELOW 3,500 FT.   BELOW 5,000 FT.

Locale: YANKEE JIMS RD. OFF I-80 EAST OF AUBURN   COMMON

The genus name is derived from the Greek *adiantos,* meaning unwetted, which refers to the way the fronds repel water. Everyone loves to see Maidenhair Fern cascading down a steep shady bank, often beside a stream. Indians used the shiny black stipe in their basket designs. Notice the fan-shaped leaf segments with the sori wrapped underneath the edge of the leaf segments. Goldback Fern is common and easy to recognize by the "gold dust" on the underside of the frond. It is fun to make a print of the leaf on the dark surface of a child's jeans. Pick a frond, press it firmly against the jeans, and say "You are my friend," and the delighted child has a print to take home. Silverback Fern, *Pityrogramma pallida*, has a silvery or white underside to its leaf.

312

SWORD FERN   WOOD FERN
Polystichum munitum   Dryopteridaceae
Height: 23-50 IN.   Fern
Habitat: FORESTS, DAMP
Elevation: BELOW 2,500 FT.
Locale: MANY

The origin of the genus name is from the Greek *polus,* many, and *stichos,* row, referring to the species that have many rows of sori. The leaves are once pinnate. Look carefully at the individual pinnae, which are crowded; they are lanceolate with a little sword hilt at the base of each. The hilt or auricle at the base of the leaf helps one to recognize this Fern. These are attractive in the garden although they die back during the winter.

GIANT CHAIN FERN
Woodwardia fimbriata
Height: 3-6 FT.   Fern

DEER FERN
Blechnaceae

Habitat: MOIST

Elevation: BELOW 5,000 FT.

Locale: YANKEE JIMS RD. OFF I-80

This Fern is unmistakable because of its size. Imagine a group of Girl Scouts cavorting under the fronds in the Giant Chain Fern Forest. They looked like elves. Look at the underside of the frond to see the chainlike arrangement of the sori along each side of the lobe midribs.

SHIELD FERN, WOOD FERN
Dryopteris arguta

WOOD FERN
Dryopteridaceae

Height: 12-24 IN.   Fern
Habitat: SHADE, DRY
Elevation: BELOW 8,000 FT.
Locale: PURDON CROSSING NEAR NEVADA CITY

Wood Fern is an attractive garden Fern, with thin pointed dark brown scales toward the base of the stipe and graceful erect fronds. The genus name is from the Greek *dryas,* oak, and *pteris,* fern. It does well in a dry shade garden and is excellent under Oaks where summer watering could attract Oak Root Rot.

315

Appendix A:
PLANT FAMILIES

* No illustration. Plant may be mentioned or is likely to be seen in the foothills.

( ) Color section in this book. *W* = white, *Y* = yellow, *P* = pink to magenta, *B* = Blue to purple, *G* = green to brown.

Family	Common Name	Botanical Name
BALD CYPRESS	Big Tree	*Sequoiadendron giganteum (G)*
BARBERRY	Oregon Grape	*Berberis aquifolium* var. *dictyota (Y)*
BEECH (G)	Chinquapin	*Castanopsis sempervirens*
	Gold Cup Oak	*Quercus chrysolepis*
	Blue Oak	*Quercus douglasii*
	Leather Oak	*Quercus durata*
	Black Oak	*Quercus kelloggii*
	Valley Oak	*Quercus lobata*
	Huckleberry Oak	*Quercus vaccinifolia*
	Interior Live Oak	*Quercus wislizeni*
BIRCH	Hazelnut	*Corylus cornuta var californica (G)*
BORAGE	Fiddleneck	*Amsinckia intermedia (Y)*
	Hound's Tongue	*Cynoglossum grande (B)*
	Popcorn Flower	*Plagiobothrys nothofulvus (W)*
BROOM-RAPE	Naked Broom-rape	*Orobanche uniflora (B)*
BUCKEYE	Buckeye	*Aesculus californica (W)*
BUCKTHORN	Buck Brush	*Ceanothus cuneatus (W)*
	Deer Brush	*Ceanothus integerrimus (W)*
	Lemmon's Ceanothus	*Ceanothus lemmonii (B)*
	Squaw Carpet	*Ceanothus prostratus (B)*
	Pine Hill Ceanothus	*Ceanothus roderickii (B)* *
	Coffeeberry	*Rhamnus californica* var. *tomentella (G)*
	Redberry, Buckthorn	*Rhamnus crocea* ssp. *ilicifolia (G)*
BUCKWHEAT	Nude Buckwheat	*Eriogonum latifolium* ssp. *nudum (W)*
	Bear Buckwheat	*Eriogonum ursinum (Y)*
BUTTERCUP	Columbine	*Aquilegia formosa (P)*
	Virgin's Bower	*Clematis lasiantha (W)*
	Hansen's Delphinium	*Delphinium hansenii (W,B,P)*
	Red Larkspur	*Delphinium nudicaule (P)*
	Spreading Larkspur	*Delphinium patens (B)*
	Royal Delphinium	*Delphinium variegatum (B)*
	Isopyrum	*Isopyrum occidentale (W)*
	California Buttercup	*Ranunculus californicus (Y)*
	Foothill Buttercup	*Ranunculus canus (Y)*
	Water Buttercup	*Ranunculus hystriculus (W)*
	Western Buttercup	*Ranunculus occidentalis (Y)*
CACAO	Flannel Bush	*Fremontia californica (Y)*

CAMPANULA	Campanula	*Campanula prenanthoides (B)* *
	Double-horn Downingia	*Downingia bicornuta (B)*
	Downingia	*Downingia ornatissima (B)*
CARROT	Eryngium	*Eryngium vaseyi* var. *vallicola (B)* *
	Cow-Parsnip	*Heracleum lanatum (W)*
	Foothill Lomatium	*Lomatium utriculatum (Y)*
	Sweet Cicely	*Osmorhiza chilensis (G)* *
	Western Sweet Cicely	*Osmorhiza occidentalis (G)* *
	Poison Sanicle	*Sanicula bipinnata (Y)*
	Purple Sanicle	*Sanicula bipinnatifida (B)*
	Gamble Weed	*Sanicula crassicaulis (Y)*
	Hartweg's Tauschia	*Tauschia hartwegii (Y)*
CAT-TAIL	Cat-tail	*Typha latifolia (Y)* *
CYPRESS	Incense Cedar	*Libocedrus decurrens (G)*
DOGWOOD	Mountain Dogwood	*Cornus nuttallii (W)*
	American Dogwood	*Cornus stolonifera (W)*
EVENING	Farewell to Spring	*Clarkia biloba (P)*
PRIMROSE	Winecup Clarkia	*Clarkia purpurea* ssp. *quadrivulnera (P)*
	Tongue Clarkia	*Clarkia rhomboidea (P)*
	Williamson's Clarkia	*Clarkia williamsonii (P)*
FERN (G)	Maidenhair Fern	*Adiantum jordanii*
	Shield Fern, Wood Fern	*Dryopteris arguta*
	Coffee Fern	*Pellaea andromedaefolia*
	Bird's Foot Fern	*Pellaea mucronata*
	Goldback Fern	*Pityrogramma triangularis*
	Silverback Fern	*Pityrogramma triangularis* var. *pallida* *
	Sword Fern	*Polystichum munitum*
	Bracken Fern	*Pteridium aquilinum* var. *pubescens*
	Giant Chain Fern	*Woodwardia fimbriata*
FIGWORT	Wavy-leaf Paintbrush	*Castilleja applegatei (P)* *
	Fuzzy Paintbrush	*Castilleja foliolosa (P)*
	Woolly Paintbrush	*Castilleja pruinosa (P)*
	Chinese Houses	*Collinsia heterophylla (P)*
	White Chinese Houses	*Collinsia tinctoria (W)*
	Sticky Monkeyflower	*Mimulus aurantiacus (Y)*
	Bicolor Monkeyflower	*Mimulus bicolor (Y)* *
	Red Monkeyflower	*Mimulus cardinalis (P)*
	Yellow Monkeyflower	*Mimulus guttatus (Y)*
	Chinless Mimulus	*Mimulus kelloggii (P)*
	Tricolor Monkeyflower	*Mimulus tricolor (P)*
	Valley Tassels	*Orthocarpus attenuatus (W)*
	Butter and Eggs	*Orthocarpus erianthus (Y)*
	Purple Owl's-clover	*Orthocarpus purpurascens (P)*
	Lousewort	*Pedicularis densiflora (P)*
	Azure Penstemon	*Penstemon azureus (B)*
	Hot Rock Penstemon	*Penstemon deustus (W)*
	Varied Leaf Penstemon	*Penstemon heterophyllus (B)*
	Beard-tongue	*Penstemon laetus (B)* *
	Pride of the Mountain	*Penstemon newberryi (P)* *

	Bee Plant	*Scrophularia californica (R)*
	Common Mullein	*Verbascum thapsus (Y)*
FUMATORY/ POPPY	Golden Ear Drops	*Dicentra chrysantha (Y)*
	Bleeding Heart	*Dicentra formosa (P)*
	Steer's Head	*Dicentra uniflora (P)*
GENTIAN	Swertia	*Frasera albicaulis* ssp. *nitida (W)*
GERANIUM	Filaree, Storksbill	*Erodium botrys (P)*
	Cranesbill	*Geranium dissectum (P)*
	Soft Cranesbill	*Geranium molle (P)*
GOOSEBERRY	Oak Gooseberry	*Ribes quercetorum (Y)*
	Sierra Gooseberry	*Ribes roezlii (P)*
	Mountain Pink Currant	*Ribes nevadense (P)*
GOURD	Wild Cucumber	*Marah horridus (W)*
GRAPE	California Wild Grape	*Vitis californica (G)*
HEATH	Madrone	*Arbutus menziesii (W)*
	Ione Manzanita rare	*Arctostaphylos myrtifolia (W)* *
	Greenleaf Manzanita	*Arctostaphylos patula (P)* *
	Whiteleaf Manzanita	*Arctostaphylos viscida (P)*
	White-veined Wintergreen	*Pyrola picta (W)* *
	Azalea	*Rhododendron occidentale (P)*
	Snow Plant	*Sarcodes sanguinea (P)*
HONEYSUCKLE	Twin Flower	*Linnaea borealis* ssp. *longiflora (P)*
	Honeysuckle	*Lonicera hispidula* var. *vacillans (P)*
	Shrub Honeysuckle	*Lonicera interrupta (W)* *
	Blue Elderberry	*Sambucus caerulea (W)*
	Creeping Snowberry	*Symphoricarpos mollis (P)*
	Snowberry	*Symphoricarpos albus* var. *laevigatus (P)* *
IRIS	Hartweg's Iris	*Iris hartwegii (Y)*
	Ground Iris	*Iris macrosiphon (B)*
	Blue-eyed Grass	*Sisyrinchium bellum (B)*
	Idaho Blue-eyed Grass	*Sisyrinchium idahoense (B)* *
LAUREL	California Bay	*Umbellularia californica (W)*
LILY	Paper Onion	*Allium amplectens (W)*
	Sierra Onion	*Allium campanulatum (P)*
	Glassy Onion	*Allium hyalinum (P)*
		Allium membranaceum (P) *
		Allium peninsulare (P)
	Appendaged Brodiaea	*Brodiaea appendiculata (B)*
	Crown Brodiaea	*Brodiaea coronaria (B)*
	Fairy Lantern	*Calochortus albus (W)*
	Golden Mariposa Lily	*Calochortus luteus (Y)*
	Yellow Star-Tulip	*Calochortus monophyllus (Y)*
	Beavertail-grass	*Calochortus coeruleus (W)*
		Calochortus elegans (W) *
	Mariposa Lily	*Calochortus venustus (W)*
	Soap Plant	*Chlorogalum pomeridianum (W)*
	Queen's Cup,	*Clintonia uniflora (W)*

	Wild Hyacinth	*Dichelostemma multiflora (B)*
	Blue Dicks	*Dichelostemma capitatum (B)*
	Twining Brodiaea	*Dichelostemma volubile (P)*
	Fairybell	*Disporum hookeri (W)*
	Fawn Lily	*Erythronium multiscapoideum (Y)*
	Tuolumne Fawn Lily	*Erythronium tuolumnense (Y)*
	Brown Bells	*Fritillaria micrantha (B)*
	Scarlet Fritillary	*Fritillaria recurva (P)*
	Humboldt Lily	*Lilium humboldtii (Y)* *
	Leopard Lily	*Lilium pardalinum (Y)*
	Washington Lily	*Lilium washingtonianum (W)*
	Odontostomum	*Odontostomum hartwegii (W)*
	Rush Lily	*Schoenolirion album (W)*
	False Solomon's Seal	*Smilacina racemosa (W)*
	Star Solomon's Seal	*Smilacina stellata (W)* *
	Wake Robin	*Trillium chloropetalum (P)*
	Bridge's Brodiaea	*Triteleia bridgesii (B)*
	Glass Lily	*Triteleia hyacinthina (W)*
	Golden Brodiaea	*Triteleia ixioides* var. *scabra (Y)*
	Ithuriel's Spear	*Triteleia laxa (B)*
	White Brodiaea	*Triteleia lilacina (W)*
	Bear-grass	*Xerophyllum tenax (W)*
	Star Lilyy	*Zigadenus fremontii (W)*
	Death Camas	*Zigadenus venenosus (W)* *
LOASA	Blazing Star	*Mentzelia lindleyi (Y)*
MADDER	Bedstraw	*Galium aparine (W)*
		Galium nuttallii (W-Y) *
MALLOW	Checker Mallow	*Sidalcea calycosa* ssp. *calycosa (P)*
	Checker	*Sidalcea hartweggii (P)* *
	Waxy Sidalcea	*Sidalcea glaucescens (P)*
MAPLE	Bigleaf Maple	*Acer macrophyllum (G)*
MEADOWFOAM	Douglas Meadowfoam	*Limnanthes douglasii (W)*
	Meadowfoam	*Limnanthes striata (W)*
MILKWEED	Purple Milkweed	*Asclepias cordifolia (B)*
MINT	Pitcher Sage	*Lepechinia calycina (W)*
	Mustang Mint	*Monardella lanceolata (B)*
	Pennyroyal	*Monardella odoratissima (B)*
	Sonoma Sage	*Salvia sonomensis (B)*
	Purple Skullcap	*Scutellaria angustifolia (B)*
	Skullcap	*Scutellaria californica (W)*
MORNING-GLORY	Sierra Morning-glory	*Calystegia malacophylla (W)* *
MUSTARD	Winter-Cress	*Barbarea orthoceras (Y)* *
	Toothwort, Milkmaids	*Dentaria californica (W)*
	Wallflower	*Erysimum capitatum (Y)*
	Mountain Jewel Flower	*Streptanthus tortuosus* var. *tortuosus (Y)*
	Lacepod, Fringepod	*Thysanocarpus curvipes (W)*
	Spokepod	*Thysanocarpus radians (W)*

NETTLE	Nettle	*Urtica holosericea (G)*
NIGHTSHADE	Jimsonweed	*Datura meteloides (W)*
	Nightshade	*Solanum xanti (B)*
OLIVE	Flowering Ash	*Fraxinus dipetala (W)*
ORCHID	Phantom Orchid	*Cephalanthera austiniae (W)*
	Coral Root	*Corallorhiza maculata (P)*
	Lady Slipper Orchid	*Cypripedium californicum (W)*
	Rattlesnake Plantain	*Goodyera oblongifolia (W)*
	Rein or Bog-Orchid	*Habenaria dilatata (W)* *
PEA	Redbud	*Cercis occidentalis (P)*
	Broom	*Genista monspessulana (Y)*
	Perennial Sweet Pea	*Lathyrus latifolia (P)*
	Sierra Nevada Pea	*Lathyrus nevadensis var. nevadensis (B)*
	Sulphur Pea	*Lathyrus sulphureus (Y)*
	Silverleaf Lotus	*Lotus argophyllus (Y)*
	Torrey's Lotus	*Lotus oblongifolius (Y)* *
	Spider Lupine	*Lupinus benthamii (B)*
	Miniature Lupine	*Lupinus bicolor (B)*
	Whorled Lupine	*Lupinus densiflorus (B)*
	Gray's Lupine	*Lupinus grayi (B)*
	Sky Lupine	*Lupinus nanus (B)*
	Harlequin Lupine	*Lupinus stiversii (P)*
	Chaparral Pea	*Pickeringia montana (P)*
	Spanish Broom	*Spartium junceum (Y)*
	Cow's Udder Clover	*Trifolium depauperatum (P)*
	Rosy Clover	*Trifolium hirtum (P)*
	Tomcat Clover	*Trifolium tridentatum (P)*
	Cow Clover	*Trifolium wormskioldii (P)* *
	Spring Vetch	*Vicia sativa (B)*
	Winter Vetch	*Vicia villosa (B)*
PEONY	Brown's Peony	*Paeonia brownii (P)*
PHLOX	Capitate Gilia	*Gilia capitata (B)*
	Bird's Eye Gilia	*Gilia tricolor (B)*
	Whisker Brush	*Linanthus ciliatus (P)*
	Evening Snow	*Linanthus dichotomus (W)*
	Mustang-clover	*Linanthus montanus (P)*
	Showy Phlox	*Phlox speciosa (P)*
PINE (G)	White Fir	*Abies concolor*
	Sugar Pine	*Pinus lambertiana*
	Yellow, Ponderosa Pine	*Pinus ponderosa*
	Gray, Ghost, Digger Pine	*Pinus sabiniana*
	Douglas Fir	*Pseudotsuga menziesii*
PINK	Sandwort	*Minuartia californica (W)*
	Indian Pink	*Silene californica (P)*
PIPEVINE	Dutchman's Pipe	*Aristolochia californica (G)*
	Hartweg's Wild Ginger	*Asarum hartwegii (G)*
POLYGALA	Milkwort	*Polygala californica (P)*
POPPY	Bush Poppy	*Dendromecon rigida (Y)*

	Caespitose, Tufted Poppy	*Eschscholzia caespitosa (Y)*
	California Poppy	*Eschscholzia californica (Y)*
	Frying Pans Poppy	*Eschscholzia lobbii (Y)*
	Cream Cups	*Platystemon californicus (Y)*
PRIMROSE	Shooting Star	*Dodecatheon hansenii (P)*
	Star Flower	*Trientalis latifolia (P)*
PURSLANE	Red Maids	*Calandrinia ciliata* var. *menziesii (P)*
	Pussy Paws	*Calyptridium umbellatum (P)*
	Cantelow's Lewisia	*Lewisia cantelovii (W)*
	Bitter Root	*Lewisia rediviva (P)*
	Dwarf Miner's Letuce	*Montia gypsophiloides (P)*
	Miner's Lettuce	*Montia perfoliata (W)*
ROSE	Chamise	*Adenostoma fasciculatum (W)*
	Service Berry	*Amelanchier pallida (W)* *
	Mountain Mahogany	*Cercocarpus betuloides (Y)*
	Mountain Misery	*Chamaebatia foliolosa (W)*
	Wild Strawberry	*Fragaria vesca (W)*
	Toyon/Christmas Berry	*Heteromeles arbutifolia (W)*
	Cream Bush	*Holodiscus discolor (W)*
	Cinquefoil	*Potentilla glandulosa (Y)*
	Sierra Plum	*Prunus subcordata (W)*
	Western Choke Cherry	*Prunus virginiana* var. *demissa (W)*
	Himalayan Blackberry	*Rubus discolor (W)*
	Western Raspberry	*Rubus leucodermis (W)*
	Thimbleberry	*Rubus parviflorus (W)*
SANDALWOOD	Bastard Toad Flax	*Comandra pallida (G)* *
SAXIFRAGE	Brook Foam	*Boykinia elata (W)*
	Alum Root	*Heuchera micrantha (W)*
	Woodland Star	*Lithophragma affine (W)*
	Indian Rhubarb	*Peltaphyllum peltatum (P)*
	California Mock Orange	*Philadelphus lewisii* ssp. *californicus (W)*
	California Saxifrage	*Saxifraga californica (W)*
	Oregon Saxifrage	*Saxifraga oregana (W)*
	Fringe Cups	*Tellima grandiflora (W)*
ST JOHN'S WORT	Tinker's Penny	*Hypericum anagalloides (Y)*
	Klamathweed	*Hypericum perforatum (Y)*
STONECROP	Live-Forever	*Dudleya cymosa (Y, P)*
	Little Sedum	*Parvisedum pumilum (Y)*
	Stonecrop	*Sedum spathulifolium (Y)*
STORAX	Snowdrop Bush	*Styrax officinalis* var. *californica (W)*
SUMAC	Poison Oak	*Rhus diversiloba (W)*
	Skunk Bush, Squaw Bush	*Rhus trilobata (Cream W)*
SUNFLOWER	Yarrow	*Achillea millefolium (W)*
	Blow Wives	*Achyrachaena mollis (Y)*
	Trail Plant	*Adenocaulon bicolor (W)*
		Agoseris grandiflora (Y) *
	Dandelion	*Agoseris heterophylla (Y)*

	Mountain Dandelion	*Agoseris retrorsa* (Y) *
	Pearly Everlasting	*Anaphalis margaritacea* (W)
	California Mugwort	*Artemisia douglasiana* (Y)
	Coyote Brush	*Baccharis pilularis* (W) pappus
	Balsamroot	*Balsamorhiza deltoidea* (Y)
	Common Blennosperma	*Blennosperma nanum* (Y)
	Star Thistle	*Centaurea solstitialis* (Y)
	Yellow-flowered Chaenactis	*Chaenactis glabriuscula* (Y)
	Chicory	*Cichorium intybus* (B)
	Thistle	*Cirsium occidentale* var. *californicum* (P) *
	Anderson's Thistle	*Cirsium andersonii* (P)
	Coreopsis	*Coreopsis stillmanii* (Y)
	Fleabane	*Erigeron foliosus* (W)
	Golden Yarrow	*Eriophyllum confertiflorum* (Y)
	Woolly Sunflower	*Eriophyllum lanatum* (Y)
	Gum Weed	*Grindelia camporum* (Y)
	California Sunflower	*Helianthella californica* var. *nevadensis* (Y)
	Hawkweed	*Hieracium albiflorum* (W)
	Goldfields	*Lasthenia californica* (Y)
	Fremont's Tidy-tips	*Layia fremontii* (Y)
	Common Madia	*Madia elegans* (Y)
	Foothill Pseudobahia	*Pseudobahia heermannii* (Y)
	Mule Ears	*Wyethia angustifolia* (Y)
	Bolander's Mule Ears	*Wyethia bolanderi* (Y)
	El Dorado County Mule Ears	*Wyethia reticulata* (Y) *
SWEET-SHRUB	Spicebush	*Calycanthus occidentalis* (P)
VALERIAN	Plectritis	*Plectritis ciliosa* (W)
VIOLA	Douglas's Violet	*Viola douglasii* (Y)
	Stream Violet	*Viola glabella* (Y)
	Pine Violet	*Viola lobata* (Y)
	Johnny-Jump-Up	*Viola pedunculata* (Y)
	Shelton's Violet	*Viola sheltonii* (Y)
WATERLEAF	Yerba Santa	*Eriodictyon californicum* (B)
	Hesperochiron	*Hesperochiron pumilus* (W) *
	Waterleaf	*Hydrophyllum occidental* (B)
	White Nemophila	*Nemophila heterophylla* (W)
	Five Spot Nemophila	*Nemophila maculata* (W)
	Baby Blue Eyes	*Nemophila menziesii* (B)
	Caterpillar Phacelia	*Phacelia cicutaria* (W)
	Varileaf Phacelia	*Phacelia heterophylla* (W/B)
	Fiesta Flower	*Pholistoma auritum* (B)
WILLOW	Fremont Cottonwood	*Populus fremontii* (G)
YEW	Yew	*Taxus brevifolia* (G)

Appendix B:
GROUPS THAT CONDUCT FIELD TRIPS

California Native Plant Society
1722 J Street, Sacramento, CA 95814; (916) 447-2677;
http://www.cnps.org
There are CNPS chapters in some of the foothill towns. Phone the main office to find out which chapter has field trips near you and to learn about spring wildflower hotlines.

U.S. Forest Service Offices
Throughout the Gold Country; they have maps, trail guides, books, and often lead field trips.

Bureau of Land Management (BLM)
63 Natoma Street, Folsom, CA 95630; (916) 985-4474

Nature Conservancy
201 Mission Street (Fourth Floor), San Francisco, CA 94105; (415) 777-0487

Sierra Club, Mother Lode Chapter
P.O. Box 1335, Sacramento, CA 95812-1335; (916) 557-1108

Lake Oroville State Recreation Area
917 Kelly Ridge Road, Oroville, CA 95965; (530) 538-2219

Plumas National Forest, Feather River Ranger District
875 Mitchell Avenue, Oroville, CA 95965; (530) 534-6500

Nevada County Land Trust
P.O. Box 2088 (418-A Broad Street), Nevada City, CA 95959; (530) 265-0430; http://www.nccn.net/~landtrst
Interesting field trips and programs concerning history, geology, flowers, birds, art, children's programs, etc.

Sequoya Challenge
P.O. Box 3166, Grass Valley, CA 95945; (530) 265-9398
Active group concerned with the Independence Trail on Highway 49; offers field trips and a newsletter.

Tahoe National Forest
631 Coyote St. Nevada City, CA 95959 (Highway 49 north of Highway 20); (530) 265-4531

Placer Land Trust and Nature Center
3700 Christian Valley Road, Auburn, CA 95602; (530) 878-6053

Auburn and Folsom State Recreation Areas
7806 Folsom-Auburn Road, Folsom, CA 95630; (916) 988-0205

El Dorado National Forest Interpretive Association (ENFIA)
3070 Camino Heights Drive, Camino, CA 95709; (530) 622-4666;
http://www.innercite.com/~enfia
Hikes, newsletter.

American River Conservancy
P.O. Box 562 (8913 Highway 49), Coloma, CA 95613; (916) 621-1224
Hikes, activities, educational shop.

Chaw'se Association, Indian Grinding Rock State Historic Park
14881 Pine Grove-Volcano Road, Pine Grove, CA 95665; (209) 296-7488

Sierra Club Tuolumne Group
P.O. Box 4440, Sonora, CA 95370
Hikes, activities, lectures, newsletter.

Tuolumne County Land Trust
P.O. Box 5362, Sonora, CA 95370; (209) 532- 6937
Conservation easement acquisition.

Groveland District Ranger Station, Stanislaus National Forest
24545 Highway 120 (8 miles east of Groveland); (209) 962-7825
Maps, hikes.

Yosemite Association
P.O. Box 230, El Portal, CA 95318; (209) 379- 2646
Offers booklet with scheduled classes, including hikes, art, and much more.

Appendix C:
NATIVE PLANT NURSERIES

It would be wise to phone first for hours or an appointment. The various California Native Plant Societies in the foothills have plant sales. To find out when and where sales are being held and to obtain a contact for your local CNPS Chapter, phone (916) 447-2677.

California Flora Nursery
P.O. Box 3, Fulton, CA 95439; (707) 528-8813

Far Star Nursery (Marcia Braga)
17395 Indian Springs Ranch Road, Grass Valley, CA 95949; (530) 273-1501

Foothill Cottage Gardens (Carolyn Singer)
13925 Sontag Road, Grass Valley, CA 95945 (off You Bet Road, near Highway 174); (530) 272-4362

Lotus Valley Nursery & Gardens
P.O. Box 859 (5606 Petersen Lane), Lotus, CA 95651; (530) 626-7021

Redbud Nursery (Dave Cox)
P.O. Box 1165, Georgetown, CA 95634; (530) 333- 2300

GLOSSARY

Achene: a dry, hard, one seeded fruit, such as a Sunflower seed.

Acuminate: tapered and pinched in to a point.

Alkaloid: slightly alkaline, which may be poisonous.

Alternate leaves: having only one leaf growing from each node; a staggered arrangement.

Annual: a plant that flowers, fruits, and dies in one year.

Anther: the pollen-containing structure at the tip of the filament.

Arrastra : a rotary contrivance of abrasive stones that move over a track powered by a mule walking in a circle; used by the Spanish Americans to crush gold-bearing quartz.

Axil: the angle between a leaf and the stem.

Banner: the upper petal of a Pea flower (see Lupine, pp. 152, 189, 286, 287, 288).

Bract: the much-reduced leaf subtending a flower or flower cluster.

Burl: a domelike growth at the base of a shrub or on the trunk of a tree.

Calyx: the outer whorl, usually green, of a flower.

Campanulate: bell-shaped.

Capitate: gathered into a head, rather ball-shaped or spherical (see Onion).

Catkin: a scaly spike or dense cluster of minute flowers that lack petals, as in alders.

Chaff: thin, dry, papery or scaly bracts in the Sunflower family.

Chaparral: term referring to the group of rigid or thorny shrubs found growing on dry slopes, such as Manzanita, Ceanothus, and Huckleberry Oak.

Ciliate: having a line of tiny hairs along the margin of a leaf, petal, or sepal.

Clasping: describing a leaf partly surrounding a stem.

Claw: a narrow, elongated base of a petal.

Climax community: the final stage of succession of plants, in which the dominant species can reseed itself in spite of deep shade; it takes fire, flood, disease, or mechanical clearing to change this stable community.

Corolla: the whorl of usually colorful petals in a flower, found outside the stamens and within the calyx.

Crest: the bumps or ridges on the ovary of the genus *Allium*.

Cultivar: a desirable form of a native plant that has been propagated vegetatively, named, and introduced into the nursery trade.

Deciduous: refers to plants that shed their leaves each fall.

Dentate: tooth-shaped margins of leaves.

Dioecious: refers to staminate and pistillate flowers on different plants.

Disk-flower: in the Sunflower family; a tubular, usually perfect flower, but lacking a raylike extension on the corolla.

Duff: the litter of leaves, bark, and other plant material that collects on the forest floor.

Entire: a leaf with smooth edges.

Estivation: summer hibernation, when certain plants lose their leaves to slow down water loss.

Evergreen: a plant that keeps its leaves all winter, such as manzanita and pines.

Exserted: extending beyond an opening, for example as the stamens of the *Phacelia* extend beyond the petals.

Family: a large group of plants with similar traits generally observed in the flower or fruit.

Fertile stamen: stamen containing an anther and pollen.

Filament: the stalk that holds the pollen sac or anther.

Follicle: a dry, elongate fruit or seed pod, such as Columbine.

Gabbro: a granular igneous rock.

Galea: the long, hoodlike upper lip of the Mint or Figwort family.

Genus: the major subdivision of plant famlies.

Glabrous: bald, hairless.

Glandular: bearing glands, or having a surface that exudes a sticky liquid.

Habitat: the general environment or location in which a plant grows.

Head: a rounded cluster of sessile flowers such as Pennyroyal.

Herb: a plant without woody stems.

Imbricate: overlapping, like shingles.

Inferior: situated below; often refers to an ovary below the other floral parts.

Inflorescence: a flower cluster.

Involucre: a whorl of bracts subtending a flower cluster.

Irregular: having different-shaped petals or sepals on the same flower (see inside front cover).

Keel: the lower two petals that are fused together on the pea flower.

Key: a method of identifying a plant by choosing characteristics that eventually will fit only a specific plant.

Leaflet: a leaflike division of a compound leaf.

Merous: having a specified number or kind of parts, such as trimerous, pentamerous, etc.

Monoecious: having stamens and pistils in separate flowers on the same plant.

Montane: of or growing in the mountains.

Node: the joint of a stem, where leaves, branches, or flowers originate.

Opposite leaves: having two leaves growing from each node on opposite sides of the stem.

Ovary: the seed-containing portion of the pistil.

Palmate: having lobes that radiate from a central point, such as the Maple leaf.

Panicle: a compound flower cluster; a branched raceme.

Pappus: the whorl or hairs, bristles, or scales at the apex of the achene in some members of the Sunflower family.

Parasitic: growing upon and deriving nourishment from another plant.

Pedicel: the stalk or stem of a flower.

Peduncle: the stalk or stem on an inflorescence, such as an umbel.

Perennial: a plant that lives for more than one year; it often has enlarged roots to store nutrients during the winter.

Perfect: having both stamens and pistils in the same flower.

Perianth: a collective term for the calyx and corolla.

Persist: wilted plant parts, generally the flower, that remain on the plant, as in Gooseberries.

Petal: one of the divisions of the corolla, usually colored, located between the stamens and the sepals.

Petiole: the stalk of a leaf.

Pinnate: describing a compound leaf with the leaflets arranged on each side of the central axis; featherlike.

Pistil: the female organ of the flower, consisting of ovary, stigma, and style.

Raceme: an elongate flower cluster with one main axis and smaller pedicels bearing one flower each, as in Lupine.

Ray-flower: a flower in the Sunflower family that bears a straplike extension on one side of the corolla; the ray-flowers are usually along the margin of the head.

Receptacle: in the Sunflower family, the fleshy base of the inflorescence in which the flowers and developing achenes sit.

Saggitate: arrowhead-shaped.

Saprophyte: a plant living on dead organic matter and thus lacking chlorophyll.

Scape: a leafless flowering stem arising from basal leaves, as in the primrose.

Sepal: the usually green outer whorl of flower parts.

Sessile: stemless; a leaf without a petiole or a flower without a pedicel; a sessile ovary is one without a stipe.

Sheath: the lower part of the leaf that is wrapped around the stem.

Shrub: a branching woody plant, usually without a distinct trunk.

Silique: a two-celled capsule, several times longer than it is wide (see *Erysimum,* page 172).

Sorus: cluster of reproductive spores of a fern generally protected on inrolled leaflet edges or the underside of leaves.

Spatulate: shaped like a spatula, with a long, narrow base and rounded at the tip.

Species: a further subdivision of genus to better define the specific plant.

Stamen: the pollen-bearing organ of a flower, consisting of a filament, an anther, and pollen.

Staminode: a sterile stamen lacking anther or pollen.

Stellate: star-shaped, often referring to hairs on Mallows or Fremontia.

Stigma: the sticky portion of the style that is receptive to pollen.

Stipe: a stalk that raises the ovary above the receptacle; also the petiole of a fern leaf.

Style: the slender portion of the pistil between the ovary and the stigma.

Succession: the progressive replacement of one plant community by another until stability is reached in the climax community; think of how a lake becomes a meadow and then a forest.

Superior ovary: one free from the calyx, above the other floral parts.

Tepal: in the Lily family, collective term for the sepals and petals composing the corolla when they are identical in color and shape.

Umbel: an inflorescence in which all the pedicels arise from the same point so as to form a flat-topped flower cluster.

BIBLIOGRAPHY AND ADDITIONAL REFERENCES

(Books marked with an asterisk (*) will enhance your enjoyment
of the Gold Country and help confirm plant identification.)

Abrams, LeRoy. *Illustrated Flora of the Pacific States*. Stanford: Stanford University Press, Vol. I, 1940; Vol. II, 1944; Vol. III, 1951; Vol. IV, with Roxanne Ferris, 1960.

Bailey, L. H. *How Plants Get Their Names*. New York: Dover Publications, 1963.

Coombes, Allen J. *Dictionary of Plant Names*. Portland: Timber Press, 1985.

*Fauver, Toni. *Wildflower Walking in Lakes Basin of the Northern Sierra*. Grass Valley, CA: Comstock Bonanza Press, 1992. (A useful guide for the area above Sierra City; same general format as this book.)

Giacomazzi, Sharon. "Briceburg, Pioneer Outpost on the Merced River," *California Explorer*, April/May 1996, Reno, NV.

Gudde, Erwin G. *California Gold Camps*. Berkeley: University of California Press, 1975.

Gudde, Erwin G. *1000 California Place Names, Their Origin and Meaning*. 2nd rev. ed. Berkeley: University of California Press, 1959.

Hart, James D. *A Companion to California*. New York: Oxford University Press, 1978.

*Hickman, James C. (ed.) *The Jepson Manual of Higher Plants of California*. Berkeley: University of California Press, 1993.

Holliday, J. S. *The World Rushed In: The California Gold Rush Experience*. New York: Simon & Schuster, 1981.

Hoover, Mildred B., and H. E. & E. G. Rensch. *Historic Spots in California*. Stanford: Stanford University Press, 1948.

Hoxie, Kathie. "Honey Run, Butte County's Historic Tri-Span Bridge," *California Explorer*, Sept./Oct. 1997, Reno, NV.

Jenkins, Olaf P. (ed.) *Geologic Guidebook along Highway 49—Sierran Gold Belt, The Mother Lode Country*. San Francisco: California Department of Natural Resources, Division of Mines, 1948.

Jokhurst, James. "Table Mountain Flora," *Madrono*, Vol. 30, No. 4, pp 1-18 (November Supplement), 1983.

Keator, Glen. *Complete Garden Guide to the Native Perennials of California*. San Francisco: Chronicle Books, 1990.

Koeppel, Elliot H. *The California Gold Country: Highway 49 Revisited*. Malakoff and Company, 1996.

Lamela, Susan, and Hank Meals. *Yuba Trails: A Selection of Historic Trails in the Yuba Watershed*. Nevada City, CA: Susan Lamela, 1993.

Mandel, Stephanie, et al. *The American River, North, Middle and South Forks*. Auburn, CA: Protect American River Canyons, 1989.

McGrew, Shana, et al. *Coyote Creek Nature Trail Guide*. Sacramento: California Bureau of Reclamation.

McPhee, John. *Assembling California*. New York: Farrar, Strauss and Giroux, 1993.

Morrison, Paul D. (ed.) *Placer Gold Deposits of the Sierra Nevada*. Baldwin Park, CA: California Gem Guides, 1997.

*Munz, P. A. *A California Flora and Supplement*. Berkeley: University of California Press, 1959. (The recognized authority on California plants. Few pictures.)

Murphey, Edith Van Allen. *Indian Uses of Native Plants*. Fort Bragg, CA: Mendocino County Historical Society, 1959.

*Niehaus, Theodore F. *A Field Guide to Pacific States Wildflowers*. Boston: Houghton Mifflin, 1976. (Many colored pictures; a good supplement to this book.)

Olmstead, John, and Eleanor Huggins. *Adventures on & off Interstate 80*. Palo Alto: Tioga Publishing Co., 1985.

Oswald, Vernon H. *Vascular Plants of Upper Bidwell Park, Chico, California*. Chico: California State University, 1996.

Parsons, Mary Elizabeth. *The Wildflowers of California*. San Francisco: California School Book Depository, 1930.

Pottenger, Dennis. "A Dalliance at Daffodil Hill," *Sierra Heritage*, March/April 1995, Auburn, CA.

*Schaffer, Jeffrey P. *The Tahoe Sierra*. Berkeley: Wilderness Press, 1975. (Detailed descriptions of all possible hikes in the Highway 49 area, with an emphasis on geology.)

Sudworth, George B. *Forest Trees of the Pacific Slope*. Washington DC: USDA Forest Service, 1908.

Sweet, M. *Common Edible and Useful Plants of the West*. Healdsburg, CA: Naturegraph Co., 1962.

INDEX TO PLANTS

INDEX TO PLANT LISTS, HIKES AND TRAILS

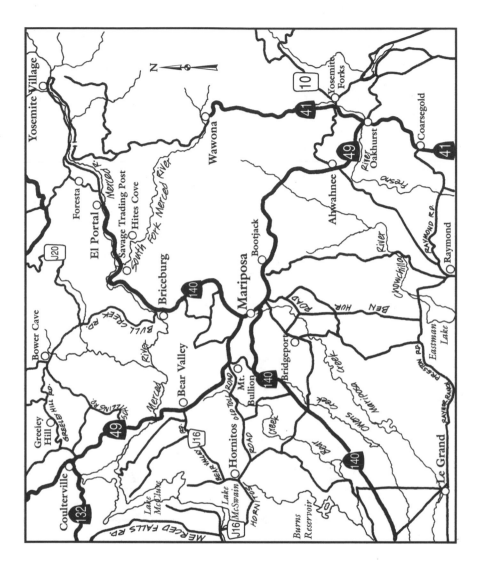

Mariposa Area

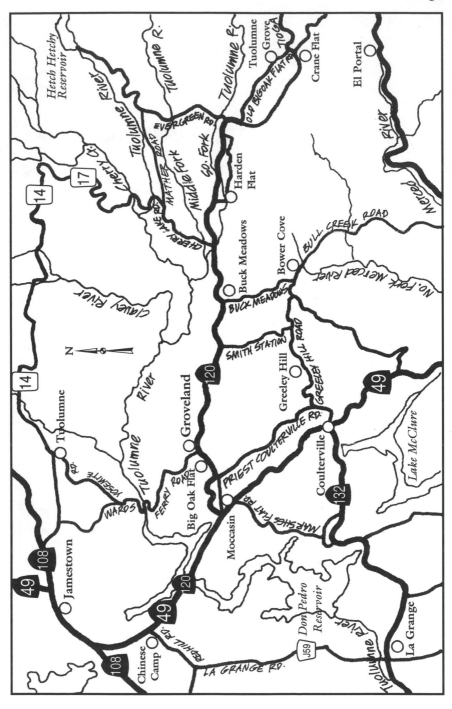

Groveland Area

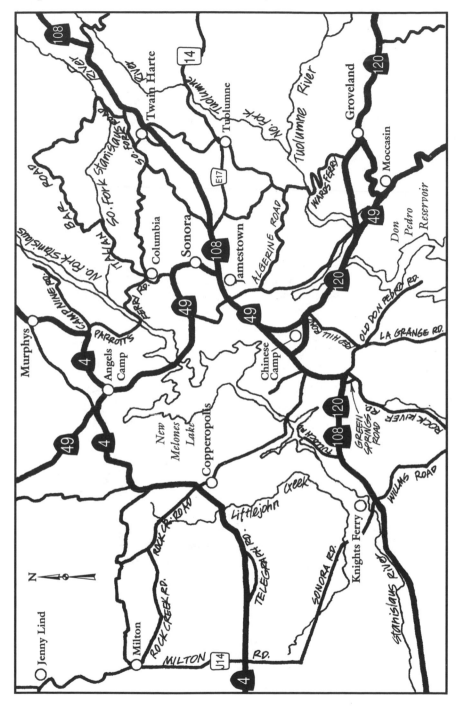

Sonora Area

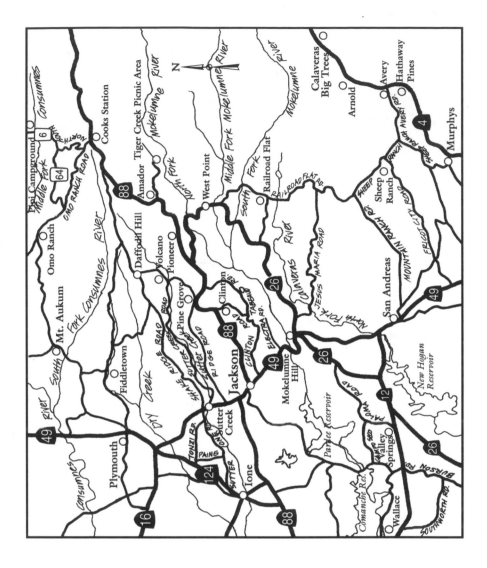

Jackson Area

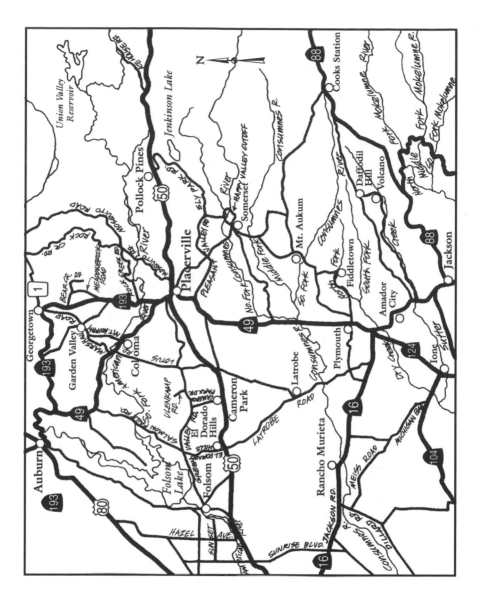

Placerville Area

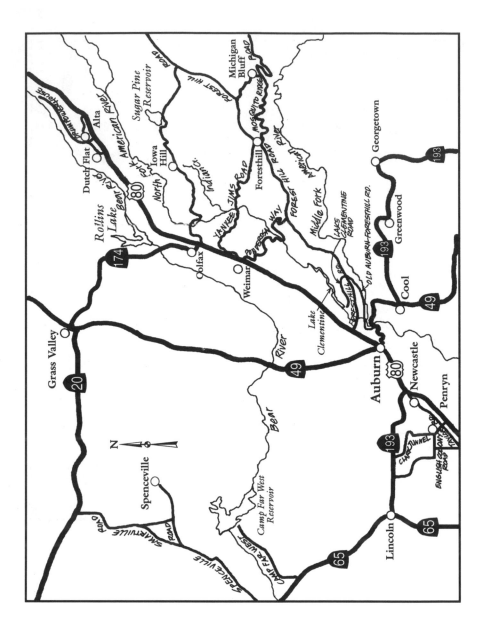

Auburn Area

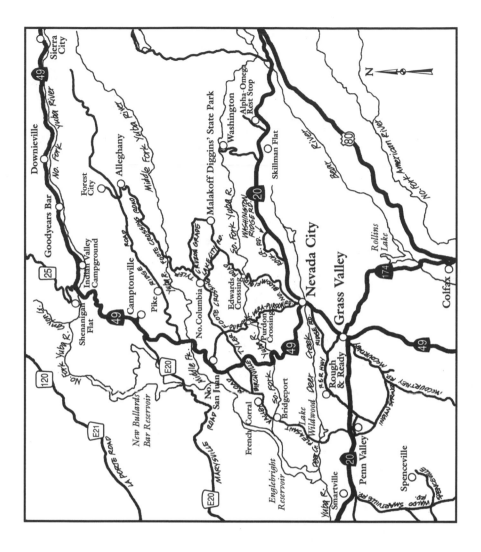

Grass Valley and Nevada City Area

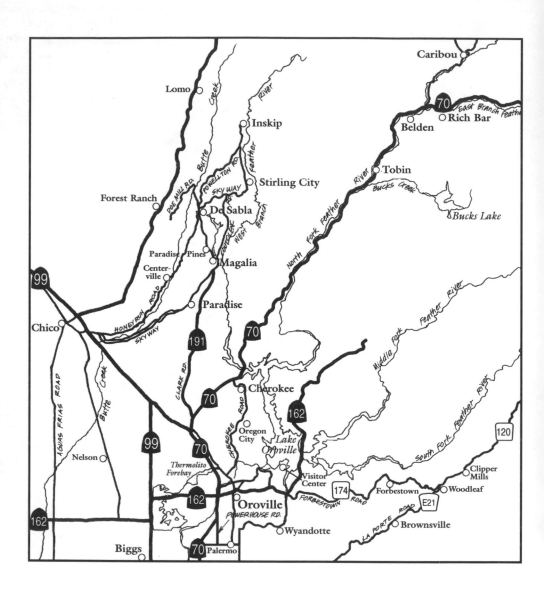

Oroville Area